Enhancing the Freedom to Flourish in Higher Education

Persistent educational, economic and social inequalities perpetuate unequal participation in higher education for a significant number of students in both developing and developed contexts, offering these students fewer opportunities to convert academic resources into equal participation. *Enhancing the Freedom to Flourish in Higher Education* explores the insight that student narratives can offer to the debate surrounding the complex reasons of why some students flourish at university while others are marginalised socially and academically. Proposing a new model of equal participation that draws not only on international comparisons, but is also embedded in the experiences of students, the book offers practical suggestions on how to enhance opportunities for equal participation.

Using South Africa as a case study, the book tracks the experiences of eight undergraduate students whose narratives illuminate the structural inequalities affecting participation in higher education. Despite the political, economic and academic factors that lead to diminished participation, the book foregrounds the resources that students used to negotiate obstacles and grounds these individual narratives in broader global debates around justice, widening participation and equality in higher education.

Enhancing the Freedom to Flourish in Higher Education brings critical social theory to the problem of unequal participation so as to challenge the invisible and implicit forms of inequality found within student narratives. It will appeal to lecturers and tutors, practitioners based in student affairs, and policy makers, as well as postgraduate students.

Talita M. L. Calitz is a Lecturer at the Department of Education Management and Policy Studies at the University of Pretoria, South Africa. She is also affiliated with the Higher Education and Human Development Research Programme at the University of the Free State, South Africa.

The Society for Research into Higher Education (SRHE) is an independent and financially self-supporting international learned Society. It is concerned to advance understanding of higher education, especially through the insights, perspectives and knowledge offered by systematic research and scholarship.

The Society's primary role is to improve the quality of higher education through facilitating knowledge exchange, discourse and publication of research. SRHE members are worldwide and the Society is an NGO in operational relations with UNESCO.

The Society has a wide set of aims and objectives. Amongst its many activities the Society:

• is a specialist publisher of higher education research, journals and books, amongst them Studies in Higher Education, Higher Education Quarterly, Research into Higher Education Abstracts and a long running monograph book series.

The Society also publishes a number of in-house guides and produces a specialist series "Issues in Postgraduate Education".

• funds and supports a large number of special interest networks for researchers and practitioners working in higher education from every discipline. These networks are open to all and offer a range of topical seminars, workshops and other events throughout the year ensuring the Society is in touch with all current research knowledge.

• runs the largest annual UK-based higher education research conference and parallel conference for postgraduate and newer researchers. This is attended by researchers from over 35 countries and showcases current research across every aspect of higher education.

SRHE *Society for Research into Higher Education*
Advancing knowledge   Informing policy   Enhancing practice

73 Collier Street   T   +44 (0)20 7427 2350
London N1 9BE   F   +44 (0)20 7278 1135
United Kingdom   E   srheoffice@srhe.ac.uk
                              www.srhe.ac.uk

Director: Helen Perkins
Registered Charity No. 313850
Company No. 00868820
Limited by Guarantee
Registered office as above

Society for Research into Higher Education Series
Series Editors:
Jennifer M. Case, *University of Vermont, USA*
Jeroen Huisman, *University of Ghent, Belgium*

This exciting new series aims to publish cutting edge research and discourse that reflects the rapidly changing world of higher education, examined in a global context. Encompassing topics of wide international relevance, the series includes every aspect of the international higher education research agenda, from strategic policy formulation and impact to pragmatic advice on best practice in the field.

Titles in the series:

Theorising Learning to Teach in Higher Education
Edited by Brenda Leibowitz, Vivienne Bozalek and Peter Kahn

Changing Pedagogical Spaces in Higher Education
Diversity, Inequalities and Misrecognition
Penny Jane Burke, Gill Crozier and Lauren Ila Misiaszek

Access to Higher Education
Theoretical Perspectives and Contemporary Challenges
Edited by Anna Mountford-Zimdars and Neil Harrison

Religion and Higher Education in Europe and North America
Edited by Kristin Aune and Jacqueline Stevenson

Reconstructing Relationships in Higher Education
Celia Whitchurch and George Gordon

Possible Selves and Higher Education
New Interdisciplinary Insights
Edited by Holly Henderson, Jacqueline Stevenson and Ann-Marie Bathmaker

Enhancing the Freedom to Flourish in Higher Education
Participation, Equality and Capabilities
Talita M. L. Calitz

For more information about this series, please visit: https://www.routledge.com/Research-into-Higher-Education/book-series/SRHE

Enhancing the Freedom to Flourish in Higher Education

Participation, Equality and Capabilities

Talita M. L. Calitz

LONDON AND NEW YORK

First published 2019
by Routledge
2 Park Square, Milton Park, Abingdon, Oxon OX14 4RN

and by Routledge
711 Third Avenue, New York, NY 10017

Routledge is an imprint of the Taylor & Francis Group, an informa business

© 2019 Talita M. L. Calitz

The right of Talita M. L. Calitz to be identified as author of this work has been asserted by her in accordance with sections 77 and 78 of the Copyright, Designs and Patents Act 1988.

All rights reserved. No part of this book may be reprinted or reproduced or utilised in any form or by any electronic, mechanical, or other means, now known or hereafter invented, including photocopying and recording, or in any information storage or retrieval system, without permission in writing from the publishers.

Trademark notice: Product or corporate names may be trademarks or registered trademarks, and are used only for identification and explanation without intent to infringe.

British Library Cataloguing-in-Publication Data
A catalogue record for this book is available from the British Library

Library of Congress Cataloging-in-Publication Data
Names: Calitz, Talita, author.
Title: Enhancing the freedom to flourish in higher education : participation, equality and capabilities / Talita Calitz.
Description: Abingdon, Oxon ; New York, NY : Routledge is an imprint of the Taylor & Francis Group, an Informa Business, [2018] | Series: Society for research into higher education series | Includes bibliographical references and index.
Identifiers: LCCN 2018008051| ISBN 9781138633827 (hbk : alk. paper) | ISBN 9781138633834 (pbk : alk. paper) | ISBN 9781315207070 (ebk : alk. paper)
Subjects: LCSH: Educational equalization—Cross-cultural studies. | Universities and colleges—Admission—Cross-cultural studies. | People with social disabilities—Education (Higher)—Cross-cultural studies. | Academic achievement—Social aspects—Cross-cultural studies.
Classification: LCC LC213 .C34 2018 | DDC 379.2/6--dc23
LC record available at https://lccn.loc.gov/2018008051

ISBN: 978-1-138-63382-7 (hbk)
ISBN: 978-1-138-63383-4 (pbk)
ISBN: 978-1-315-20707-0 (ebk)

Typeset in Galliard
by Florence Production Ltd, Stoodleigh, Devon, UK

Printed by CPI Group (UK) Ltd, Croydon CR0 4YY

For the Earth and its citizens — human and non-human — who long for freedom.

Contents

List of abbreviations xii
List of illustrations xiii
Acknowledgements xiv

1 **Inequality in higher education** 1

   Inequality and the lives of students 2
   　Mapping unequal participation in international higher education 3
   　Overview of inequality in international higher education 3
   　Inequality and higher education 4
   　Inequality and higher education in the global South 7
   Inequality, massification and South African higher education 7
   　Trade-offs and resources 8
   　The dysfunctional public school system 10
   　Race, institutional demographics and transformation 10
   　Individual deficit or structural inequality? 13
   Researching inequality and student lives 15
   Navigating the book chapters 16

2 **Structures of unequal participation** 23

   Structural inequality in global higher education 23
   Structural inequality in South African higher education 25
   The deficit approach, resources and massification 26
   　The deficit approach and South African higher education 28
   A deficit approach and academic provision 29
   　Teaching and learning constraints 30
   　Academic support programmes 31
   Resisting a deficit approach 32
   　Structural relations of power 33

Recognising student resources and agency 33
The intersection of race, gender, class and participation 35
Conclusion 36

3 The capability approach and inequality in higher education 45

The capability approach and structural injustice 45
    A capability approach to higher education research 46
    A capability critique of neoliberal higher education 47
Capability framework 47
    Capabilities and functionings 48
    Education as freedom 50
    Democratic participation 51
    Agency 52
    Conversion factors 54
    Adaptive preference 55
    Well-being 55
Freire and education as freedom 56
    Resisting the banking system 57
Fraser and the capability approach 58
    Redistribution 59
    Recognition 60
    Representation 61
Conceptual framework for narrative analysis 61

4 Introducing student narratives 67

Listening to student experiences 67
    Introducing the participants 68
    Student experiences at school 69
    Inequality and South African schooling 70
    Resources and recognition at school 73
Developing aspirations 83
    School and identity 86
    Family resources and aspirations 86
Summary of themes 92

5 Structural constraints to participation 96

Individualising failure 96
Uncritical engagement with knowledge 102
Lack of participation in decision-making 107

Alienation from lecturers 113
Misrecognition 116
Transformation and structural constraints 121

6   **Student agency in higher education**   127

   Enabling affiliation with lecturers 127
   Enabling affiliation with peers 132
   Creating platforms for student voice 136
   Distributing access to knowledge 138
   Recognising student capabilities 142
   Transformation and student agency 145

7   **Capabilities for equal participation**   147

   From exclusion to capability development? 147
   Designing capability praxis 149
       Resources and pedagogy 150
   Capabilities for equal participation in pedagogy 151
       Practical reason 152
       Critical literacies 153
       Student research 155
       Deliberative participation 156
       Critical affiliation 158
       Values for the public good 160
   Conclusion 162

8   **Creating just universities**   168

   From deficit discourse to enabling structures in higher education 169
   Implementing a resource threshold 170
   Equalising opportunities 172
       Equal opportunities for commuter students 173
   Restructuring academic support programmes 174
       Transforming knowledge and institutional cultures 175
   Cultivating recognition 177
       Undergraduate research 177
       Participatory decision-making 178
   Inequality and transforming higher education 179
   Transforming higher education 180

   Index   185

Abbreviations

ANC: African National Congress
CHE: Council on Higher Education
CHET: Centre for Higher Education Transformation
DHET: Department of Higher Education and Training
HESA: Higher Education South Africa
NSFAS: National Student Financial Aid Scheme
SRC: Student Representative Council
USAf: Universities South Africa

Illustrations

Figures

3.1 Working definition of equal participation 62
3.2 Conceptualising education as the practice of freedom 62

Tables

4.1 Participant biographical information 69
4.2 Organisation of analytical codes 70
7.1 Capabilities emerging from student narratives and literature 149
8.1 A minimum resource threshold 171

Acknowledgements

My colleagues and friends have played an invaluable role in the completion of this book. Melanie Walker and Merridy Wilson-Strydom shaped my thinking around social justice and human development during my five years at the Centre for Research on Higher Education and Development (CRHED) at the University of the Free State. I am profoundly grateful to the rigorous space for intellectual development created for the doctoral students at CRHED. Members of the HDCA community were generous with their time and input, in particular Elaine Unterhalter, Monica McLean, Sandra Boni and Veronica Crosbie. It was a privilege to work within a thriving community at CRHED, and to refine my thinking in conversations with peers, in particular with Mikateko Höppener, Oliver Mutanga, Tendayi Marovah, Thandi Lewin, Sonja Loots and Carmen Martinez-Vargas.

This book would not have been possible without generous funding from the National Research Foundation, the Department of Science and Technology Chair in Higher Education and Human Development and the Centre for Research in Higher Education and Development (CRHED) at the University of the Free State. I am grateful to Johnathan Jansen for the vibrant research climate at the University of the Free State, and for creating opportunities for international collaboration and publishing. At the University of Pretoria, I have also received developmental support from the Dean's Young Scholars Programme, and funding from the Research Development Grant and the Department of Education Management and Policy Studies.

In June/July of 2017, Enrica Chiappero-Martinetti at the University of Pavia offered me the wonderful intellectual space through the CICOPIS scholarship to work on the book. I am very grateful to both Enrica and Melanie Walker for making these opportunities available to the CRHED community. Emily Henderson helped me secure a visit at the University of Warwick's Institute of Advanced Study, which was an exciting space to share my work and to build networks. Early in my career, my colleagues at the University of the Free State's Institute for Reconciliation and Social Justice Andre Keet, Lihlumelo Toyana, Nangamso Koza and Andrew Westover shaped my ideas around social justice, the public good and education. I am grateful for the many thought-provoking conversations with Wynoma Michaels, who has offered me sound advice and mentorship during this project.

I have received invaluable support and mentorship from my Dean at the University of Pretoria, Chika Sehoole, my Head of Department at Education Management and Policy Studies Everard Weber, and colleagues who have enabled me to write when there was much work to be done! Thank you especially to Maitumeleng Nthontho and Chaya Herman for your encouragement and mentorship.

I am grateful for a lifetime of love and support from my parents Anton and Riana Calitz, and my sister Adéle Calitz, who encouraged my curiosity, and assured me that there would always be plenty of new books to read. Toy Janse van Rensburg and our golden beasts offered their loving presence, which sustained me during the writing process. Cornelis Muller's friendship, intellectual acuity, and humour kept me sane. Janeke Thumbran, whose friendship has gifted over two decades of grace, growth and love, has profoundly shaped my way of being in the world.

To every student who shared their experiences and participated in constructing narratives and disrupting hierarchies, this research would not have been possible without your courage. *Ke a le boa.*

Chapter 1

Inequality in higher education

A walk across a South African university campus reveals glaring inequalities. As you cross the parking lot where managers park their cars, you will see expensive sport models and SUVs. Students entering campus walk from their accommodation, or use public transport from informal settlements located outside the city. Other students drive onto campus with new Mini Coopers, some with less expensive cars. At lunchtime, the campus restaurant serves a buffet that caters exclusively to academics and their guests. If you look through the windows of the restaurant, students gather on the outskirts of the student centre, sharing food brought from home, others do not have anything to eat. Some students study at the library with their own laptops and smartphones, while others queue to use the university labs. You will see the latest fashion, shoes and accessories, and also students who wear the same outfit to class every week. At the end of the day, many students wait at the taxi rank to take them back home to the still-segregated urban and rural settlements created by apartheid, while lecturers walk to their cars and drive home to manicured suburbs and gated communities.

These inequalities have become the new normal in post-apartheid South Africa, where obscene wealth exists alongside extreme poverty. But what is the cost of this inequality for the most vulnerable students at South Africa universities? What do student experiences reveal about the public university in an age of dwindling state support? What happens when higher education, with its roots in the colonial and apartheid past, exists within a global space where democracy, citizenship and livelihoods come up against competing corporate interests (Chomsky & Polychroniou 2017; Giroux 2013)? In an increasingly competitive system, how do students use their agency to navigate university life with limited personal resources and academic preparation? Despite significant personal and structural obstacles, what is the individual able to achieve using her agency?

To help me answer these questions, I designed a research project that tracked the lives of Black, working-class, first-generation undergraduate students at a South African university. Drawing on the narratives that emerged from the research, the book explores how institutional and pedagogical arrangements enabled and constrained students' freedom to participate in the academic and social life of the university. The narratives reveal how students used their agency to navigate personal and institutional resource scarcity, and to find innovative responses to individual and structural barriers. This book examines student participation in light of broader issues of resource scarcity in South Africa, within the context of historical, economic and socio-political challenges that shape higher education in the global South. In both developing and developed contexts, exclusion, unequal access and diminished equality of participation are urgent issues on higher education agendas. A capability approach to higher education research informed my analysis of expanding student numbers and diversifying student demographics as inadequate indicators of equity and transformation in higher education (Boni & Walker 2013; Walker & McLean 2013; Wilson-Strydom 2015).

Inequality and the lives of students

Many young South Africans born into democracy nurture aspirations for a university education that could increase the possibility of employment[1] and social mobility. Despite relatively low participation rates, an increasing number of South Africans are gaining access to higher education. For the 19 per cent who qualify for university entrance (CHE 2016), securing a place at one of South Africa's 26 public universities is an extraordinary feat of resilience, agency and determination. However, access is the first of many hurdles. Once admitted, structural inequalities often diminish the freedom of students to participate and succeed (Bozalek & Boughey 2012; Mthethwa 2013; Department of Education (DoE) 2008). Students from poor and emergent middle-class families navigate the reality that, despite its mineral wealth and relatively strong economy on the African continent, South Africa is the fourth most unequal country in the world, with a Gini coefficient of 0.70, and a youth employment rate of 67 per cent[3] (STATS SA 2017). This intensifies higher education's unequal playing field, since many students pursue their studies without reliable social services such as health, housing and nutrition (DHET 2014). Poverty and unemployment in a student's family and extended relative structure also make it difficult to cover tuition fees and living costs.

A university degree has high stakes in a country where approximately 14 million (40.3 per cent) South Africans between the ages of 15 and 24 are not in any form of education, employment or training (DHET 2017). The World Bank estimates that 52.7 per cent of South Africans between the ages of 15 and 24 are unemployed (World Bank 2017). In contrast, the unemployment rate for graduates is relatively low at 7 per cent (Broekhuizen & Van der Berg 2013) and some university graduates have a better chance to access decent work and social mobility (DHET 2013). From a human capital perspective, a low higher education participation rate and a shortage of high-level skills is detrimental to national economic growth (DHET 2015), keeping in mind that economic growth does not guarantee equal economic or social freedoms for all citizens (Fioramonti 2017; Robeyns 2016). Nevertheless, from a human capital and a human development perspective, unequal access, participation, and outcomes in higher education diminish an individual's freedom to contribute meaningfully to her society. Compared with students who drop out before completion, university graduates could have enhanced opportunities to respond to social challenges such as poverty, to attain social mobility, and to contribute towards sustainable human development.

Mapping unequal participation in international higher education

At universities in both developing and developed contexts, the challenges associated with inequality and participation are a growing concern in higher education research (Archer, Hutchings, & Ross 2005; Armstrong & Hamilton 2013; Berg 2016; Brown & Hoxby 2015; Burke 2012; Carpentier & Unterhalter 2011; David 2013; David *et al.* 2009; David & Naidoo 2013; Finnegan, Merrill, & Thunborg 2014; Goldrick-Rab 2016; Harwood, Hickey-Moody, & McMahon 2016; Jacob & Holsinger 2008; King, Marginson, & Naidoo 2011; Mettler 2014; Morley & Lugg 2009; Mullen 2011; Naidoo 2010; Reay & Ball 2005; Stuart 2002; Unterhalter 2010; Unterhalter 2017). Some international literature concerned with inequality and higher education pays particular attention to the impact of neoliberal economic policies on higher education, which I discuss in Chapter 2, and the role of globalisation in reshaping the aims of higher education. There is also debate about the impact of massification, especially in developing contexts, and the tension between higher education framed as a private and a public good, summarised as follows: 'The growing emphasis on cost recovery, higher tuition and university-industry links distracts from the traditional social role and service function of higher education that are central to contemporary society' (Altbach, Rumble, & Reisberg 2009: xii).

Because of the 'more or less global capture of higher education by economic arguments and neoliberal policy' (Boni & Walker 2013: 15; Nussbaum 2012; Giroux 2013; Altbach *et al.* 2009), higher education institutions and structures not only maintain existing socioeconomic inequalities, but in some instances deepen such inequalities (Armstrong & Hamilton 2013; Berg 2016; Naidoo 2010).

Overview of inequality in international higher education

Despite important nuances between the global North and South, a number of factors define patterns of inequality in higher education. With over 26 per cent of the age cohort enrolled in higher education globally (Altbach *et al.* 2009), more people than ever before have access to expanded opportunities for development, innovation and research. Under globalisation, higher education has developed much potential for social mobility (Carpentier & Unterhalter

2011). Yet globalisation also brings complex risks and new layers of inequality (Naidoo 2010; Zajda, Biraimah, & Gaudelli 2008). For instance, despite significant expansion in access for poor and working-class students, many young people in the poorest countries have little chance of accessing higher education, and many struggle to succeed (Berg 2016; Ilie & Rose 2016; Unterhalter 2010).

Carpentier and Unterhalter (2010) situate inequality in higher education as a global phenomenon entangled with social crises such as poverty and extreme income inequality across national and regional contexts (see also Unterhalter 2012). Higher education in the global North and South faces resource scarcity, as competing national priorities shrink public spending and state investment in higher education. While public universities with large endowments and private institutions may not be as severely affected, public universities that rely on inadequate state subsidy face serious challenges, especially in the global South (Habib 2016; Mamdani 2007).

Although globally access to higher education has increased, some developing regions have very low rates of participation. Sub-Saharan Africa has the lowest participation rate for higher education at only 6 per cent (Unterhalter 2017). While many universities have a diverse student population and programmes to address disadvantage (Altbach *et al.* 2009), there are still marked differences between access, participation and outcomes across indicators of race, gender and socioeconomic status. Given widening socioeconomic inequalities, poor and middle-class students attend university alongside elite students from well-resourced schools. Yet even in well-resourced, high-participation contexts such as the United States, participation rates for ethnic minority students are much lower, while socioeconomic status remains a primary indicator of degree attainment (Altbach *et al.* 2009; Berg 2016; Jerrim & Vignoles 2015).

Inequality and higher education

Research in the global North traces the historical, economic and social causes of persistent injustice in higher education. In the United States, with its established system of massified higher education (Altbach *et al.* 2009), and an undergraduate participation rate of around 45 per cent (Jerrim & Vignoles 2015), glaring inequalities permeate the system. Positioned in contrast to South Africa's developing economy, and a participation rate of roughly 19.5 per cent (CHE 2016), the scale and intensity of inequality in the US system is markedly different. Nevertheless, research on working-class and/or first-generation university students in the United States, especially from African American and indigenous communities, reveals challenges also faced by South African students. These include the transition from secondary school to university, inadequate academic preparation, limited family support and inadequate finances (Berg 2016; Brown & Hoxby 2015; Jerrim & Vignoles 2015). Once admitted, there are also similarities in structural constraints that diminish student participation, including racism and class-based discrimination, difficulty integrating into academic and social life, the pressure to work while studying, family responsibilities, and inadequate financial support to fund studies to completion (Armstrong & Hamilton 2013; Berg 2016; Mettler 2014; Mullen 2011). Strikingly similar to the South African context is the large number of undergraduate drop outs in the US, with an almost 50 per cent attrition rate (Jerrim 2013; see also DHET 2013).

Socioeconomic class remains an indicator of the equality of access, participation and success in higher education across the global North. Student poverty is complicated by the rising cost of tuition and living expenses, and in some countries the shift from free education to privately funded models or loan systems disadvantages the most economically vulnerable students (Altbach *et al.* 2009; Berg 2016; Goldrick-Rab 2016). A convergence of factors inside and outside the institutions makes social mobility increasingly unattainable for low-income students (Berg 2016). Low-income students in the United States have more precarious access to higher education, while also experiencing what Berg terms a 'reduced impact' even when they manage to overcome structural and personal constraints (Berg 2016). Another US-based study concludes that higher education is more likely to benefit affluent students whose class position gives them preferential access, while being more likely to reproduce their parents' class positon, compared with less privileged students who leave university with reduced freedom for social mobility and future life chances (Armstrong & Hamilton 2013). Research into class, gender and inequality in the US system shows patterns of inequality in which affluent students at elite universities develop themselves personally and intellectually, while students at non-elite institutions often need to work to fund their studies and are more likely to follow vocational trajectories (Mullen 2011).

At the point of entry, there has been some levelling of inequality, with working-class students and ethnic minorities increasingly represented in higher education (Croxford & Raffe 2014). Yet social inequalities persist for working-class students who enter the system (Bathmaker, Ingram, & Waller 2013). Students from disadvantaged backgrounds are still 'significantly underrepresented in the undergraduate population, particularly within high-status institutions' (Jerrim 2013). This is because within the same system, the same institution and even the same degree programme, marked differences in participation are evident, depending on the student's access to resources, level of preparation, family support, and capitals. Working-class students are still disadvantaged in complex ways, both before and after entry into higher education (Iannelli 2007). Differences in race, gender and class influence the degrees and subjects that students choose (Iannelli 2007). Young people from disadvantaged backgrounds in the United States and the UK are less likely to develop the advanced cognitive and social skills demanded by elite higher education (Jerrim 2013). In terms of class difference, young people in the United States and Australia with professional parents are more likely to gain access to an elite university compared with young people from working class families (Jerrim & Vignoles 2015). Yet increased equity at the point of entry and quantified outcomes such as success or graduation do not tell us enough about disadvantaged and vulnerable students' quality and equality of participation, and their actual life chances beyond university.

Mapping the spectrum of university experience, including the formation of aspirations for higher education and the process of university selection (Marks, Turner, & Osborne 2003; Reay & Ball 2005), research in the UK nuances the inequalities associated with class and higher education. This includes the complex reasons why working-class students are less likely to choose or access an elite university, how they struggle to claim identity, integration and belonging in the same way as their middle-class and elite peers (Leathwood & O'Connell 2003; Read, Archer, & Leathwood 2003; David & Naidoo 2013; David 2013; Lister 2010 Harwood *et al.* 2016) and why inequalities persist despite widening participation policies. Differences in social class are also reinforced by racial inequalities in access when it comes to choosing a university, thus deepening social stratification (Reay & Ball 2005).

Research also suggests that higher education does not always have positive outcomes for working-class students, because '[t]he balance between the potential benefits as weighed against the risks and costs of participation are differently structured across social class . . . with the result that working-class students face greater risks of failure and and uncertain rewards' (Archer 2003: 119).

In research conducted into student voices and inequalities in European higher education (Finnegan *et al.* 2014), the experiences of 'non-traditional' students across a number of regional contexts nuance the contemporary challenges of inequality in higher education, including how student agency is negotiated despite these challenges (see also Garaz & Torotcoi 2017).

The intersection of race and inequality resonates with race-sensitive critiques of exclusion in North American and European research where ethnic and racial minority students struggle against institutional invisibility, and exclusion. This also reflects an importance historical resonance, particularly as decolonial debates across the global North and South resist the dominance of Eurocentric epistemologies and pedagogical approaches (Ahmed 2012; Mirza 2016; Smith 2012. Similar examples of institution inequalities are found in the Indian context, where questions of inclusion and ethnic quotas remain, despite transformation (Deshpande 2009). In the Indian context, multiple layers of vulnerability such as class and caste reduce the possibility of accessing higher education (Krishna 2014). Parental education and income are also important indicators of participation in higher education, with students marginalised due to class, caste, gender, religion less likely to participate (Pramanik 2015; Subramanian 2015). A key issue in both the international and South Africa scholarship is that demographic diversity, such as representation of race, class or gender, however important, is an incomplete indicator of equal participation.

In conclusion, despite vastly different socioeconomic structures and higher education systems, South Africa and North America, both highly unequal societies, share concerns about inequality in higher education, which include but are not limited to stratification in access, participation and outcomes. In tracing inequality in developed and developing contexts, family income, race, gender, quality of primary and secondary schooling, and socioeconomic status influence the freedom to gain access to and benefit from higher education. Across higher education systems, poorly prepared, disadvantaged students from low-income families – often racial and ethnic minorities – remain concentrated in the lower rungs of higher education institutions, enrolled in community, technical or vocational colleges, or in large generic degree courses with fewer career possibilities than professional degrees. Even when taking into account differences in historical trajectories and complexities across national higher education contexts, structural inequality prevents low-income, working-class and academically underprepared students from accessing high-status degree programmes like medicine at selective universities, attaining the same outcomes, or from benefitting equally from university, when compared with more privileged peers.

Inequality and higher education in the global South

Given the complexities in international higher education above, the book offers a case study of a higher education in the global South, where structural constraints and widening socioeconomic inequalities impact on students' freedom to participate. While I have pointed out important similarities between the global North and South, developing countries negotiate the expanding demand for higher education with comparatively weak infrastructure and a dwindling supply of highly specialised and qualified academics (Altbach *et al.* 2009; Habib 2016). Universities also compete for resources, as national budgets are split into multiple urgent social priorities. Despite different infrastructure and resources, there is mounting pressure to compete for rankings and funding, despite fewer universities in the global South being positioned as centres of knowledge production (Connell 2014; Mbembe 2017). Socioeconomic scarcity intersects with the demands of twenty-first century higher education, where the resources and technology needed to participate are increasingly privatised and unequally distributed (Boni & Walker 2013; Carpentier & Unterhalter 2011). I now turn to the South African context, which despite its unique historical and political trajectory shares many challenges facing higher education in the developing world.

Inequality, massification and South African higher education

While inequalities in higher education are found across systems in the global North and South, the South African landscape presents a complex cluster of entangled historical, social, individual, and institutional factors. These present an intensified situation of inequality within universities. South Africa's transition to democracy in the aftermath of colonial rule and apartheid has been complicated by its legacy of an 'elitist, racially and ethnically fragmented, and inefficient higher education system' (Habib 2016: 43).

Many universities in the global South are transitioning from elite systems with participation rates of under 15 per cent, to massified systems with participation of up to 50 per cent of the age cohort. Although overall participation in higher education on the African continent is still comparatively low, demand in South Africa has increased dramatically, with the national participation level at around 19.5 per cent, compared with the average rate of 6 per cent in sub-Saharan Africa (Unterhalter 2012; DHET 2015. While massified systems offer a much larger percentage of the population access to higher education, this achievement is complicated by the fact that expanding student numbers have in many cases not been met with sufficient resources to maintain academic quality. Across systems in the global South and North, massification brings particular challenges, as demand for higher education expands beyond available capacity (Mok & Wu 2016; Ahunanya, Chineze, & Nnennaya 2013; Rossi 2010; Mamdani 2007). Obvious problems linked to massification are insufficient infrastructure, high staff to student ratios, and the decline of academic quality (Altbach *et al.* 2009; Giannakis & Bullivant 2016; Taylor & Bedford 2004).

The challenges associated with massification and resource scarcity in the South African higher education system are not unique. However, structural constraints associated with expanding demand intersect with poverty, unemployment and income inequality, which affect the majority of South Africa's population (STATS South Africa 2017). Massification has coincided with the need for universities to contribute to sustainable economic growth and institutional transformation (Akoojee & Nkomo 2007; Habib 2016). In South Africa, these challenges contribute to a higher eduaction system that is not sufficiently productive or competitive compared with other developing countries (Habib 2016).

Trade-offs and resources

South African universities are faced with four equally important policy goals, which are equity, efficiency, democratic participation and development (Habib 2016). The implementation challenge has been trying to address these goals simultaneously, within a national context of resource constrains and competing national priorities. Overall, South African state subsidy for higher education has been declining in real terms, which means that while student numbers have increased dramatically, state funding has not increased in relation to the growing student body (Cloete 2016; USAf 2016). South Africa higher education receives about 40 per cent (ZAR 22 billion, ZAR 37 billion) less funding through state subsidies than that which is needed to reach the global average needed to sustain the system (Habib 2016; CHE 2016; Bozzoli 2015; DHET 2013). The percentage of GDP allocated to higher education in South Africa was 0.72 per cent in 2015/2016, which falls short of African and global resource commitments to higher education (Cloete 2016). Moreover, South Africa allocates only 12 per cent of its total expenditure on education to higher education, while other African and OECD countries contribute 20 per cent and 23.4 per cent to higher education respectively (Bozzoli 2015). Because state subsidy has decreased from 49 per cent to the current 40 per cent of total funding in the past 20 years (Cloete 2016), universities have become more reliant on funding from tuition fees and relatively unstable third stream income, which creates uneven endowments across the sector (Altbach *et al.* 2009; Lynch 2005). In South Africa, this has exacerbated the gulf between historically white institutions that are able to align their mandates with the push for international research, and historically Black, rural and underfunded institutions that focus mostly on teaching (Habib 2016).

In response to reduced state subsidy, many institutions have raised tuition fees, which have led to national-wide student protests. Because many students depend on funding and scholarships to afford tuition and basic living costs, escalating fees increase the likelihood of financial exclusion (Mngomezulu, Dhunpath, & Munro 2017). Due to the rising demand for higher education, South Africa's national bursary scheme, the National Student Financial Aid Scheme (NSFAS), is unable to assist all eligible students. Providing bursaries for poor and working-class university students would require an investment of R36-billion from the current R4-billion, while nationally a total of R51-billion would be needed to fund university and college students who qualify for admission (Khosi 2015; Nkopo 2015). Given South Africa's precarious financial situation, the source of such significant additional funding is unknown. The Heher report released in November 2017 suggests income-contingent bank loans as a funding model, which raises serious questions about the impact on the most vulnerable students (Heher 2017). At the beginning of 2018 free higher education was announced for poor and middle-class students, but the feasibility and sustainability of this model would have to be measured over time.

To contextualise the position of undergraduate students, it is also necessary to consider how state funding is distributed at South African universities. Keeping in mind South Africa's high attrition rate, and the fact that only a small percentage of graduates continue to postgraduate studies, state funding for undergraduate teaching input is still significantly higher than funding allocation for teaching outputs or graduations (DHET 2013; Woodiwiss 2008). At the same time, the teaching output grant – i.e. state funding introduced to incentivise increased graduations – is only weighted at 16 per cent (DHET 2013). This means that over 60 per cent of state funding is allocated for enrolments:

> The South African higher education system has, for years, operated a 'win win' situation. Universities admit students who they say are not adequately prepared for higher education. At least 50% of these students fail. But universities take the subsidy (more than 80% of the total government allocation) and blame the school system for the failure. In other words, they keep the money and displace the blame.
>
> (Cloete 2011)

While arguably all students and staff are affected by institutional resource constraints, students with resource insecurity, who are forced to work while studying, are particularly vulnerable to exclusion. Inadequate funding results in poor living conditions and insufficient support needed to adjust to the academic and social demands of university (DHET 2013). In contrast, students from wealthier families can afford basic needs such as tuition and textbooks, and are more likely to possess the academic and social resources and mobility that enable them to navigate the institution.

A lack of resources not only constrains the ability of individual students to cover tuition costs or the institutional commitment to assist poor students. Universities running on insufficient budgets with growing student numbers also face operational constraints that can affect the quality of teaching and learning, the retention of qualified staff, infrastructure, and a basic threshold of resources that poor students need for equal participation (Bozzoli 2015). Under the pressures of an expanding higher education system, persistent patterns of historical inequality, and the need to sustainably fund universities, what is the impact on academically underprepared and socioeconomically vulnerable undergraduate students' freedom to participate once they gain entry into the system?

The dysfunctional public school system

International research confirms that quality of basic and secondary schooling has a direct impact on access to and participation in higher education (Jerrim & Vignoles 2015; Berg 2016). In South Africa, one of the most glaring legacies of the apartheid government is its unequal public school system, which I discuss within the context of student lives in Chapter 4. Scholars agree that many Black, poor and rural South Africans are being denied the right to a basic education, while basic conditions of safety and dignity are absent at many schools (Bloch 2009; DHET 2013). South Africa's segregated legacy has affected its secondary schooling provision for students, most of whom are Black and poor. As an urgent area of research, public schooling requires long-term restructuring and massive investments in infrastructure and capacity building. In the meantime, the intake into higher education from schools that have left many academically capable students underprepared for the academic and social demands of university has increased dramatically at a time when higher education's resources and capacity are being stretched to their limit (Wilson-Strydom 2015).

Race, institutional demographics and transformation

In addition to resource constraints and concerns about schooling, the South Africa sector faces a number of embedded institutional hierarchies, cultures and practices that exclude and marginalise students. During the transition to democracy, higher education policy in South Africa was committed to creating transformed institutions where 'the doors of learning would be open to all'

(ANC 1955). In 1997, the Department of Education's White Paper 3 outlined a programme of transformation and South Africa began constructing its democracy. White Paper 3 stipulated some of higher education's strategic functions as the following:

> To meet the learning needs and aspirations of individuals through the development of their intellectual abilities and aptitudes throughout their lives. Higher education equips individuals to make the best use of their talents and of the opportunities offered by society for self-fulfilment. It is thus a key allocator of life chances and an important vehicle for achieving equity in the distribution of opportunity and achievement among South African citizens.
>
> (MoE 1997: 3)

Since the 1990s, the higher education sector has moved through a number of major transitions in pursuit of these strategic goals. The Department of Higher Education and Training (DHET) has made progress in addressing historical injustices by providing education and training opportunities for young people and adults excluded from participation in the social and economic life (DHET 2013: xi). Since 1994, the university system has a more racially representative cohort of students and graduates (DHET 2013). Yet increased student numbers have transformed the institutional demographic only in absolute numbers, and the overall participation rate of Black[3] students remains low. During the transition to democracy in the early 1990s, and in particular after 1994, the student demographic expanded to include a higher percentage of Black students, which grew from 53 per cent to 67 per cent of the national student population between 1996 and 2010 (CHE 2013). In 2015, when disaggregated by race, only 16.5 per cent of Black students and 14.5 per cent of Coloured students were participating, while a much higher 48.9 per cent of Indian students and 54.7 per cent of white students enrolled (CHE 2017. Even though there has been some improvement in the enrolment rate, there is still evidence of low racial representation for Black and Coloured students. In response to patterns of unequal access, the DHET aims to increase participation to 25 per cent by 2030 (DHET 2013: 30).

These persistent racial disparities in participation do not give a complete picture of the extent of inequality in higher education. A report by the Council on Higher Education (2013) found that as many as 55 per cent of undergraduate students drop out, while only 5 per cent of Black and Coloured students completed their qualifications (CHE 2013). The report found that for the 2006 cohort, 35 per cent graduated within 5 years, while it is estimated that 55 per cent of the intake will never graduate, which means that 70,000 students drop out (CHE 2013: 52).The CHE cites this staggering reality as 'an unacceptable failure to develop the talent in the groups where realisation of potential is most important' (CHE 2013: 51). More recently, disaggregated data on race and gender for the 2012 cohort showed that Black and Coloured males had a 37.5 per cent and 39.5 per cent chance of drop out respectively, while 10.1 per cent of white females were likely to drop out, which also reminds us of the stark historical patterns of inequality along racial lines (DHET 2015: 21).

While racial disparities remain a serious concern, the rise of a racially diverse middle class suggests that an over-simplified analysis of race and participation can downplay the intersectionality of race and class. At issue is the way that resource insecurity and identity misrecognition associated with socioeconomic class are blurred when historically disadvantaged students are treated as a homogenous group. The intersection of race and class provides a more nuanced understanding of the multidimensional nature of unequal participation. The White Paper on the Post-School Sector summarises the intersection of race and class as the following:

> A growing Black middle class has been empowered by the new conditions created by the arrival of democracy, and its members have managed to transform their lives in many ways. However, the majority of South Africans have still to attain a decent standard of living. Most Black people are still poor; they are still served by lower quality public services and institutions (including public educational institutions) than the well-off.
> (DHET 2013: 4)

Persistently low graduation rates at the intersection of race and class require structural conditions that enable equal participation for students who experience intersectional vulnerability.

Universities have invested in re-designing teaching and learning structures to enable equitable access to knowledge. However, transformation is spread unevenly across institutions and deep forms of pedagogical and curricular transformation have been slow to take hold (CHE 2016). Earmarked funding and infrastructure in dedicated access, support and foundational programmes have afforded places at universities to students who would not previously have been admitted. Interventions to address the needs of underprepared students include, for example, curriculum development, staff support and student mentoring, and resources have been allocated to improve the quality of undergraduate teaching and learning (DHET 2013).

The inequalities mapped out above reproduce and deepen the injustices that policies for expanded access, participation and success seek to address. Thus, while the *doors* of learning might be open to more students, there is much concern about what happens within the *walls* of higher education (see also Fataar 2017). Working from the assumption that there are significant differences between policy goals and lived experiences of students and staff in higher education (Bozalek & Boughey 2012), complex structural inequalities are found in 'the subtext of the organisational life even as institutions seek to transform' (CHE 2010: 179).

Individual deficit or structural inequality?

Within the context of these systemic challenges, the concern in this book is how the benefits of higher education are distributed across the student body. Once students gain access to higher education, with its potential to increase employability and address structural inequalities, how are real opportunities to participate and benefit distributed, and how do working-class, rural and Black students in non-elite degree courses benefit? Under the pressures of an expanding higher education system and persistent patterns of historical inequality, concerns about unsustainable student to staff ratios (DHET 2013), the need to adequately fund universities, and the pressure to conduct research, what is the impact on academically underprepared and socioeconomically vulnerable undergraduate students' freedom to participate once they gain entry into the system?

Having crossed multiple economic and social hurdles to gain access to university, students enter and navigate higher education institutions that are fraught with structural inequalities. Students are likely to enter institutions that are unprepared to afford them the equal freedoms they need to negotiate academic, financial, psychological, social and personal challenges (Barnett 2007; Otto *et al.* 2017). Instead of equal access to resources and opportunities, students are likely to face intersectional discrimination such as racism, classism and sexism, untransformed institutional structures, and epistemologies that reflect colonial and apartheid-era legacies (Department of Education (DoE) 2008). Instead of being welcomed into a community of emerging scholars and citizens, Black, working class and rural undergraduate students in particular are more likely to be treated as outsiders, problems or outliers, while students' resources and capabilities are less likely to be assimilated into the institutional culture.

For a tangible micro-analysis of such structural inequality, consider the following two scenarios for a Black, female, first-generation[4] student. In the first scenario, the student does not have reliable access to basic needs like nutritious food, decent housing, transport, and money for photocopies and textbooks. Her family is poor and her bursary does not cover living costs and academic expenses like books. She spends a lot of time worrying about money, walking long distances to unsafe accommodation where a landlord threatens to evict her if she cannot pay her rent. She enters an institution that measures her potential with standardised entry scores. When this student appears to disengage in the classrooms or performs poorly in exams, her lack of skills is then addressed as the primary obstacle to her success. She is assigned to a foundational programme to address her academic and social 'deficits'. The programme is based on generic study and language skills, separated from the mainstream cohort, and misaligned with the academic demands of her degree programme. These courses perpetuate low expectations and remind her of her status as an outsider. Most of her classes are crowded; there are few opportunities for lecturer interaction or small group tutorials. Because of meritocratic selection criteria, she does not have the opportunity to participate in extracurricular or leadership programmes.

In the classroom, she is frequently reminded of how 50 per cent of students will never graduate, and of her inability to pass challenging modules. Around her she notices peers who are confident and seem to be doing well, but she does not know what their 'secret to success' could be. She tries to study harder and spends a lot of time alone at the library, but she barely passes tests and assignments, feels lonely and overwhelmed, and is always worried about money for food transport and textbooks. She was expecting university to be an amazing experience, but she feels like an outsider.

Now imagine this same individual in a different environment. Her family is poor but she has access to a bursary that covers all her basic living costs with enough money to buy nutritious food. She has reliable access to the Internet and is able to afford textbooks for her course. She lives on campus in an integrated residence where she receives social support and opportunities for development. She is not placed on a foundational programme that separates her from her peers. Instead, foundational support is embedded in her department as discipline-specific support structures available to all students on her degree course. Her department offers a capacity-building programme staffed with dedicated senior students and postgraduate students to mentor undergraduates in the discourses and theoretical traditions of the discipline. Her degree programme has a tutorial system for every subject that does not teach students to memorise content for the next test, but offers research-based projects around pertinent questions in the discipline. The tutorials encourage critical reading and writing development on a weekly basis in line with challenging academic content.

There is a discipline-specific programme taught by lecturers and professors in her subject area that focuses on developing academic literacies and capabilities for practical reasoning. Her time studying is not alone in the library or in her room, but with undergraduate peers working on interdisciplinary projects. These projects bring knowledge and practice together in finding research-based solutions to problems relevant to their discipline. Although the environment is challenging, she is reminded frequently of her potential, encouraged to challenge herself and reminded that, despite being a 'beginner' at the institution, she has the ability and necessary support to succeed. There are regular opportunities for social support, and a counsellor dedicated to her faculty that is available to address psychosocial needs. She is part of a cohort of students and lecturers from her first year until graduation. She is busy, challenged, and often stressed, but she feels integrated into her department, has good relationships with peers and staff members, and has a sense of belonging to her department and the institution.

Now imagine the equality of participation in these two different scenarios. The student immersed in either scenario might graduate, and despite facing the first scenario, some students do graduate. But this reveals nothing about the capabilities that the institution enabled them to cultivate. If the student in the first scenario fails to graduate, we are likely to attribute this to her lack of preparation, literacy, social capital, motivation, poor schooling, home environment, effort or talent. What would undergraduates be capable of achieving if enabling pedagogical and institutional structures were equally available across degree programmes and institutions?

Researching inequality and student lives

In this chapter, I have mapped out South African higher education as a complex landscape marked by uneven freedoms and opportunities, and the historical inequalities that characterise the country's economic and social segregation. While universities may offer knowledge, employment and social mobility, they are also complex spaces where resources and opportunities are unequally distributed. Unequal participation is also rooted in historical and persistent injustices that require rigorous technical innovation, theoretical engagement, and pedagogical redesign. I applied a capability approach to analyse student experiences of participation at the intersection of distributional inequality, misrecognition, institutional cultures and pedagogical arrangements. The capability framework enabled an analysis of injustices while retaining a focus on the agency and resources that students bring to higher education. Given the structural constrains discussed above, how do students convert available pedagogical and institutional arrangements and resources into participation?

While data on access and outcomes are important, they do not sketch the entire landscape of structural and individual complexities and tensions embedded within South Africa's low participation and high drop-out system, and we still know relatively little about in-depth student experiences. For this reason, I designed the research as a longitudinal, participatory project that included students as co-investigators of their experiences. I collected student narratives to deepen my understanding of how inequalities enable or contain the freedom to participate at university. Student experiences include socioeconomic, academic, emotional and community dimensions. The book offers a nuanced, critical and narrative account of how individual students navigate the academic and social spaces of a public South African university[5] with fewer resources and opportunities. Participant narratives represent a small slice of everyday, structural inequalities, and illustrate the trade-offs that students make to achieve participation. Their narratives suggest that far from being passive, disengaged victims of poverty, individuals negotiate structural inequalities with agency and resistance.

Drawing on the student narratives, I present a capability-informed praxis for undergraduate students based on the student narratives. This praxis conceptualised equal participation on a spectrum where on the one end, equality means access to the resources, opportunities and arrangements needed to achieve valued outcomes aligned with student capabilities, agency and aspirations. On the other end of the spectrum, unequal participation refers to students positioned precariously at the institution, who are vulnerable to drop out, face resource scarcity, and do not have sustained access to pedagogical or institutional arrangements that enable them to convert available resources into the freedom for equal participation. I conceptualised six capabilities for equal participation based on the student narratives.

Navigating the book chapters

The chapters are designed to be read together as a research narrative, moving from the context, to the conceptual framing, and analysis of student narratives, and culminating in the capability-informed praxis.

In Chapter 1, I map out inequality in higher education, and give an overview of challenges in the South African higher education landscape. The chapter explores the impact of structural inequality on the lives of individual students.

The second chapter is a critical overview of structural inequality in higher education, drawing on relevant research used to construct the research problem. In this review, I focus on two primary approaches to student participation: the first approach addresses unequal participation using a remedial approach to student problems; while the other, more critical cluster takes a structural approach to unequal participation.

In the third chapter, I introduce the capability approach and critical social theory as the conceptual framework used to collect and analyse student narratives. The capability approach is founded on the principles of social justice and human development, which focus on both agency and structure in addressing unequal arrangements.

Chapter 4 is an introduction to student narratives before their entry into higher education. I focus on how schooling reproduces inequalities and cultivates aspirations, and how students navigate these challenges using their agency.

Chapter 5 focuses on pedagogical and institutional arrangements that constrain the freedom for equal participation. I distil five conversion factors that constrain unequal participation.

In Chapter 6, I explore conversion factors that enable participation in higher education.

Chapter 7 draws on narratives to suggest praxis for higher education based on the development of six capabilities and more fair and equal distribution of resources in higher education.

Chapter 8 interrogates how universities could cultivate arrangements that enable the most vulnerable students to convert available resources and opportunities into capabilities for equal participation.

Notes

1 We must scrutinise the promise that 'education leads to skills, skills lead to employment, employment leads to economic growth, economic growth creates jobs and is the way out of poverty and inequality' (Klees 2014; see also Allen *et al.* 2013). While some graduates do find employment, many who enter the system never complete a degree, and join the millions of South Africans who are unemployed and unable to access real

opportunities for education or training. The assumption that higher education can provide access to the market system 'places the burden of responsibility squarely on individuals and their "deficits" while obscuring the real obstacles to procuring decent and remunerative employment' (Vally & Motala 2014: 6).
2   The statistic is based on the expanded definition of unemployment, which includes discouraged job seekers.
3   In this chapter, Black as a racial category does not depict a homogenous identity or experience, but reflects the persistence of racialized classification due to apartheid legislation.
4   The definition of first-generation students used in this book is students who are the first person in their family to attend university.
5   The student participants were situated at a historically white, urban university. Despite having comparatively more resources than historically Black, rural South African universities, the institution is under pressure from an expanding student body. The institution also faces specific transformation challenges, as it struggles to overcome its racialised legacy (Habib 2016). Another challenge is that as an institution traditionally focused on teaching, the university is also positioning itself as increasingly competitive in terms of research outputs in the national context.

References

Ahmed, S., 2012. *On Being Included: Racism and Diversity in Institutional Life*. Durham, NC: Duke University Press.

Ahunanya, S., Chineze, U., & Nnennaya, I., 2013. Massification of University Education in Nigeria: Private Participation and Cost Challenges. *Africa Education Review* 10, 65–79.

Akoojee, S., & Nkomo, S., 2007. Access and Quality in South African Higher Education: The Twin Challenges of Transformation. *South African Journal of Higher Education* 21, 385–399.

Allen, K., Quinn, J., Hollingworth, S., & Rose, A., 2013. Becoming Employable Students and 'Ideal' Creative Workers: Exclusion and Inequality in Higher Education Work Placements. *British Journal of Sociology of Education* 34, 431–452. https://doi.org/10.1080/01425692.2012.714249

Altbach, P.G., Rumbley, L., & Reisberg, L., 2009. Trends in Global Higher Education: Tracking an Academic Revolution (UNESCO 2009 World Conference on Higher Education). United Nations Educational, Scientific and Cultural Organization, Paris.

ANC 1955. The Freedom Charter: www.sahistory.org.za/article/freedom-charter

Archer, L., 2003. Social Class and Higher Education. In Archer, L., Hutchings, M., & Ross, A. (Eds), *Higher Education and Social Class: Issues of Exclusion and Inclusion*. London and New York: Routledge, pp. 5–44.

Archer, L., Hutchings, M., & Ross, A., 2005. *Higher Education and Social Class: Issues of Exclusion and Inclusion*. London and New York: Routledge.

Armstrong, E.A., & Hamilton, L.T., 2013. *Paying for the Party: How College Maintains Inequality*. Cambridge, MA: Harvard University Press.

Barnett, R., 2007. *A Will to Learn: Being a Student in an Age of Uncertainty*. New York: McGraw-Hill.

Bathmaker, A.-M., Ingram, N., & Waller, R., 2013. Higher Education, Social Class and the Mobilisation of Capitals: Recognising and Playing the Game. *British Journal of Sociology of Education* 34, 723–743.

Berg, G.A., 2016. *Low-Income Students and the Perpetuation of Inequality: Higher Education in America*. London and New York: Routledge.

Bloch, G., 2009. *The Toxic Mix: What's Wrong with South Africa's Schools and How to Fix It*. Tafelberg: Cape Town.

Boni, A., & Walker, M., 2013. *Human Development and Capabilities: Re-imagining the University of the Twenty-first Century*. London and New York: Routledge.

Bozalek, V., & Boughey, C., 2012. (Mis)framing Higher Education in South Africa. *Social Policy & Administration* 46(6), 688–703. https://doi.org/10.1111/j.1467-9515.2012.00863.x

Broekhuizen, H., & Van der Berg, S., 2013. How High Is Graduate Unemployment in South Africa? A Much Needed Update. (RESEP (Research on Socio-economic Policy), Department of Economics). University of Stellenbosch.

Brown, J.R., & Hoxby, C.M., 2015. *How the Financial Crisis and Great Recession Affected Higher Education*. Chicago, IL: University Of Chicago Press.

Brown, R.N., 2009. *Black Girlhood Celebration: Toward a Hip-hop Feminist Pedagogy*. New York, NY: Peter Lang.

Burke, P.J., 2012. *The Right to Higher Education: Beyond Widening Participation*. London and New York: Routledge.

Carpentier, V., & Unterhalter, E., 2011. Globalization, Higher Education, and Inequalities: Problems and Prospects. In King, R., Marginson, S., & Naidoo, R. (Eds), *Handbook on Globalization and Higher Education*. Cheltenham: Edward Elgar Publishing.

CHE, 2010. *Access and Throughput in South African Higher Education: Three Case Studies*. Higher Education Monitor. Pretoria: Council on Higher Education.

CHE, 2013. *A Proposal for Undergraduate Curriculum Reform in South Africa: The Case for a Flexible Curriculum Structure*. Council on Higher Education, Pretoria, South Africa. www.che.ac.za/sites/default/files/publications/Full_Report.pdf

CHE, 2016. *South African Higher Education Reviewed – Two Decades of Democracy*. Council on Higher Education, Pretoria, South Africa.

CHE, 2017. *Vital Stats. Public Higher Education 2015*. Council on Higher Education, Pretoria, South Africa.

Chomsky, N., & Polychroniou, C.J., 2017. *Optimism over Despair: On Capitalism, Empire, and Social Change*. Chicago, IL: Haymarket Books.

Cloete, N., 2011. South Africa: Radical New Plan for Higher Education. *University World News*, 4 December 2011, 200. www.universityworldnews.com/article.php?story=2011120222252975

Cloete, N., 2016. *The Ideology of Free Higher Education in South Africa: The Poor, the Rich and the Missing Middle*. Pretoria: Council on Higher Education.

Connell, R., 2014. Rethinking Gender from the South. *Feminist Studies* 40, 518–539.

Croxford, L., & Raffe, D., 2014. Social Class, Ethnicity and Access to Higher Education in the Four Countries of the UK: 1996–2010. *International Journal of Lifelong Education* 33, 77–95.

David, M., 2013. Equity and Diversity: Towards a Sociology of Higher Education for the Twenty-first Century? In Naidoo, R., & David, M. (Eds), *The Sociology of Higher Education: Reproduction, Transformation and Change in a Global Era*. London and New York: Routledge.

David, M., Bathmaker, A.-M., Crozier, G., Davis, P., Ertl, H., Fuller, A., Hayward, G., Heath, S., Hockings, C., Parry, G., Reay, D., Vignoles, A., & Williams, J., 2009.

Improving Learning by Widening Participation in Higher Education. London and New York: Routledge.

David, M., Naidoo, R., 2013. *The Sociology of Higher Education: Reproduction, Transformation and Change in a Global Era*. London and New York: Routledge.

Department of Education (DoE). (2008). Report of the Ministerial Committee on Transformation and Social Cohesion and the Elimination of Discrimination in Public Higher Education Institutions: Final Report. Pretoria, South Africa: DoE. www.voced.edu.au/content/ngv:61442

Deshpande, S., 2009. Inclusion versus Excellence: Caste and the Framing of Fair Access in Indian Higher Education. *South African Review of Sociology* 40, 127–147.

DHET, 2012. *Staffing South Africa's Universities Framework: A Comprehensive, Transformative Approach to Developing Future Generations of Academics and Building Staff Capacity*. Pretoria, South Africa.

DHET, 2013. *White Paper on Post School Training: Building an Expanded, Effective and Integrated Post-school System*. Pretoria: Department of Higher Education and Training, Republic of South Africa.

DHET, 2014. *Ministerial Statement on University Funding: 2015/16 AND 2016/17*. Pretoria: Department of Higher Education and Training, Republic of South Africa.

DHET, 2015. *Are We Making Progress with Systemic Structural Transformation of Resourcing, Access, Success, Staffing and Researching in Higher Education: What Do the Data Say?* Pretoria: Department of Higher Education and Training, Republic of South Africa., 2nd National Higher Education Summit 15–17 October 2015.

DHET, 2017. Fact Sheet on 'NEETS' (Persons who are not in employment, education or training). Pretoria: Department of Higher Education and Training, Republic of South Africa.

Fataar, A., 2017. Decolonising Education in South Africa: An Interview with Aslam Fataar. Litnet. www.litnet.co.za/decolonising-education-south-africa-interview-aslam-fataar/

Finnegan, F., Merrill, B., & Thunborg, C., 2014. *Student Voices on Inequalities in European Higher Education: Challenges for Theory, Policy and Practice in a Time of Change*. London and New York: Routledge.

Fioramonti, L., 2017. *Wellbeing Economy: Success in a World without Growth*, 1st edn. Johannesburg: Pan Macmillan.

Garaz, S., & Torotcoi, S., 2017. Increasing Access to Higher Education and the Reproduction of Social Inequalities: The Case of Roma University Students in Eastern and Southeastern Europe. *European Education* 49, 10–35. https://doi.org/10.1080/10564934.2017.1280334

Giannakis, M., & Bullivant, N., 2016. The Massification of Higher Education in the UK: Aspects of Service Quality. *Journal of Further and Higher Education* 40, 630–648.

Giroux, H.A., 2013. Public Intellectuals against the Neoliberal University. 29 October, 2013. *Truthout*. www.truth-out.org/opinion/item/19654-public-intellectuals-against-the-neoliberal-university

Goldrick-Rab, S., 2016. *Paying the Price: College Costs, Financial Aid, and the Betrayal of the American Dream*. Chicago, IL: University Of Chicago Press.

Habib, A., 2016. Transcending the Past and Reimagining the Future of the South African University. *Journal of Southern African Studies* 42, 35–48. https://doi.org/10.1080/03057070.2016.1121716

Harwood, V., Hickey-Moody, A., & McMahon, S., 2016. *The Politics of Widening Participation and University Access for Young People: Making Educational Futures.* London and New York: Routledge.

Heher, J., 2017. *Interim Report of The Commission into the Feasibility of Fee-Free Higher Education and Training. Commission for Inquiry into Higher Education*, Pretoria, South Africa.

Iannelli, C., 2007. Inequalities in Entry to Higher Education: A Comparison over Time between Scotland and England and Wales. *Higher Education Quarterly* 61, 306–333.

Ilie, S., & Rose, P., 2016. Is Equal Access to Higher Education in South Asia and Sub-Saharan Africa Achievable by 2030? *Higher Education* 72, 435–455. https://doi.org/10.1007/s10734-016-0039-3

Jacob, W.J., & Holsinger, D.B., 2008. Inequality in Education: A Critical Analysis. In Holsinger, D.B., & Jacob, W.J. (Eds), *Inequality in Education*, CERC Studies in Comparative Education. Springer Netherlands, pp. 1–33. https://doi.org/10.1007/978-90-481-2652-1_1

Jerrim, J., 2013. Family Background and Access to 'High Status' Universities. Sutton Trust. https://www.raeng.org.uk/publications/other/family-background-and-access-to-high-status-univer

Jerrim, J., & Vignoles, A., 2015. University access for disadvantaged children: a comparison across countries. *High Education* 70, 903–921. https://doi.org/10.1007/s10734-015-9878-6

Khosi, B. 2015. State Leaves Students High and Dry. 23 January 2015. *Mail & Guardian.* https://mg.co.za/article/2015-01-23-state-leaves-students-high-and-dry

King, R., Marginson, S., & Naidoo, R., 2011. *Handbook on Globalization and Higher Education.* Cheltenham: Edward Elgar Publishing.

Klees, 2014. Neoliberal Policies Destroy Human Potential and Devastate Education. *Mail & Guardian.* 18 July 2014. https://mg.co.za/article/2014-07-18-neoliberal-policies-destroy-human-potential-and-devastate-education

Krishna, A., 2014. Examining the Structure of Opportunity and Social Mobility in India: Who Becomes an Engineer? *Development & Change* 45, 1–28. https://doi.org/10.1111/dech.12072

Leathwood, C., & O'Connell, P., 2003. 'It's a Struggle': The Construction of the 'New Student' in Higher Education. *Journal of Education Policy* 18, 597–615. https://doi.org/10.1080/0268093032000145863

Lister, R., 2010. Ladder of Opportunity or Engine of Inequality? *The Political Quarterly* 77, 232–236.

Lynch, K., 2006. Neo-Liberalism and Marketisation: The Implications for Higher Education. *European Educational Research Journal* 5, 1–17.

Macheke, 2015. To Be Young, Privileged & Black: A Word on the Mimicry & Assimilation of White Hegemony. The Suburban Zulu. https://suburbanzulu.wordpress.com/2015/05/01/mimickingwhitehegemony/

Mamdani, M., 2007. *Scholars in the Marketplace. The Dilemmas of Neo-Liberal Reform at Makerere University, 1989–2005.* African Books Collective.

Marks, A., Turner, E., & Osborne, M., 2003. 'Not for the Likes of Me': The Overlapping Effect of Social Class and Gender Factors in the Decision Made By Adults Not to Participate in Higher Education. *Journal of Further and Higher Education* 27, 347–364. https://doi.org/10.1080/0309877032000128064

Mbembe, A., 2017. *Critique of Black Reason.* Durham, NC: Duke University Press.

Mettler, S., 2014. *Degrees of Inequality: How the Politics of Higher Education Sabotaged the American Dream.* New York, NY: Basic Books.
Mirza, H.S., 2016. Decolonizing Higher Education: Black Feminism and the Intersectionality of Race and Gender. *The Journal of Feminist Scholarship* 7–8, 1–6.
Mngomezulu, S., Dhunpath, R., & Munro, N., 2017. Does Financial Assistance Undermine Academic Success? Experiences of 'At Risk' Students in a South African University. *Journal of Education* 68, 131–148.
MoE, 1997. Education White Paper 3 – *A Programme for the Transformation of Higher Education.* Pretoria: South African Ministry of Education.
Mok, K.H. & Wu, A.M., 2016. Higher Education, Changing Labour Market and Social Mobility in the Era of Massification in China. *Journal of Education and Work* 29, 77–97.
Morley, L., & Lugg, R., 2009. Mapping Meritocracy: Intersecting Gender, Poverty and Higher Educational Opportunity Structures. *Higher Education Policy* 22, 37–60. https://doi.org/10.1057/hep.2008.26
Mthethwa, N., 2013. 'How Could I Have Failed Varsity'? *Mail & Guardian.* http://mg.co.za/article/2013-01-11-how-could-i-have-failed-varsity
Mullen, A.L., 2011. *Degrees of Inequality: Culture, Class, and Gender in American Higher Education.* Johns Hopkins University Press, Baltimore, MD; Bognor Regis.
Naidoo, R., 2010. Global Learning in a NeoLiberal Age: Implications for Development. In Unterhalter, E. (Ed.), *Global Inequalities and Higher Education: Whose Interests Are You Serving?* London: Palgrave Macmillan.
Nkopo, A., 2015. We still don't belong here. *The Star.* 8 September, 2015. https://www.iol.co.za/the-star/we-still-dont-belong-here-1912238
Nussbaum, M.C., 2012. *Not for Profit: Why Democracy Needs the Humanities.* With a New afterword by the author. Princeton University Press, Princeton, NJ; Woodstock.
Nwadeyi, L., 2017. Decolonising the Curriculum: Justice, Humanisation and Healing through Education. University of Pretoria. www.up.ac.za/en/department-of-university-relations/calendar/event-info/2422146/public-lecture-series-decolonising-the-curriculum-justice-humanisation-and-healing-through-education
Otto, H.-U., Pantazis, S., Ziegler, H., & Potsi, A., 2017. *Human Development in Times of Crisis – Renegotiating Social Justice.* London: Palgrave.
Pramanik, S., 2015. The Effect of Family Characteristics on Higher Education Attendance in India: A Multivariate Logit Approach. *Higher Education for the Future* 2, 49–70.
Read, B., Archer, L., & Leathwood, C., 2003. Challenging Cultures? Student Conceptions of 'Belonging' and 'Isolation' at a Post-1992 University. *Studies in Higher Education* 28, 261–277. https://doi.org/10.1080/03075070309290
Reay, D., & Ball, S.J., 2005. *Degrees of Choice: Class, Race, Gender and Higher Education.* London: Trentham Books.
Robeyns, I., 2016. Having Too Much (SSRN Scholarly Paper No. ID 2736094). Social Science Research Network, Rochester, NY.
Rossi, F., 2010. Massification, Competition and Organizational Diversity in Higher Education: Evidence from Italy. *Studies in Higher Education* 35, 277–300. https://doi.org/10.1080/03075070903050539
Smith, L.T., 2012. *Decolonizing Methodologies: Research and Indigenous Peoples*, 2nd edn. London: Zed Books.
STATS South Africa. 2017. Quarterly Employment Statistics (QES) June 2017.

Stuart, M., 2002. *Collaborating for Change? Managing Widening Participation in Further and Higher Education*. Leicester: National Institute of Adult Continuing Education (NIACE).

Subramanian, A., 2015. Making Merit: The Indian Institutes of Technology and the Social Life of Caste. *Comparative Studies in Society & History* 57, 291–322. https://doi.org/10.1017/S0010417515000043

Taylor, J.A. & Bedford, T., 2004. Staff Perceptions of Factors Related to Non-completion in Higher Education. *Studies in Higher Education* 29, 375–394. https://doi.org/10.1080/03075070410001682637

Unterhalter, E., 2010. *Global Inequalities and Higher Education: Whose Interests Are You Serving?* London: Palgrave Macmillan.

Unterhalter, E., 2017. Global: What is Wrong with Global Inequality in Higher Education? In *Understanding Global Higher Education, Global Perspectives on Higher Education*. SensePublishers, Rotterdam, pp. 1–7. https://doi.org/10.1007/978-94-6351-044-8_1

USAf, 2016. *Universities Funding in South Africa; A Fact Sheet.* Universities South Africa.

Vally, S., & Motala, E., 2014. *Education, Economy & Society.* Pretoria: Unisa Press.

Walker, M. & McLean, M., 2013. Professional Education, Capabilities and the Public Good: The Role of Universities in Promoting Human Development, 1st edn. ed. London and New York: Routledge.

Wilson-Strydom, M., 2015. *University Access and Success: Capabilities, Diversity and Social Justice.* London and New York: Routledge.

Woodiwiss, A.J., 2012. Publication Subsidies: Challenges and Dilemmas Facing South African Researchers. *Cardiovascular Journal of South Africa* 23, 421–427.

World Bank, 2017. Unemployment, Youth Total (% of total labour force ages 15–24) (modelled ILO estimate). http://data.worldbank.org/indicator/SL.UEM.1524.ZS

Zajda, J., Biraimah, K., & Gaudelli, W., 2008. *Education and Social Inequality in the Global Culture.* New York, NY: Springer Science & Business Media.

Chapter 2

Structures of unequal participation

Building onto my overview of global and South African inequalities in higher education, this chapter focuses on the impact of economic policies on pedagogical arrangements in higher education, and the impact on vulnerable students. The first section analyses macro-economic policies that contribute towards resource scarcity and institutional constraints in higher education. In the second section, I discuss how such policies have contributed to a deficit approach to vulnerable students, especially in undergraduate academic support programmes.[1] The second section examines how the combination of systemic constraints and the deficit approach permeates academic programmes designed to increase vulnerable students' participation and success in higher education. In the final section, I offer an analysis of literature that resists a deficit approach within pedagogy and support programmes.

Structural inequality in global higher education

Despite important differences in national and international contexts, scholars in the global North and South agree that significant changes in the management of public higher education can be attributed in part to neoliberal policies (Lynch 2006. In the global North, four decades of economic neoliberalism have had a profound impact on higher education policies (Altbach, Rumbley, & Reisberg 2009; Deem 2001; Giroux 2013; Gray 2016; le Grange 2011; Lynch 2006). Giroux situates neoliberalism as a logic that widens existing inequalities and clusters advantage for the benefit of political elites (Giroux 2014). A neoliberal logic erodes collective responsibility, public values and a concern with the public good and replaces these with individualism, in which personal responsibility is held as the primary indicator of achievement (Giroux 2014; see also Brennan & Naidoo 2008; Naidoo 2010).

Neoliberal policies have a profound yet uneven effect on the function and structure of higher education, which is evident in pedagogy and institutional cultures at universities (Marginson 2011; Naidoo 2011; Pennington *et al.* 2017; Vally & Motala 2013; Walker 2012):

Neoliberalism, by shifting educational policy away from the local level, turning education into a competitive market, and using testing and test scores as a management technique, creates [institutions] where students and teachers rarely focus on the relationship they have with one another and with the human and ecological community in which they are situated.

(Henderson & Hursh 2014: 169)

Such policies have shaped universities against the backdrop of national and institutional contexts, which produce unique challenges, opportunities and risks across the higher education system (Naidoo 2010). With higher education framed as a global commodity, its traditional role as a public good has been eroded, which poses risks for the broader goals of human development and well-being (Boni & Walker 2013; Marginson 2011; Naidoo 2010; Naidoo & Williams 2015; Nussbaum 2012).

Globally, the dominant narrative in higher education is that universities are drivers of economic development in a knowledge economy (Naidoo 2010). However, high-skills knowledge economies are unevenly cultivated in developing contexts, where human development and high-skill jobs are scarcer and more precarious, despite the attainment of higher education (Naidoo 2010). The promise of a knowledge economy, with its autonomous, socially mobile, and creative knowledge workers, is less likely to take hold in developing contexts such as South Africa, where much knowledge work is likely to be characterised by 'routinization, surveillance, and exploitation' (Naidoo 2010: 69; see also Vally & Motala 2014). Critical perspectives thus question the promise that higher education is able to provide high-level skills, technical expertise and decent employment across the system (Valley & Motala 2014). Such criticism foregrounds the distinction between students who have access to a rich bundle of marketable degrees, professional networks and academic participation, in contrast to vulnerable students who have limited opportunities to achieve the same capabilities.

Another risk facing higher education is that instead of leading the way to sustainable solutions that resist neoliberal policies, universities then become a significant part of the problem (Boni & Walker 2013). For instance, corporate interests embedded into universities risk overshadowing the urgency of distributional justice within and between nations (Robeyns 2016; Nussbaum 2012; Feldman & Gellert 2010). Higher education institutions that compromise their position as an ethical voice in transformation and economic redistribution suggest that 'the notion of social justice has been appropriated into a neoliberal strategy for growing competitive economics' (Singh 2011: 482; see also Akoojee & Nkomo 2007; Bauman 2009). Such instrumentalism of higher education is evident in the failure to consider how market-driven skills acquisition erodes the construction of higher education as a public good, and stifles the contributions of critical academic and student voices (Giroux 2005). As universities in the global North are pressured to become increasingly corporate, 'the narrower economic policies of neoliberals have caused not only great harm in how we think about ourselves and our relationship with one another and the natural world, but also to our educational system' (Henderson & Hursh 2014: 168).

Structural inequality in South African higher education

In a developing economy such as South Africa, higher education is not structured explicitly for individual or corporate profit, as is evident in critiques of academic capitalism in the global North (Johnson & Hirt 2010; Olssen & Peters 2005; Slaughter & Rhoades 2011). Yet despite its commitment to equity in a post-apartheid context, South Africa is not immune to the international neoliberalising shifts (Habib 2016; le Grange 2011; Pennington *et al.* 2017; Vally & Motala 2014; Boni & Walker 2013). Global trends under a neoliberal logic identified in both developed and developing higher education, particularly relevant to South African universities, include the following: increased tuition fees and diminishing state funding (Altbach *et al.* 2009; Brock-Utne 2003; Habib 2016; Lynch 2006); the introduction of intensive managerial and efficiency measures (Besley & Peters 2006; Giroux 2014; Gray 2016; Maistry 2012; Mbembe 2016); degrees that are increasingly orientated to market demands (Mamdani 2007; Naidoo & Williams 2015; Nussbaum 2010; Shrivastava & Shrivastava 2014); the erosion of intellectual autonomy (Cini & Guzmán-Concha 2017; Labaree 2017); and precarious employment conditions for university staff (Altbach 2013; Johnson & Hirt 2010; Pennington *et al.* 2017).

In the global South, the risks associated with neoliberal policies – the erosion of intellectual culture, unsustainable workloads, disproportionate power given to corporate interests, and the declining status of teaching as compared to research – are compounded by systemic challenges such complex inequalities, and widespread poverty and unemployment. As part of the pressure on developing countries to compete internationally and become more efficient, 'managerial practices and accountability mechanisms from the corporate sector have been unthinkingly imported into public institutions and universities' (Habib 2016: 45; see also Deem 2001). To this end, the power of decision-making has shifted from academics to administrators and managers, as '[u]niversities are increasingly treated as business entities' where '[p]rofitability rather than sustainability seems to be the driving ethos' (Habib 2016: 46). In protests across Europe, Latin America and Africa, students are resisting socioeconomic and political processes such as funding cuts, outsourcing, and managerialisation (Cini & Guzmán-Concha 2017). In South Africa, students and scholars have used the #FeesMustFall protest movement to resist 'the dangerous construction of higher education as a big business' (McKenna *et al.* 2015). This reflects a growing concern about the integrity of public universities, as expressed by academics: '[A]s students fees escalate, along with student debt, as workers are outsourced to private companies, large bonuses are paid to senior administrators, and academic life is increasingly corporatized' (McKenna *et al.* 2015).

Scholars working in African universities have critiqued policies that reduce funding for academic programmes that are less productive, reduced budgets for departments that are less able to align their academic project with marketable outputs, and for framing students as customers of academic commodities (Mamdani in Gooch & Ruderman 2016; see also Deem 2001; Johnson & Hirt 2010; Habib 2016; Nussbaum 2010; Lynch 2006; Mbembe 2016).

As an emerging economy, South Africa faces multiple global and local pressures, such as the historical legacy of uneven institutional development due to racialised segregation, which has left historically Black, rural higher education institutions 'under-developed' and under-resourced (Habib 2016; Bozalek & Boughey 2012). Another critique is that an expanding private higher education sector intensifies managerial practices that frame students as 'clients' (Naidoo & Williams 2015; Zepke 2016). While committed in theory to equity, South African universities navigate the pressure to compete for international funding, rankings and publications, expanding research and innovation, and responding to a huge demand for undergraduate teaching. This pressure has led to efficiency measures such as contract-based teaching and incentives for research output that diminish the quality and efficiency of the academic programmes that underprepared students need to succeed (DHET 2013).

Critics of neoliberal influences in South Africa higher education cite the rise of an audit culture, state influence, and quality assurance as reflective of broader social pressures (le Grange 2011). At issue is how these new forms of managerialism complicate the precarious position of underprepared, disadvantaged students in higher education. What is the impact on the most vulnerable students when acadmeic staff are scrambling to meet deadlines, publish in internatinal journals, raise third-stream income, and teach large undergraduate classes while supervising graduate students; which of these is less likely to garner resources, time and energy, in the way that teaching, researching and fund raising are incentivised?

The deficit approach, resources and massification

It is inevitable that the macro pressures of structural inequality, massification, and the resource crisis will filter into the academic life of the university. In the following section, I explore how macro institutional pressures and constraints contribute to the construction of a deficit approach to vulnerable students. A deficit approach is an overemphasis on the individual student's responsibility to succeed, despite social inequalities and unjust structural arrangements in higher education. A deficit discourse has also been defined as:

> the growing dominance of a neo-liberal culture emphasising individual competitiveness and responsibility spreading through society. . . . A meritocratic

ideology is central to this culture, bringing with it the message that your problems are all your fault. And similarly, your privileges are all your own achievement.

(Brennan & Naidoo 2008: 90)

A deficit approach blames individual students for their failure without equal attention given to the role of institutional structures in enabling participation. The assumption that the individual is solely responsible for the motivation, academic effort and social adjustment needed to make the transition from school to university misframes students as academically underprepared, demotivated or culturally deficient. A deficit approach frames poor participation as a 'reflection of the underperforming [student] rather than some reflection of the underperforming system' (Spaull & Kotze 2015: 15).

The deficit approach 'problematize(s) students from non-traditional backgrounds, rather than the educational institutions responsible for their progress' (Bowl 2001). A deficit approach works to 'blame individuals for their lack of "investment" in human capital, for their not attending school, for their dropping out of school, for their not studying the "right" fields, for their lack of entrepreneurship' (Klees 2014).

Focusing on fixing individual deficits deflects attention from such structural inequalities, which complicates the boundary between individual and institutional responsibility within conditions of extreme injustice. A deficit approach individualises failure and misrecognises student potential while reproducing systemic injustices, and misaligning resource provision to student capabilities (Fraser 2009; Leibowitz 2011). For example, while being a university student positions an individual as relatively advantaged, Black, working-class students are vulnerable to exclusion, since the university's resources, energy and time commitment will be less likely to trickle down to enable participation. At the same time, many students pursue a degree while working, adjusting to the university environment, dealing with the burden of racism and classism, and facing disconnection from family and community (Berg 2016).

At this point, it is important to reiterate that individual responsibility is an important part of university life, and that the individual must contribute her available talent, time, effort and resources to succeed in her studies. However, when structural conditions within and outside the university are extremely unequal, it becomes more difficult to distinguish between different reasons for an individual student's academic struggle and failure. When both the institution and the individual face resource constraints, the institutional response to student struggle is also more complex in that available academic and support structures may be less accessible to vulnerable students. At an institutional level, designing and maintaining sustainable support structures that take into account historical exclusion while simultaneously being sensitive to current pressures is an ongoing challenge.

Closely aligned to a deficit approach is the meritocracy at the core of selection processes in higher education. Meritocracy in higher education is critiqued as 'an ever-evolving, moving target that simultaneously shapes and is shaped by power relations in a given society' and that is powerfully influenced by values of elites (Rivera 2015: 6; Armstrong & Hamilton 2013). While meritocracy in academic institutions has been adopted for its potential to reduce class inequalities, this optimistic view downplays the fact that many students do not benefit from the selection processes at a university (Goldthorpe 2003; Morley & Lugg 2009). In a meritocratic system, failure and exclusion are characteristic of systemic constraints that fail to provide equal opportunities for all its members. This is evident in arrangements that position some first-generation students as vulnerable to unequal participation. Given South Africa's history, meritocracy is complicated by the misrecognition associated with race, gender, class and other identity-specific hierarchies. While all students and staff may be affected by a meritocratic ethos, undergraduate students are particularly vulnerable to an environment where resources and cultural capitals are vital to academic success.

The deficit approach and South African higher education

A deficit appraoch to vulnerable students in the South African context is an unintended consequence of massification, the funding crisis, international pressure to compete with well-resourced and stable systems, the dysfunctional school system and the ongoing transformation of South African univerities. In the South African context, implicit assumptions about student incompetence are a complex intersection of staff frustration about students' poor academic preparation, the impact that poor academic and social preparation has on teaching and learning, increased teaching loads, and the pressure to conduct internationally competitive research within the new management framework of the public university. Individual struggle amplifies a deficit logic, where a focus on the individual's shortcomings – academic, social or psychological – overshadows a systemic analysis that identifies and responds to structural weaknesses. When insufficient resources are available to enable equal participation, a 'sink or swim' logic to student success may work for some, while leaving others vulnerable (Taylor & Bedford 2004).

Under conditions of constrained resources, it is increasingly difficult to negotiate participation for students perceived as less likely to contribute towards institutional profit and economic growth. Black, working-class and/or first-generation students who enter higher education thus face historically embedded inequalities, while also being framed as underprepared in a system that understandably prioritises excellence, achievement, innovation, research and postgraduate outputs (see also Taylor & Bedford 2004; Cross & Carpentier 2009). In light of these constraints, how could an underfunded higher education system in the global South manage the trade-offs between research and innovation, and the resources, staff development and institutional transformation needed to enable equal participation? Where do working-class, first-generation students facing resource scarcity fit into pedagogical arrangements at institutions striving to become globally competitive producers of knowledge? The lower status of undergraduate teaching means that postgraduate teaching and supervision are more attractive because of the associated status and career advancement (Mouton, Louw, & Strydom 2013). As a result, undergraduates are less likely to attract the academic support or resources needed for meaningful participation and academic engagement (Lewin & Mawoyo 2014; Scott 2009).

Given these contradictory pressures, how are undergraduate students positioned as vulnerable outsiders, and what is the impact on student experience? Although many students begin their studies as outsiders in an unfamiliar education system, economically vulnerable undergraduates who are also first-generation students may occupy a particularly precarious position. When students are misframed at the intersection of economic, cultural and political injustice, they may have less secure access to resources or recognition to make justice claims (Fraser 2013).

A deficit approach and academic provision

The institutional and academic response to underprepared students has been extensive, from projects that track academic behaviour and performance (Engle & Tinto 2008; Kuh 2003; Strydom & Mentz 2013; Upcraft, Gardner, & Barefoot 2004; Zepke & Leach 2013) to pedagogical interventions that work with student resources and agency (Bathmaker Ingram, & Waller 2013; Fataar 2017; Kemmis, McTaggart, & Nixon 2013; Wilson-Strydom 2015). While more established higher education systems in the global North have been able to respond to non-traditional students with well-established pedagogical structures, there are significant concerns even in well-resourced contexts about the limitations and risks associated with academic programmes aimed at vulnerable students. In the section below, I explore challenges that filter into academic programmes.

In both the international and South African literature, academic access or bridging programmes are contentious sites that some argue could perpetuate a deficit approach to vulnerable students. This is due to conflicting pressures that leave insufficient resources to respond to vulnerable undergraduate students, and the competing pressures discussed in previous sections. Under systemic constraints, approaches aimed at 'correcting inequitable outcomes of social arrangements without disturbing the underlying framework that generates them' (Fraser 2008: 82) are likely to flourish. One limitation of interventions based on an affirmative approach is that they foreground a 'skills' model focused on remediation or technical solutions without attention to the epistemological and structural assumptions underlying structural inequality. For example, research that focuses on important individual traits like resilience may downplay contextual factors that constrain student participation, and may perpetuate a pathologising view of underprepared students as lacking resilience (McKay & Devlin 2016; Shields, Bishop, & Mazawi 2004; Theron & Theron 2010; Valencia 2010).

Teaching and learning constraints

Vulnerable students are dependent on the quality of the institutional response to underprepared students, on an institution's pedagogical and social response, where under-qualified teaching staff, lack of research and under-developed infrastructure limit the developmental potential of intervention programmes (Boughey 2010; Leibowitz & Bozalek 2015; Tinto 2014). Although there is great diversity amongst higher education systems, it is unlikely that the least prepared students will be matched with the most well-qualified staff and the best resourced pedagogical spaces at the university, especially at institutions that are historically under-resourced. In the developing context, higher education faces a decline in academic staff qualifications, where many university staff only have a bachelor's degree and are employed part-time, raising serious concerns about academic quality (Altbach *et al.* 2009; DHET 2012). In South Africa, financial constraints constrain pedagogical interventions and limit the research and staff development needed to develop sustainable and high-quality interventions (Leibowitz & Bozalek 2015). There is also generally weak support for the professional development of undergraduate teaching staff (DHET 2013).

Crowded classrooms deepen the strain on a rapidly growing sector on the African continent, where Mamdani (2007) describes a Ugandan university in which student numbers expanded from 6,000 to over 50,000 in a couple of decades. Without concomitant resources and infrastructure in response to this rapid growth, the quality of teaching and learning deteriorated rapidly. In other developing countries, some academics are forced to work at more than one institution in order to make ends meet, while academics in the global South are attracted to the higher salaries and improved conditions overseas, which leads to brain drain in their own countries (Altbach *et al.* 2009). In South Africa, the ability to retain talented academic staff is an urgent part of efforts to transform universities, and to create a more racially representative professoriate (Habib 2016; DHET 2012).

The effects of massification are not evenly spread across higher education institutions. Some disciplines, especially STEM, have been more successful in obtaining sufficient funding to enable teaching and research. Other disciplines, such as the Arts and Humanities face a range of challenges that diminish quality of participation for vulnerable students. These challenges include large class sizes in disciplines that have traditionally required in-depth engagement between academics and students. Due to staffing shortages, there is an increasing reliance on standardised assessment, online content and generic programmes. As teaching and learning models have adapted to growing demand, one risk is that vulnerable students have a diminished opportunity to participate. While such trends affect many students, those who are less prepared for university may be more vulnerable to the consequences of constrained systems.

Academic support programmes

Where funds are available for the development of undergraduate teaching, there are concerns about how effective academic support programmes are in enhancing participation for vulnerable students (Lewin & Mawoyo 2014; Walton, Bowman, & Osman 2015; Tinto 2014). Interventions based on remediating students' problems are at times ineffective and in some cases have been unable to develop the skills and knowledge that students lack when they enter university (Boughey & Niven 2012; Boughey 2007; Gilmour, Christie, & Soudien 2012; Hlalele 2010; Parkinson *et al.* 2008; Tinto 2014). Ineffective programmes are a barrier to pedagogy and curricula in that they 'hinder rather than facilitate student potential' (Scott, Hendry, & Yeld 2007: 44). While lack of resources is often cited as the reason for structural problems such as capacity development and adequate staff provision (Scott *et al.* 2007; see also Boughey 2010), financial investments are not sufficient to ensure that academic support programmes are effective (Walton *et al.* 2015). In South Africa, while funds are allocated to academic support programmes, persistent inequalities in participation have been connected to the 'proliferation and fragmentation of interventions which do not ultimately have systemic impact' (Walton *et al.* 2015: 263; see also Hlalele 2010; Boughey 2007a). International scholars have similarly critiqued support programmes as an ineffective 'laundry list of actions, one disconnected from another' (Tinto 2012: 5; Kahu 2013). Academic environments that communicate deficit beliefs about students' intelligence, language, race and class fail to provide a pedagogical space where students are able to engage deeply with knowledge (Boughey 2010; see also MacFarlane 2012).

One specific constraint has been the effectiveness of academic support programmes that are situated outside of the degree programme (Hlalele 2010; Leibowitz & Bozalek 2015; Pearce *et al.* 2015; Walton *et al.* 2015; Wingate 2006). In the South African context, this concern is complicated by the history of academic support models that were introduced to address the academic needs of first-generation students. This created an unintentional yet racialised academic support approach that fuelled suspicion and resistance from Black students who framed their experiences as agentic instead of seeing themselves as 'victims who needed to be pitied and helped' (Tema in Boughey 2010: 10; Hlalele & Alexander 2012; Leibowitz & Bozalek 2015). An academic approach that separates students based on academic ability creates homogeneous pedagogical environments in which

> students are generally segregated and stigmatised [and] treated as a separate group that accessed university somewhat 'illegitimately' was found to have a negative effect on social inclusion and diversity, while producing damaging stereotypes and detracting from the development these programmes were meant to offer.
>
> (Hlalele & Alexander 2012: 497)

A deficit view of students is also associated with a crisis discourse that focuses on extreme cases of student underpreparedness to justify remedial interventions. A crisis discourse is strengthened by a homogenised view of all students struggling with the same problems, instead of nuancing individual and structural limitations (Wilson-Strydom 2015). For these reasons, despite progress, '[e]xamples of older academic support models, in which "gaps are filled", "bridges are built" and missing "skills" are somehow "added on" to students who are deemed to be poorly equipped for university study . . . sadly persist' (Boughey & Niven 2012).

In South Africa, a crisis discourse has been criticised in academic language interventions that focus on students' deficits as second language speakers, instead of incorporating 'theory which takes into account literacy as a socially embedded phenomenon' (Boughey 2010: 6; see also Street & Lea 2006; Leibowitz 2011). From a multiple literacies perspective, an individual has differential access to literacies based on systems of privilege that value formal academic literacy over a student's home language. At the same time, the social and professional literacies that students use outside of universities are sometimes misunderstood, creating a distorted perspective of illiteracy based on narrow institutional privilege (Archer 2012; Gee & Hayes 2011). This devalues student agency by failing to 'incorporate the capabilities that students bring to the university (Leibowitz 2011: 223; Ivanič et al. 2009; Jacobs 2005).

Another limitation of academic development programmes is the uncritical adoption of academic support models from the global North. The need for cost-effective systems increases the use of generic courses taught by contract workers, which has an adverse impact on academic quality (Altbach et al. 2009). Technical approaches reflect market-driven values that favour quantifiable solutions to address study skills and time management. While such skills are crucial as part of a holistic support model, a skills approach may ignore 'attitudes, values and norms embodied within the socially prestigious forms of literacy [that are] are seen to be neutral and apolitical and therefore above question' (McKenna 2010: 11). For example, literacy interventions could be based on normative assumptions about language, culture and racial identity, while presenting literacy as a value-neutral skill (Bock & Gough 2002; Gee & Hayes 2011; Kapp & Bangeni 2011).

Resisting a deficit approach

In the global North, critical responses to a deficit ideology suggest that instead of trying to 'fix' students affected by inequality, more resources should be invested in addressing structural inequalities (Gorski 2011). Scholars who resist a deficit approach to students in higher education focus particularly on students more likely to be marginalised by poverty and discrimination (Taylor & Bedford 2004; Iverson 2007; Williams 2014; Allen et al. 2013; McKay & Devlin 2016; Stich 2012; Shields et al. 2004; Valencia 2010; Burke 2013; Ninnes, Aitchison, & Kalos 1999; Ladson-Billings 2007; Devlin 2013). In the section below, I explore research that resists a deficit approach to teaching and learning in higher education.

Structural relations of power

Instead of focusing on how to 'fix' the student, critical research assumes that material, affective, agentic and structural arrangements should be re-organised to expand freedom for participation (Brown & Kwakye 2012; Bauman 2009; Bok 2009; Mirza 2016; Yosso 2005). Relationships of power and decision-making structures are also important factors that enable or constrain participation (Archer, Hutchings, & Ross 2005; Gorski 2008; Giroux 2001; Mann 2008; Morley 2003). Anti-deficit approaches focus on the significance of student–lecturer alliances and student agency, emancipatory pedagogy and student aspirations (Bathmaker *et al.* 2013; Shay & Peseta 2016; Sayer 2005; Wilkins & Burke 2015). Instead of pathologising the individual, this approach is cognizant of cultures and practices that are 'underprepared for the task of embracing the diversity that would characterise student populations following a shift to democracy' (Boughey & Niven 2012). In contrast to research that assumes that education is value-neutral, a structural critique is reflexive about how embedded values and cultures marginalise and exclude student and scholars that resist a deficit approach (Davies, Safarik, & Banning 2003; Hill, Tinker, & Catterall 2010; Lawrence 2003; McKay & Devlin 2016).

Recognising student resources and agency

Studies that challenge a deficit approach investigate what institutional arrangements would look like if universities worked *with* the agency, resources and capabilities that students bring to higher education. Based on the findings of her research on first-year students' transition from high school to university, Wilson-Strydom (2015) argues that a more nuanced view of student preparedness is needed, in which we recognise that first-year students enter the university with different level of preparation in academic and social aspects of participation. Valuing existing student capitals is a necessary step towards de-individualising student failure while also taking into account the ways in which institutions can be alienating to students (Case 2013; Mann 2008). At the same time, it is important to be aware that students may have limited freedom to 'press justice claims against a system that has not prepared them adequately for tertiary study' (Bozalek & Boughey 2012: 699). An overemphasis on individual factors such as individual academic ability shifts attention to individual failure instead of how higher education is underprepared to respond to diverse students (Bozalek & Boughey 2012).

Another way to resist a deficit approach is to recognise the resources and agency that students bring to higher education (Fataar 2017). This approach is empowering in that it 'recognize(s) and build(s) upon the capabilities that students bring with them into higher education' (Scott *et al.* 2007: 45). For instance, a critical approach to student literacy has challenged the power imbalance in practices required for access to university knowledge (Archer 2012; Banda 2003; Kapp & Bangeni 2011; Leibowitz 2011; Nomdo 2006). Acknowledging diverse student literacies as an important cluster of resources has the potential to disrupt the privileging of dominant languages (Henderson & Hirst 2007; Gee 2011; Street & Lea 2006). This means acknowledging the 'interim literacies' that English second language speakers bring to the university and utilising them within pedagogy (Paxton 2012), while highlighting the importance of an academic literacy pedagogy that helps students gain access to the discourses of the academic community (Van Schalkwyk, Bitzer, & Van der Walt 2009).

A number of researchers have used in-depth narrative and biographical methodologies to establish the material, cognitive and affective issues that influence teaching and learning for vulnerable students (Gachago *et al.* 2014; Leibowitz 2009; Marshall & Case 2010). An approach that focuses on students' background would take into account academic and social needs. Understanding student biography can also reframe the struggle that students face in accessing higher education. For example, taking into account the lack of resources at schools offers insight into the resource scarcity that students face while drawing on the capabilities they have developed (Janse van Rensburg & Pym 2015).

Individual case studies show that even when students face barriers in higher education, they bring agency and reflexivity to the institution as they learn to negotiate new ways of thinking and being (Leibowitz & Bozalek 2015; Walton *et al.* 2015). These qualitative studies have drawn attention to the impact of individual agency by resisting 'simplistic, anecdotal, sociologically ungrounded characterisations of young adults in the post-apartheid context' (Marshall & Case 2010: 493). Pym and Kapp (2013) suggest that higher education institutions should be unapologetic about the fact that some students require more support than others; they should offer developmental support to students without reinforcing a deficit discourse.

The issue of student voice is particularly contentious within institutional hierarchies where the legitimacy to speak increases with qualification, status and measurable success (Fraser 2008). This means that vulnerable students may be silenced because they do not *yet* have access to the resources and education needed to make a legitimate and articulate contribution. In addition, their status as first-generation students who are vulnerable to drop out and unlikely to contribute towards institutional funding or prestige means that they may be less likely to receive the resources that could help them develop a legitimate voice before they face failure. At the same time, the struggle to cope with academic demands coupled with resource scarcity means that the most vulnerable students are unlikely to have the freedom to develop a legitimate voice. In response to this problem, some participatory approaches have focused on students developing an independent and critical voice (Brooman, Darwent, & Pimor 2014; Burke 2012; Cook-Sather 2006; McLeod 2011; Sellar & Gale 2011).

The intersection of race, gender, class and participation

Another critical cluster of research uses an intersectional analysis of race, gender and class to foreground how cultural capitals, resource inequality and privilege alienate students from the institution (Archer & Hutchings 2000; Bathmaker *et al.* 2013; Burke 2012; Hart 2012; Sayer 2005; Skeggs 2004; Reay & Ball 2005). Research on social class and exclusion has found that 'participation is an inherently more risky, costly and uncertain "choice" for working-class groups than for middle-class groups' (Archer 2003: 17; Vally & Motala 2014). Access to resources and recognition decrease or expand students' opportunities to participate. The freedom to have control over the environment means that students who have access to sufficient resources, such as parents' financial assistance, or bursaries and loans, which provide money for accommodation, textbooks, proper nutrition and transportation for students living off-campus, have greater freedom for equal participation (Mthethwa 2013). Class-based analyses integrate recognition and distributional justice to suggest that inequality has normative significance and demands an ethical response beyond resource distribution (Sayer 2005). In relation to first-generation student participation, this means that the structure of inequality is entrenched in the way resources and opportunities are unfairly distributed amongst students. At the same time, the relational, dispositional and cultural aspects of learning have a profound effect on students' ability to participate as equal members in 'a competition which [working-class students] have effectively lost before they have begun to play' (Sayer 2005: 35). The integration of material resources and the individual need for recognition by valued others is pertinent to the experiences of first-generation students who need not only epistemological access but also recognition of their potential to succeed (Sayer 2005; see also Walker 2008).

Class-based analyses of student participation have also produced a critical response to normative ideals around higher education as an unquestioned good (Burke 2012; Bathmaker *et al.* 2013). By questioning how education can be alienating to a diverse student body, this critical approach questions the assumption that low skill or ability is the primary barrier to academic access:

> Those who scorn the demands of socially excluded groups for respect or esteem, on the grounds that they have clearly not earned it, callously overlook the need of such groups for both resources to be able to achieve much and unconditional recognition of their needs and powers as human beings.
> (Sayer 2005: 62)

The expectations of time, energy, commitment and investment in undergraduate students speak to the absence of recognition for Black, working-class students who are perceived as less deserving of institutional time and commitment while being vulnerable to the 'unspoken messages of contempt or disrespect transmitted to marginal groups within hierarchical relationships' (Sayer 2005:

64). Recognition is therefore not only visible in distributional inequality, but in the forms of status injury and misrecognition that may erode the freedom for equal participation.

Conclusion

The chapter has given an overview of the complex challenges that university students face when they begin their studies with constrained resources and academic preparation. In the global South, inequalities reflect historical forces, massification and global macro-economic trends. The everyday reality of inequality filters into the macrocosm of university life, into classrooms and power dynamics, where a deficit approach to individual struggle and failure has been one response. Critical responses recognise the resources and agency that students bring to higher education.

Notes

1 Academic support programmes are implemented across disciplines to help students make the transition from school to higher education. For additional examples in the South Africa context, see Andrews 2015; Eybers 2015; Krige & Bezuidenhout 2015; Louw & de Villiers 2015; Lubben *et al.* 2010; Mashiyi 2015; Marshall & Case 2010; Slabbert 2015; Volkwyn *et al.* 2014.

References

Ahmed, S., 2012. *On Being Included: Racism and Diversity in Institutional Life.* Durham, NC: Duke University Press.

Akoojee, S., & Nkomo, S., 2007. Access and Quality in South African Higher Education: The Twin Challenges of Transformation. *South African Journal of Higher Education* 21, 385–399.

Alexander-Floyd, N.G., 2012. Disappearing Acts: Reclaiming Intersectionality in the Social Sciences in a Post-Black Feminist Era. *Feminist Formations* 24(1), 1–25.

Allen, K., Quinn, J., Hollingworth, S., & Rose, A., 2013. Becoming Employable Students and "Ideal" Creative Workers: Exclusion and Inequality in Higher Education Work Placements. *British Journal of Sociology of Education* 34, 431–452. https://doi.org/10.1080/01425692.2012.714249

Altbach, P.G., Rumbley, L., & Reisberg, L., 2009. Trends in Global Higher Education: Tracking an Academic Revolution (UNESCO 2009 World Conference on Higher Education). United Nations Educational, Scientific and Cultural Organization, Paris.

Altbach, P., 2013. The Complex Roles of Universities in the Period of Globalization (Synthesis of Higher Education in the World), in *Report Higher Education in the World 3.* New York: Palgrave McMillan.

Andrews, D., 2015. Redress for Academic Success: Possible 'Lessons' for University Support Programmes from a High School Literacy and Learning Intervention: Part 2. *South African Journal of Higher Education* 29(1), 354–372.

Archer, L., 2003. Social Class and Higher Education. In Archer, L., Hutchings, M., & Ross, A. (Eds), *Higher Education and Social Class: Issues of Exclusion and Inclusion.* London: RoutledgeFalmer, pp. 5–44.

Archer, A., 2012. Writing as Design: Enabling Access to Academic Discourse in a Multimodal Environment. *South African Journal of Higher Education* 26, 411–421.

Archer, L., & Hutchings, M., 2000. 'Bettering Yourself'? Discourses of Risk, Cost and Benefit in Ethnically Diverse, Young Working-Class Non-participants' Constructions of Higher Education. *British Journal of Sociology of Education* 21, 555–574. https://doi.org/10.1080/713655373

Archer, L., Hutchings, M., & Ross, A., 2005. *Higher Education and Social Class: Issues of Exclusion and Inclusion*. London and New York: Routledge.

Armstrong, E.A., & Hamilton, L.T., 2013. *Paying for the Party: How College Maintains Inequality*. Cambridge, MA: Harvard University Press.

Banda, F., 2003. A Survey of Literacy Practices in Black and Coloured Communities in South Africa: Towards a Pedagogy of Multiliteracies. *Language, Culture and Curriculum* 16, 106–129.

Bathmaker, A.-M., Ingram, N., & Waller, R. 2013. Higher Education, Social Class and the Mobilisation of Capitals: Recognising and Playing the Game. *British Journal of Sociology of Education* 34, 723–743. https://doi.org/10.1080/01425692.2013.816041

Bauman, Z., 2009. *Does Ethics Have a Chance in a World of Consumers?* Cambridge, MA: Harvard University Press.

Berg, G.A., 2016. *Low-Income Students and the Perpetuation of Inequality: Higher Education in America*. New York and London: Routledge.

Besley, A.C., & Peters, M.A., 2006. Neoliberalism, Performance and the Assessment of Research Quality. *South African Journal of Higher Education* 20, 814–832.

Bock, Z., & Gough, D., 2002. Social Literacies and Students in Tertiary Settings: Lessons from South Africa. *Australian Review of Applied Linguistics* 25, 49–58.

Bok, D., 2009. *Universities in the Marketplace: The Commercialization of Higher Education*. Princeton, NJ: Princeton University Press.

Boni, A., & Walker, M., 2013. *Human Development and Capabilities: Re-imagining the University of the Twenty-first Century*. London and New York: Routledge.

Boughey, C., 2007. Marrying Equity and Efficiency: The Need for Third Generation Academic Development. *Perspectives in Education* 25(3), 1–11.

Boughey, C., 2010. Academic Development for Improved Efficiency in the Higher Education and Training System in South Africa. *Development Bank of Southern Africa*.

Boughey, C., & Niven, P., 2012. Common Sense Fails Our Students. *Mail & Guardian*. http://mg.co.za/article/2012-08-10-common-sense-fails-our-students

Bowl, M., 2001. Experiencing the Barriers: Non-traditional Students Entering Higher Education. *Research Papers in Education* 16, 141–160. https://doi.org/10.1080/02671520110037410

Bozalek, V., & Boughey, C., 2012. (Mis)framing Higher Education in South Africa. Social *Policy & Administration* 46, 688–703. https://doi.org/10.1111/j.1467-9515.2012.00863.x

Brennan, J., & Naidoo, R., 2008. Higher Education and the Achievement (and/or Prevention) of Equity and Social Justice. *Higher Education* 56, 287–302. https://doi.org/10.1007/s10734-008-9127-3

Brock-Utne, B., 2003. Formulating Higher Education Policies in Africa: The Pressure from External Forces and the Neoliberal Agenda. *Journal of Higher Education in Africa*/Revue de l'enseignement supérieur en Afrique 1, 24–56.

Brooman, S., Darwent, S., & Pimor, A., 2014. The Student Voice in Higher Education Curriculum Design: Is There Value in Listening? *Innovations in Education and Teaching International* 1–12. https://doi.org/10.1080/14703297.2014.910128

Brown, R.N., & Kwakye, C.J. (Eds). 2012. *Wish to Live: The Hip-hop Feminism Pedagogy Reader.* New York: Lang Publishing.

Burke, P.J., 2012. *The Right to Higher Education: Beyond Widening Participation.* London and New York: Routledge.

Case, J.M., 2013. *Researching Student Learning in Higher Education: A Social Realist Approach.* London and New York: Routledge.

Cini, L., & Guzmán-Concha, C., 2017. Student Movements in the Age of Austerity. The Cases of Chile and England. *Social Movement Studies* 16(5), 623–628. https://doi.org/10.1080/14742837.2017.1331122

Cook-Sather, A., 2006. Sound, Presence, and Power: 'Student Voice' in Educational Research and Reform. *Curriculum Inquiry* 36, 359–390.

Cross, M., & Carpentier, C., 2009. 'New Students' in South African Higher Education: Institutional Culture, Student Performance and the Challenge of Democratisation. *Perspectives in Education* 27, 6–18.

Davies, T.G., Safarik, L., & Banning, J.H., 2003. The Deficit Portrayal of Underrepresented Populations on Community College Campuses: A Cross Case Analysis. *Community College Journal of Research and Practice* 27, 843–858. https://doi.org/10.1080/713838275

Deem, 2001. New Managerialism and the Management of UK Universities. Economic and Social Research Council. http://www.leeds.ac.uk/educol/documents/189420.pdf

Devlin, M., 2013. Bridging Socio-cultural Incongruity: Conceptualising the Success Of Students from Low Socio-economic Status Backgrounds in Australian Higher Education. *Studies in Higher Education* 38, 939–949. https://doi.org/10.1080/03075079.2011.613991

DHET, 2012. Staffing South Africa's Universities Framework: A Comprehensive, Transformative Approach to Developing Future Generations of Academics and Building Staff Capacity. Pretoria, South Africa.

DHET, 2013. *White Paper on Post School Training: Building an Expanded, Effective and Integrated Post-school System.* Pretoria: Department of Higher Education and Training, Republic of South Africa.

Engle, J., & Tinto, V., 2008. Moving Beyond Access: College Success for Low-Income, First-Generation Students. Pell Institute for the Study of Opportunity in Higher Education.

http://eric.ed.gov/?id=ED504448Eybers, O. 2015. From Mechanist to Critical Realist Interrogations of Academic Literacy Facilitation in Extended Degree Programmes. *South African Journal of Higher Education* 29, 79–90.

Fataar, A., 2017. Towards a Teacher Education Pedagogy of Recognition as a Response to the Decolonizing Education Imperative. In Decolonization of Teacher Education and Educational Research. Potchefstroom Campus, NWU.

Feldman, S., & Gellert, P., 2006. The Seductive Quality of Central Human Capabilities: Sociological Insights into Nussbaum and Sen's Disagreement. *Economy and Society* 35, 423–452. https://doi.org/10.1080/03085140600845008

Fraser, N., 2008. *Adding Insult to Injury: Nancy Fraser Debates Her Critics.* New York: Verso Books.

Fraser, N., 2009. Feminism, Capitalism and the Cunning of History. *New Left Review* 56, 97–117.

Fraser, N., 2013. *Fortunes of Feminism: From State-Managed Capitalism to Neoliberal Crisis.* New York, NY: Verso Books.

Gachago, D., Condy, J., Ivala, E., & Chigona, A., 2014. 'All Stories Bring Hope Because Stories Bring Awareness': Students' Perceptions of Digital Storytelling for Social Justice Education. *South African Journal of Education* 34(4), 1–12.

Gee, J.P., & Hayes, E.R., 2011. *Language and Learning in the Digital Age.* New York, NY: Taylor & Francis.

Gilmour, D., Christie, P., & Soudien, C., 2012. *The Poverty of Education.* Presented at the Strategies to Overcome Poverty and Inequality: Towards Carnegie III, University of Cape Town.

Giroux, H.A., 2001. *Theory and Resistance in Education: Towards a Pedagogy for the Opposition.* Westport, CT: Greenwood Publishing Group.

Giroux, H.A., 2005. The Terror of Neoliberalism: Rethinking the Significance of Cultural Politics. *College Literature* 32, 1–19. https://doi.org/10.2307/25115243

Giroux, H.A., 2013. Public Intellectuals against the Neoliberal University. 29 October, 2013. *Truthout.* www.truth-out.org/opinion/item/19654-public-intellectuals-against-the-neoliberal-university

Giroux, H.A., 2014. *Neoliberalism's War on Higher Education.* Chicago, IL, Haymarket Books.

Goldthorpe, J., 2003. The Myth of Education-based Meritocracy. *New Economy* 10, 234–239. https://doi.org/10.1046/j.1468-0041.2003.00324.x

Gooch, C.D., & Ruderman, A., 2016. A Conversation with Mahmood Mamdani. *disClosureA A Journal of Social Theory* 25, 178–180.

Gorski, P., 2008. The Myth of the 'Culture of Poverty'. https://www.inflexion.org/the-myth-of-the-culture-of-poverty/

Gorski, P.C., 2011. Unlearning Deficit Ideology and the Scornful Gaze: Thoughts on Authenticating the Class Discourse in Education. *Counterpoints* 402, 152–173.

Gray, B., 2016. Neoliberalising Higher Education: Language and Performing Purpose in Corporatised Universities. *Critical Arts: A South-North Journal of Cultural & Media Studies* 30, 745–750. https://doi.org/10.1080/02560046.2016.1269237

Habib, A., 2016. Goals and Means: Reimagining the South African University and Critically Analysing the Struggle For Its Realisation. *Transformation: Critical Perspectives on Southern Africa* 90, 111–132. https://doi.org/10.1353/trn.2016.0006

Hart, C.S., 2012. *Aspirations, Education and Social Justice: Applying Sen and Bourdieu.* London: Bloomsbury.

Henderson, J.A., & Hursh, D.W., 2014. Economics and Education for Human Flourishing: Wendell Berry and the 'Oikonomic' Alternative to Neoliberalism. *Educational Studies* 50, 167–186.

Henderson, R., & Hirst, E., 2007. Reframing Academic Literacy: Re-examining a Short-course for 'Disadvantaged' Tertiary Students. *English Teaching: Practice and Critique* 6, 25–38.

Hill, P., Tinker, A., & Catterall, S., 2010. From Deficiency to Development: The Evolution of Academic Skills Provision at One UK University. *Journal of Learning Development in Higher Education* 2.

Hlalele, D., & Alexander, G., 2012. University Access, Inclusion and Social Justice. *South African Journal of Higher Education* 26, 487–502.

Hlalele, D.J., 2010. Do Learning Skills Acquired in the University Access Programme Enhance Participation in Academic Practice? *South African Journal of Higher Education* 24(1), 98–110,

hooks, B., 1994. *Teaching to Transgress: Education as the Practice of Freedom*. New York: Routledge.

Ivanič, R., Edwards, R., Barton, D., Martin-Jones, M., Fowler, Z., Hughes, B., Mannion, G., Miller, K., Satchwell, C., & Smith, J., 2009. *Improving Learning in College: Rethinking Literacies across the Curriculum*. New York: Routledge.

Iverson, S.V., 2007. Camouflaging Power and Privilege: A Critical Race Analysis of University Diversity Policies. *Educational Administration Quarterly* 43, 586–611. https://doi.org/10.1177/0013161X07307794

Jacobs, C., 2005. On Being an Insider on the Outside: New Spaces for Integrating Academic Literacies. *Teaching in Higher Education* 10, 475–487.

Janse van Rensburg, V., & Kapp, R., 2015. 'So I Have to Be Positive, No Matter How Difficult It Is': A Longitudinal Case Study of a First-Generation Occupational Therapy Student. *South African Journal of Occupational Therapy* 44, 29–33.

Johnson, A.T., & Hirt, J.B., 2010. Reshaping Academic Capitalism to Meet Development Priorities: The Case of Public Universities in Kenya. *Higher Education* 61, 483–499. https://doi.org/10.1007/s10734-010-9342-6

Kahu, E.R., 2013. Framing Student Engagement in Higher Education. *Studies in Higher Education* 38, 758–773. https://doi.org/10.1080/03075079.2011.598505

Kapp, R., & Bangeni, B., 2011. A Longitudinal Study of Students' Negotiation of Language, Literacy and Identity. *Southern African Linguistics and Applied Language Studies* 29, 197–208.

Kemmis, S., McTaggart, R., & Nixon, R., 2013. *The Action Research Planner: Doing Critical Participatory Action Research*. New York, NY: Springer Science & Business Media.

Klees, 2014. Neoliberal Policies Destroy Human Potential and Devastate Education. *Mail & Guardian*. https://mg.co.za/article/2014-07-18-neoliberal-policies-destroy-human-potential-and-devastate-education

Krige, D., & Bezuidenhout, J. 2015. Philosophy and Role Reflection of Teaching Practices in the Communication Science Extended Degree Programme. *South African Journal of Higher Education* 29, 132–149.

Kuh, G.D., 2003. What We're Learning about Student Engagement from NSSE: Benchmarks for Effective Educational Practices. *Change: The Magazine of Higher Learning* 35, 24–32. https://doi.org/10.1080/00091380309604090

Labaree, D., 2017. *A Perfect Mess: The Unlikely Ascendancy of American Higher Education*. Chicago, IL: University of Chicago Press.

Ladson-Billings, G., 2007. Pushing Past the Achievement Gap: An Essay on the Language of Deficit. *The Journal of Negro Education* 76, 316–323.

Lawrence, J., 2003. The 'Deficit-Discourse' Shift: University Teachers and Their Role in Helping First Year Students Persevere and Succeed in the New University Culture. UltiBASE.

Le Grange, L., 2011. [Re]thinking [Trans]formation in South African [higher] Education. *Perspectives in Education* 29, 1–9.

Leibowitz, B., 2011. Academic Literacy as a Graduate Attribute: Implications for Thinking about 'Curriculum'. In Bitzer, E., & Botha, N. (Eds), *Curriculum Inquiry in South*

African Higher Education: Some Scholarly Affirmations and Challenges. Stellenbosch: SUN MeDIA, pp. 221–236.

Leibowitz, B., & Bozalek, V., 2015. Foundation Provision – A Social Justice Perspective: Part 1: Leading Article. *South African Journal of Higher Education* 29(1), 8–25.

Lewin, T., & Mawoyo, M., 2014. Student Access and Success: Issues and Interventions in South African Universities. Inyathelo: The South African Institute for Advancement.

Louw, A., & de Villiers, A., 2015. Teaching First Aid in High Schools: The Impact on Students in the Health Sciences Extended Degree Programme. *South African Journal of Higher Education* 29, 198–210.

Lubben, F., Davidowitz, B., Buffler, A., Allie, S., & Scott, I., 2010. Factors Influencing Access Students' Persistence in an Undergraduate Science Programme: A South African Case Study. *International Journal of Educational Development* 30, 351–358.

Lynch, K., 2006. Neo-Liberalism and Marketisation: The Implications for Higher Education. *European Educational Research Journal* 5, 1–17.

Macfarlane, B., 2012. Re-framing Student Academic Freedom: A Capability Perspective. *Higher Education* 63(6), 719–732.

Maistry, S.M., 2012. Confronting the Neo-Liberal Brute: Reflections of a Higher Education Middle-level Manager. *South African Journal of Higher Education* 26, 515–528.

Mamdani, M., 2007. Scholars in the Marketplace. *The Dilemmas of Neo-Liberal Reform at Makerere University, 1989–2005*. African Books Collective.

Mann, S., 2008. *Study, Power and the University*. London: McGraw-Hill Education.

Marginson, S., 2011. Higher Education and Public Good. *Higher Education Quarterly* 65, 411–433.

Marshall, D., & Case, J., 2010. Rethinking 'Disadvantage' in Higher Education: A Paradigmatic Case Study Using Narrative Analysis. *Studies in Higher Education* 35, 491–504. https://doi.org/10.1080/03075070903518386

Mashiyi, F.N., 2015. Embedding Graduate Attributes into The Foundation Programme: Reflections on Process and Product: Part 1. *South African Journal of Higher Education* 29(1), 181–197.

Mbembe, A., 2016. Decolonizing the University: New Directions. *Arts and Humanities in Higher Education* 15, 29–45. https://doi.org/10.1177/1474022215618513

McKay, J., & Devlin, M., 2016. 'Low Income Doesn't Mean Stupid and Destined for Failure': Challenging the Deficit Discourse around Students from Low SES Backgrounds in Higher Education. *International Journal of Inclusive Education* 20, 347–363. https://doi.org/10.1080/13603116.2015.1079273

McKenna, S., 2010. Cracking the Code of Academic Literacy: An Ideological Task. In Hutchings, C., & Garraway, J. (Eds), *Beyond the University Gates: Provision of Extended Curriculum Programmes in South Africa*. Rhodes University.

McKenna, S., 2015. Five Trends South Africa's Universities Must Reject if They Really Want Change. *The Conversation*. 20 October 2015. https://theconversation.com/five-trends-south-africas-universities-must-reject-if-they-really-want-change-49452

McLeod, J., 2011. Student Voice and the Politics of Listening in Higher Education. *Critical Studies in Education* 52, 179–189. https://doi.org/10.1080/17508487.2011.572830

Mirza, H.S., 2016. Decolonizing Higher Education: Black Feminism and the Intersectionality of Race and Gender. *The Journal of Feminist Scholarship* 7–8, 1–6.

Morley, L., 2003. *Quality and Power in Higher Education*. London: McGraw-Hill Education.

Morley, L., & Lugg, R., 2009. Mapping Meritocracy: Intersecting Gender, Poverty and Higher Educational Opportunity Structures. *Higher Education Policy* 22, 37–60. https://doi.org/10.1057/hep.2008.26

Mouton, N., Louw, G., & Strydom, G., 2013. Present-Day Dilemmas and Challenges of The South African Tertiary System. *International Business & Economics Research Journal* 12, 285–300.

Mthethwa, N., 2013. How Could I Have Failed Varsity? *Mail & Guardian*, 11 January 2013. https://mg.co.za/article/2013-01-11-how-could-i-have-failed-varsity

Naidoo, R., & Williams, J., 2015. The Neoliberal Regime in English Higher Education: Charters, Consumers and the Erosion of the Public Good. *Critical Studies in Education* 56, 208–223. https://doi.org/10.1080/17508487.2014.939098

Naidoo, R., 2010. Global Learning in a NeoLiberal Age: Implications for Development. In Unterhalter, E. (Ed.), *Global Inequalities and Higher Education: Whose Interests Are You Serving?* New York, NY: Palgrave Macmillan.

Naidoo, R., 2011. Rethinking Development: Higher Education and the New Imperialism. In King, R., & Marginson, S. (Eds), *Handbook on Globalization and Higher Education*. Cheltenham, UK: Edward Elgar Publishing.

Naidoo, R., & Williams, J., 2015. The Neoliberal Regime in English Higher Education: Charters, Consumers and the Erosion of the Public Good. *Critical Studies in Education* 56, 208–223. https://doi.org/10.1080/17508487.2014.939098

Ninnes, P., Aitchison, C., & Kalos, S., 1999. Challenges to Stereotypes of International Students' Prior Educational Experience: Undergraduate Education in India. *Higher Education Research & Development* 18, 323–342. https://doi.org/10.1080/0729436990180304

Nomdo, 2006. Identity, Power and Discourse. In van Pletzen, E., & Thesen, L. (Eds), *Academic Literacy and the Languages of Change*. London: Continuum.

Nussbaum, M.C., 2012. *Not for Profit: Why Democracy Needs the Humanities*. Princeton, NJ: Princeton University Press.

Olssen, M., & Peters, M.A., 2005. Neoliberalism, Higher Education and the Knowledge Economy: From the Free Market to Knowledge Capitalism. *Journal of Education Policy* 20, 313–345. https://doi.org/10.1080/02680930500108718

Parkinson, J., Jackson, L., Kirkwood, T., & Padayachee, V., 2008. Evaluating the Effectiveness of an Academic Literacy Course: Do Students Benefit? *Per Linguam* 24, 11–29.

Paxton, M., 2012. Student Voice as a Methodological Issue in Academic Literacies Research. *Higher Education Research & Development* 31, 381–391. https://doi.org/10.1080/07294360.2011.634382

Pearce, H., Campbell, A., Craig, T.S., le Roux, P., Nathoo, K., & Vicatos, E., 2015. The Articulation Between the Mainstream and Extended Degree Programmes in Engineering at the University of Cape Town: Reflections and Possibilities. *South African Journal of Higher Education* 29, 150–163.

Pennington, A., Mokose, M., Smith, M.N., & Kawanu, Z., 2017. Neoliberalism and the Crisis in Higher Education in South Africa: Student Voice. *New Agenda: South African Journal of Social and Economic Policy* 64, 28–32.

Pym, J., & Kapp, R., 2013. Harnessing Agency: Towards a Learning Model for Undergraduate Students. *Studies in Higher Education* 38, 272–284. https://doi.org/10.1080/03075079.2011.582096

Read, B., Archer, L., & Leathwood, C., 2003. Challenging Cultures? Student Conceptions of 'Belonging' and 'Isolation' at a Post-1992 University. *Studies in Higher Education* 28, 261–277. https://doi.org/10.1080/03075070309290
Reay, D., & Ball, S.J., 2005. *Degrees of Choice: Class, Race, Gender and Higher Education.* London: Trentham Books.
Rivera, L.A., 2015. Pedigree: *How Elite Students Get Elite Jobs.* Princeton, NJ: Princeton University Press.
Robeyns, I., 2016. Having Too Much (SSRN Scholarly Paper No. ID 2736094). Social Science Research Network, Rochester, New York.
Sayer, A., 2005. *The Moral Significance of Class.* Cambridge: Cambridge University Press.
Scott, I., 2009. Academic Development in South African Higher Education. In *Higher Education in South Africa: A Scholarly Look Behind the Scenes.* Stellenbosch: AFRICAN SUN MeDIA.
Scott, I., Hendry, N., & Yeld, J., 2007. Higher Education Monitor: A Case for Improving Teaching and Learning in South African Higher Education. Council on Higher Education.
Sellar, S., & Gale, T., 2011. Mobility, Aspiration, Voice: A New Structure of Feeling for Student Equity in Higher Education. *Critical Studies in Education* 52, 115–134. https://doi.org/10.1080/17508487.2011.572826
Shay, S., & Peseta, T., 2016. A Socially Just Curriculum Reform Agenda. *Teaching in Higher Education* 21, 361–366. https://doi.org/10.1080/13562517.2016.1159057
Shields, C.M., Bishop, R., & Mazawi, A.E., 2004. *Pathologizing Practices: The Impact of Deficit Thinking on Education.* New York: Peter Lang.
Shrivastava, M., & Shrivastava, S., 2014. Political Economy of Higher Education: Comparing South Africa to Trends in the World. Higher Education: *The International Journal of Higher Education and Educational Planning* 67, 809–822.
Singh, M., 2011. The Place of Social Justice in Higher Education and Social Change Discourses. *Compare: A Journal of Comparative and International Education* 41, 481–494.
Skeggs, B., 2004. Exchange, Value and Affect: Bourdieu and 'The Self'. *The Sociological Review* 52, 75–95. https://doi.org/10.1111/j.1467-954X.2005.00525.x
Slabbert, R., 2015. Extended Curriculum Programme Evolution: A Road Map to Academic Success? Part 1. *South African Journal of Higher Education* 29(1), 45–59.
Slaughter, S., & Rhoades, G., 2011. Markets in Higher Education: Trends in Academic Capitalism. In Altbach, P.G., Gumport, P.J., & Berdahl, R.O. (Eds), *American Higher Education in the Twenty-First Century: Social, Political, and Economic Challenges.* Baltimore, MD: Johns Hopkins University Press, pp. 433–464.
Spaull, N., & Kotze, J., 2015. Starting Behind and Staying Behind in South Africa. *International Journal of Educational Development* 41, 13–24.
Stich, A.E., 2012. *Access to Inequality: Reconsidering Class, Knowledge, and Capital in Higher Education.* New York, NY: Lexington Books.
Street, B., & Lea, M.R., 2006. The 'Academic Literacies' Model: Theory and Applications. *Theory into Practice* 45, 368–377.
Strydom, J.F., & Mentz, M. 2013. Enhancing a Culture of Evidence: Using Student Engagement to Identify Problem Areas which Institutions Can Do Something About. *South African Journal of Higher Education* 27, 401–418.
Taylor, J.A., & Bedford, T., 2004. Staff Perceptions of Factors Related to Non-Completion in Higher Education. *Studies in Higher Education* 29, 375–394. https://doi.org/10.1080/03075070410001682637

Theron 2011
Tinto, V., 2012. *Completing College: Rethinking Institutional Action*. Chicago, IL: University Of Chicago Press.
Tinto, V., 2014. Access without Support is Not Opportunity. *Community College Week* 26, 4–4.
Upcraft, M.L., Gardner, J.N., & Barefoot, B.O., 2004. *Challenging and Supporting the First-Year Student: A Handbook for Improving the First Year of College*. San Francisco, CA: Jossey-Bass.
Valencia, R.R., 2010. *Dismantling Contemporary Deficit Thinking: Educational Thought and Practice*. London and New York: Routledge.
Vally, S., & Motala, E., 2014. *Education, Economy & Society*. Pretoria: Unisa Press.
Van Schalkwyk, S., Bitzer, E., & Van der Walt, C., 2009. Acquiring Academic Literacy: A Case of First-Year Extended Degree Programme Students. *Southern African Linguistics & Applied Language Studies* 27, 189–201. https://doi.org/10.2989/SALALS.2009.27.2.6.869
Volkwyn, T., Marshall, D., Conana, H., & Maclons, H.M., 2014. Becoming a Physicist': The Implementation of a Research Based Physics Course in an Extended Curriculum Programme. Presented at the ASSAf STEM 'Mind the Gap' Forum.
Walker, M., 2008. Widening Participation; Widening Capability. *London Review of Education* 6, 267–279. https://doi.org/10.1080/14748460802489397
Walker, M., 2012. A Capital or Capabilities Education Narrative in a World of Staggering Inequalities? *International Journal of Educational Development* 32, 384–393. https://doi.org/10.1016/j.ijedudev.2011.09.003
Walton, E., Bowman, B., & Osman, R., 2015. Promoting Access to Higher Education in an Unequal Society: Part 2 – Leading Article. *South African Journal of Higher Education* 29(1), 8–25.Wilkins, A., & Burke, P.J., 2015. Widening Participation in Higher Education: The Role of Professional and Social Class Identities and Commitments. *British Journal of Sociology of Education* 36, 434–452. https://doi.org/10.1080/01425692.2013.829742
Williams, R.A., 2014. *Men of Color in Higher Education: New Foundations for Developing Models for Success*. Sterling, VA: Stylus Publishing.
Wilson-Strydom, M., 2015. *University Access and Success: Capabilities, Diversity and Social Justice*. London and New York: Routledge.
Wingate, U., 2006. Doing Away With 'Study Skills'. *Teaching in Higher Education* 11, 457–469. https://doi.org/10.1080/13562510600874268
Yosso, T.J., 2005. Whose Culture has Capital? A Critical Race Theory Discussion of Community Cultural Wealth. *Race Ethnicity and Education* 8, 69–91. https://doi.org/10.1080/1361332052000341006
Zepke, N., 2016. *Student Engagement in Neoliberal Times: Theories and Practices for Learning and Teaching in Higher Education*. New York, NY: Springer.
Zepke, N., & Leach, L., 2010. Improving Student Engagement: Ten Proposals for Action. *Active Learning in Higher Education* 11, 167–177. https://doi.org/10.1177/1469787410379680

Chapter 3

The capability approach and inequality in higher education

In this chapter, I outline the capability framework used to analyse student narratives. Drawing on a combination of the capability approach and social theory, I construct a critique of institutional arrangements that situates student participation at the nexus of individual freedom and structural arrangements in higher education. The first section of this chapter introduces the capability approach as a theoretical alternative to a deficit approach to underprepared students in higher education. The next section explores key concepts of the capability approach that I used to conceptualise equal participation. In the final section, I explore the notion of education as the expansion of human freedom, which combines the capability approach with Nancy Fraser's and Paulo Freire's theories.

The capability approach and structural injustice

The capability approach integrates concepts of freedom, agency and human development to make evaluations about the quality of life as 'a broad normative framework for the evaluation and assessment of individual well-being and social arrangements, the design of policies, and proposals about social change in society' (Robeyns 2005: 94; Nussbaum 2011). With its expansive view of human well-being, the capabilities approach prioritises well-being outcomes for individuals in the pursuit of the public good (Sen 1992; Boni & Walker 2013).

Within the context of South Africa's higher education landscape, I applied this normative approach to justice and equality to investigate structural arrangements embedded in higher education. When held up against the standard of individual achievement in higher education, the capability approach is an egalitarian alternative that I used to focus on the arrangements that enable students to convert resources into capabilities for equal participation. In framing my research, the capability approach offered a multidimensional analytical tool to examine comparative freedoms and opportunities available to students positioned precariously in higher education. Instead of a deficit view of students, the capability approach enabled an evaluation of structural injustice alongside individual agency and freedom. I used the capability approach to investigate the social contexts in which students participate, exercise their agency and convert resources into capabilities. In contrast to a deficit view of students, the capability approach prioritises the structures in which every individual is valued for their inherent worth and not merely for their instrumental value as consumer or 'client' (Walker 2008). In resistance to pathologising views of the individual student, I am concerned about 'whether the circumstances in which people choose from their opportunity sets are enabling and just' (Robeyns 2005: 99).

A capability approach to higher education research

The capability approach is a methodologically flexible approach that has been theorised and operationalised in higher education research and policy (Crosbie 2013; Walker 2006; Walker & McLean 2013; Wilson-Strydom 2015; Walker & Wilson-Strydom 2016; Walker & Fongwa 2017). Capability scholars have applied the approach to seek:

> [A]nswers to practical educational questions about what knowledge to teach, using what pedagogy, and to whom, [to] express judgments about which aspects of existing forms of social life ought to be reproduced and to be transformed if all [students] are to be prepared for the world of the future.
> (Walker 2006: 90)

Capability research has been used to analyse teaching, learning, curriculum and assessment as conditions that ought to equalise education opportunities but which 'acknowledges that some [students] may benefit more than others from the same quantity of educational experience' (Hart 2009: 396). Capability-informed analyses show that educational practices and policies diminish student freedom (Lozano et al. 2012; Unterhalter 2003).

Capability scholars agree that education counts as a basic freedom that should expand an individual's access to fertile opportunities (Sen 1999; Nussbaum 2011; Wolff & de-Shalit 2007). For example, expanded literacy could allow an individual the freedom to communicate, which could enable their contribution to the well-being of a community (Robeyns 2006). I have applied the approach as an evaluative framework based on comparative freedoms between individuals positioned within higher education to draw attention to inequalities within a relatively privileged academic space. Even though a student who has access to university may have more opportunities than an individual who only completed a few years of primary school, I evaluate a student's freedom for equal participation by looking critically at both enablers and constraints to participation (Walker & McLean 2013).

A capability critique of neoliberal higher education

The capability approach is located within a human development paradigm and promotes the values of participation, sustainability, equity and productivity (Deneulin & Shahani 2010: 29–30; ul Haq 2003). These values take into account the economic, environmental, political and social consequences for human development. The human development prioritises well-being, and argues that income and Gross Domestic Product (GDP) are important yet insufficient indicators of development because of growing economic disparities within nations and groups (ul Haq 2003; Sen 1999).

While a human capital model quantifies 'skills' as commodities as the 'main criteria of human success' (Sen 2009: 233), a human development model reframes success as the freedoms an individual needs to pursue a meaningful life, which includes but is not limited to economic resources (Boni 2012; Walker 2012). A human capital approach that prioritises education as skills and knowledge 'as an investment in the productivity of the human being as an economic production factor' (Robeyns 2006: 72) is limiting because it constricts the function of education to an instrumental good. This is also an unreliable measure of development because it downplays the way that education often fails to benefit people in the same way (Hart 2012; Walker 2008a; Unterhalter 2010). When this instrumentalism is combined with the logic of a neoliberal university, vulnerable students who seem less likely to offer a return on investment then fall to the bottom of the institutional hierarchy (Catlaks 2013).

The human development approach offers philosophical and practical alternatives to the complex problems facing twenty-first century higher education. Instead of reducing university education to mostly the accumulation of private benefits, a human development approach calls for structural arrangements that enable more citizens to benefit from public resources (Deneulin 2014). The human development approach offers 'alternatives to the narratives of consumerism, and corresponding alternative channels for improving well-being' (Gasper 2013: 101–102). From a human development perspective, the individual is enabled to cultivate empathy, reasoned thinking and critical imagination (Nussbaum 2012; Flores-Crespo 2007). To this end, social justice should enable human capabilities in resistance to the view of higher education as business for the sake of profit (Boni & Walker 2013: 1–2; see also McLean, Abbas, & Ashwin 2013, Walker 2008a). In contrast, socially just pedagogical arrangements would expand human freedom and choice (Walker 2009).

Capability framework

In this section, I outline the foundational concepts of capability approach which I used to interpret and analyse student narratives. I framed equal participation using an intersection of theoretical approaches to social justice, equality and education with a particular focus on the capability approach, Freire's critical education and Nancy Fraser's redistributive theory of justice. The theories are aligned with two core assumptions. The first is that a more just justice demands a redistribution of resources and opportunities amongst members of the institution. Unlike the 'trickle down' logic of neoliberal policies, a redistributive approach is explicit about ensuring that the most excluded and vulnerable groups are given access to resources and opportunities that enable capabilities and functionings.

A second assumption draws on Ingrid Robeyns' limitarian approach, which is that extreme individual privilege and wealth are not defensible in the context of 1) global poverty, 2) urgent unmet needs, such as basic education for women and girls and 3) collective crises such as environmental damage and global warming (Robeyns 2016). Given that all three conditions are met in most parts of the world, and particularly in South Africa, I use the limitarian approach to argue that it is unjust that because of luck and inherited privilege some students have real access to all the facilities, opportunities and resources offered by the university, and are able to convert these into capabilities and functionings. Because of social inequality, economically vulnerable students at the same institution have access to a comparatively impoverished experience of higher education with comparatively fewer or none of the benefits enjoyed by their privileged peers.

Capabilities and functionings

Capabilities and functionings are foundational units of analysis in the capability approach. Human development is evaluated not as utilities or primary goods, but as the 'substantive freedoms – the capabilities – to choose a life one has reason to value' (Sen 1999: 74). According to Sen (1999) the combination of functionings indicates an individual's achievements, while a capability set shows the actual *freedom* that an individual has to achieve these functionings. Both capabilities as *freedoms* and functionings as *achievements* are important to understanding individual agency and freedom to participate.

The notion of a capability expands the idea of what someone is able to achieve because of birth or natural talent: 'capabilities are not just abilities residing inside a person but also the freedoms or opportunities created by a combination of personal abilities and the political, social and economic environment' (Nussbaum 2011: 20). Nussbaum distinguishes between combined capabilities, which are the substantial freedoms that an individual has for 'choice and action in her specific political, social and economic situation', and internal capabilities, which are 'trained or developed traits and abilities, developed, in most cases, in interaction with the social, economic, familial, and political environment' (Nussbaum 2011: 21). A capability is cultivated within an individual's social environment. Combined and internal capabilities must be produced together; for example, developing the internal capability for a reasoning voice requires the combined capabilities, or freedoms, to express this voice in an environment where dissent, free speech and participation are valued and protected (Nussbaum 2011).

Making judgments about capability development in student experiences focuses on what students are able to do and be within structural arrangements. From a social justice perspective, the 'attitude towards people's basic capabilities is not a meritocratic one – more innately skilled people get better treatment... but the opposite: those who need more help to get above the threshold get more help' (Nussbaum 2011: 24). In the example above, an individual whose school, cultural or familial environment does not nurture her basic capability for confident speech would not be labelled as inarticulate and excluded from public platforms, but would rather be given appropriate support, external conditions and resources to develop her internal capability for voice.

Once the individual has the capability for voice as a cluster of capabilities that gives her the freedom to express her voice, she can then transition from the freedom to the actual being or doing. The realisation of capability is therefore a *functioning* (Nussbaum 2011). Functioning could be an active 'doing', such as using the capability for voice to speak confidently in a classroom full of people. But functioning is also a state of being in which a capability has been realised, such as being a critically educated citizen. Again, freedom of choice is central to functionings in that people should be free to choose the functionings that they have reason to value (Nussbaum 2011). The student in the example above would not be forced to speak in public once she has the capability for voice; the important thing is that she has the freedom to speak, and real opportunities to speak if she chooses to do so. While capabilities must be prioritised as equal access to opportunities, people should be free to choose from a number of available possibilities (Robeyns 2006).

Fertile functioning works accumulatively to expand well-being (Wolff & de-Shalit 2007). For example, the ability to be educated could lead to decent employment, to better health and nutrition. A fertile functioning is determined by 'the interaction of your internal resources with the social and material structures within which you find yourself [which] determines your genuine opportunities for secure functionings' (Wolff & de-Shalit 2007: 173). Corrosive disadvantages on the other hand cluster and have negative effects on other functionings (Wolff & de-Shalit 2007: 121). The idea of a fertile or corrosive capability has important implications for the analysis since being aware of corrosive disadvantage could also clarify 'the causal relations between disadvantages, to try to understand why patterns of disadvantage form and persist' (Wolff & de-Shalit 2007: 121). Corrosive disadvantage can also point to areas that require intervention and transformation.

A critical distinction is that structural arrangements that create capability deprivation should be eliminated instead of making judgments about the inherent ability of individuals who occupy these environments. This reframes freedom within the context in which an individual must choose and act by examining the actual opportunities available for capability development. Injustice is exacerbated when arrangements are aligned with individual deprivation instead of challenging structural inequalities.

Education as freedom

A capability-informed interpretation of freedom is another aspect of my theoretical framework. Economist Amartya Sen, founder of the capability approach, states that 'greater freedom enhances the ability of people to help themselves and to influence the world' (Sen 1999: 18) while expanding people's choices (ul Haq 2003). Education has a complicated history of complicating individual freedom and imposing values and information onto students as 'passive' recipients (Gandin & Apple 2002; Freire 1970; Leach & Moon 2008). Although an expanding body of scholarship resists the socialisation of people into docile workers and citizens, this oppressive legacy is finding new expressions under a neoliberal ethos. Under the creeping logic neoliberalism, the market-driven university increases standardisation and an uncritical assimilation of knowledge (Vally & Motala 2014; Giroux 2013: Chomsky 2017).

As an egalitarian alternative, I use Sen's notion of development as freedom to frame education as freedom: education as a process of freedom (the everyday participation) and freedom as an end (outcomes, a degree, income, social mobility) (Sen 1999). If universities hope to expand students' freedom as both a process and an outcome, then evaluating the quality and equality of individual participation makes more sense than only measuring outcomes. Sen's notion of freedom as process and outcome suggests a shift away from some established practices in higher education. As a starting point, Sen argues that development depends on instrumental freedoms that advance individual capacity. These freedoms include political freedoms, economic facilities, social opportunities, transparency guarantees and protective security (Sen 1999). These freedoms are interconnected by individual well-being: for instance, an individual should not have to wait to be adequately nourished before having access to a platform where she can criticise her leaders, nor should she wait to become educated before she can choose who should govern her country. Applied to student participation at university, instrumental freedoms would ensure that pedagogical and institutional arrangements enable equal participation. In this way, education as freedom enables a student to participate in designing arrangements while she is developing her capability for voice. Instead of assuming that students cannot decide for themselves, Sen's view insists that even the most vulnerable individuals must participate in the planning of their own lives. In my analysis of student narratives, I use the idea of education as freedom to mean that vulnerability should not be used to exclude students from contributing to arrangements that diminish their participation. For instance, instead of requiring participation in literacy interventions of first-generation students who do not have access to formal academic discourses, students would have equitable access to platforms that cultivate academic discourses. In this way, resources and opportunities would be redistributed to students who do not have the freedom for equal participation (Nussbaum 2011).

Democratic participation

Development as freedom resists educational structures that are implemented without rigorous processes of democratic participation, which is the second human development value in my conceptual framework. A freedom-based approach would enable deliberative processes that include students in decision-making (Crocker 2008). This participatory focus would replace a top-down approach to first-generation students. Sen defines the political freedoms required for democratic participation as:

> the opportunities that people have to determine who should govern and on what principles, and also include the possibility to scrutinize and criticize authorities, to have freedom of political expression and an uncensored press, to enjoy the freedom to choose between different political parties and so on.
>
> (Sen 1999: 38)

A human development perspective requires an expansion of choice and alternatives as a condition of development as freedom. According to Sen, freedom of choice is concerned with 'our ability to decide to live as we would like and to promote the ends that we may want to advance' (Sen 2009: 228; Nussbaum 2011: 18). Instead of bureaucratic processes that fail to include people as decision-makers, deliberative processes require access to critical knowledge to help people understand the costs and consequences of arrangements (Sen 1999). Democratic participation requires the development of practical reason as a capability that is woven into other freedoms (Nussbaum 2010).

If such freedoms are applied to micro processes in the classroom, students would be involved as actors who contribute to decision-making. Instead of being consumers of knowledge, students would be free to engage in a process of decision-making that shapes the structural conditions in which they learn and the outcomes that this learning enables (Sen 1999; see also Fraser in Bozalek 2012: 148). Walker's (2006: 47–48) application of democratic participation to higher education argues that, in:

> developing a capability-based policy for teaching and learning at university, those affected by the policy – lecturers, students, support staff . . . should be participants and agents. They would collectively decide on the selection of relevant capabilities, and the institutional conditions should support such participation.

Sen addresses the tension between economic and political freedoms, which I found particularly relevant to addressing the financial and academic vulnerability of first-generation students, since 'the intensity of economic needs adds to – rather than subtracts from – the urgency of political freedoms' (Sen 1999: 148): 'An attempt to choke off participatory freedoms on grounds of traditional values ... simply misses the issue of legitimacy and the need for people affected to participate in deciding what they want and what they have reason to accept' (Sen 1999: 32). Socioeconomic vulnerability therefore makes it more important for students to have a platform for participation in political rights, because 'freedom of expression and discussion, are not only pivotal in inducing social responses to economic needs, they are also central to the conceptualization of economic needs themselves' (Sen 1999: 154).

I look carefully at the degree of freedom that students have in determining the conditions of their own learning and whether pedagogical arrangements offer an opportunity to learn and practise their democratic rights (Sen 1999; see also Deneulin 2014):

> If people are well-nourished [or educated] but not empowered to exercise practical reason and planning with regard to their health and nutrition [or education and learning], their situation is not fully commensurate with human dignity: they are being taken care of the way we take care of infants.
> (Nussbaum 2011: 39)

In combination with platforms for resistance, I was interested in whether students who face significant resource constraints are able to access deliberative platforms for shared decision-making. An important step to remediating injustices and redistributing resources would be to facilitate and support the public platforms that students need to identify injustices and act to enable 'the capacity to influence the range of available choices and the social settings in which choices are made and pursued' (Bauman 2009: 189). These platforms could empower student voices to design workable support structures and to contribute towards institutional transformation (Hart 2012; Walker 2012). The freedom to partici--pate as critical and engaged members of the institution is '[t]o promote areas of freedom, and this is not the same as making people function in a certain way' (Nussbaum 2011: 25). I focus my analysis not only on whether students have the freedom to contribute to decision-making, but at what point a student gains entry into these processes. According to Crocker's model of participation, the earlier the individual entry into decision-making, the higher the quality of participation and agency (see Crocker 2008).

Agency

I used a capability framework to examine the significance of agency and structural inequality in contributing towards student participation. Instead of technical interventions, the capability approach contributes a theory of justice that prioritises the involvement of people in their own development, in order to shift the focus from deficit to agency. From this agency-orientated lens, higher education could be 'fostering first generation participation in higher education by building aspirations, confidence and educational capabilities' (Marginson 2011: 34), while being cognizant of equal participation for all students (Walker 2008b). Framed in this way, I evaluated whether the arrangements and opportunities offered by higher education enable vulnerable students to achieve valued capabilities.

Because unjust structures have the potential to entrench inequality when they erode individual freedom to participate in deliberative processes (Deneulin 2014), my analysis requires a simultaneous focus on the individual agent who navigates these structures. In the capability approach, agency is concerned with the freedom that an individual has to make autonomous choices. Sen (1992: 56–57) distinguishes between agency *achievement* as 'the realization of goals and values she has reasons to pursue' and agency *freedom* as 'one's freedom to bring about the achievements one values and which one attempts to produce'.

A capability approach respects individual freedom to make choices, since people have different conceptions of what a valued life entails (Robeyns 2005: 101; Crocker & Robeyns 2010: 76). While most people have the potential for agency, 'the freedom to actually become an active agent also depends on social, political, and economic opportunities available to us' (Sen 1999: xii). In the analysis of student experiences, it was crucial to show how students who accessed university despite structural constraints demonstrated agency (Pym & Kapp 2013). For this reason, I focused on the degree of agency freedom that students have to act and make choices in the years leading up to university and during their undergraduate years at university.

Amplifying agency as the *recognition* of equal human worth, dignity and potential has been an important response to a deficit approach to first-generation students, while being sensitive to the fact that they might require more resources and support to participate equally. Instead of 'pathologizing Black student experiences and creating a notion of victimhood' (Pym & Kapp 2013: 273), my analysis focuses on how individuals used agency as resistance despite structural and personal barriers. The strength of the capability approach is therefore its focus on structural inequality, while not neglecting the individual conversion factors, adaptive preference and agency faced by university students (Walker 2005).

Because the participants in this research are working-class and/or first-generation students who occupy stratified racial, ethnic and language hierarchies in South Africa's post-apartheid society, an agency-focused approach recognised the challenges of students negotiating misrecognition within institutions. The focus on individual agency is cautious about:

> the twin assumptions that ... you can be whatever you want to be; and therefore ... if anything bad happens to you, it's no one's fault but your

own. . . . We are thought to be in control of our own lives, even in situations where circumstances are not in our favour.

(Cederström & Spicer 2015: 6)

Recognition could offer the platform that enables students to cultivate the autonomous and confident identities as scholars and citizens (Christie, Munro, & Wager 2008).

Conversion factors

Conversion factors are well-aligned to a redistributive analysis of structures (Sen 1999: 72–73; see also Sen 2009: 66). According to the capability approach, conversion factors are personal, social and environmental differences that explain why individuals benefit differently from the same resource bundle or arrangements (Robeyns 2005). These factors point to the diverse conditions in which people make choices and to the internal factors and external circumstances affecting these choices. Because the capability approach takes into account how personal and socio-environmental factors influence the conversion of commodities into capabilities and functionings (Robeyns 2005: 99), this opens up an interpretative space to investigate how conversion factors can be either enabling or constraining. In resistance to the deficit view of 'underprepared' students explored in Chapter 2, conversion factors could explain why some individuals flourish in a particular environment while others experience capability deprivation. From a social justice perspective, although education is an intrinsic good in itself, it can also 'contribute to capability deprivation . . . through existing inequalities' (Tikly & Barrett 2011: 7; see also Stromquist 2006; Hart 2009).

In the analysis of student experiences, I used social or structural conversion factors that interact with an individual's existing resources and capabilities. It is not sufficient to ensure that students have a fair share of resources unless structural arrangements also equally distribute the opportunities to convert resources into functionings (Tikly & Barrett 2011: 4; see also Freire 1970: 66–67). The distinction between goods and capabilities frames a participatory trajectory that requires a basic threshold in combination with enabling conditions (Robeyns 2005: 96–97). For example, an unsafe walk from home to campus as a conversion factor could explain why some students do not use the library or computer laboratories after dark. Because of this environmental factor, a student is not free to convert a resource (e.g. books at the library) into engagement with knowledge. Unless resources like books and Internet access are accompanied by development structures that enable students to convert resources into opportunities, these resources fail to address inequality (Pick & Sirkin 2010). Understanding how conversion factors work within *pedagogical* arrangements was important to determine not only whether students attend lecturers or tutorials (which offer educational 'resources' as information), but how teaching and learning conditions constrained or enabled a student's freedom to convert information into actual participation in critical learning.

Adaptive preference

In the analysis of student experiences, I also used the idea of adaptive preference, defined by capability scholars as:

> deprived people [who] tend to come to terms with their deprivation because of the sheer necessity of survival, and they may, as a result, lack the courage to demand any radical change, and may even adjust their desires and expectations to what they unambitiously see as feasible.
> (Sen 1999: 63; see also Nussbaum 2001; Bridges 2006).

Because the capability approach prioritises the protection of human freedom and agency, the idea that we can evaluate someone's choice as 'deformed' has received significant criticism. It has also been defended by scholars who have attempted to find a balance between values that seek the empowerment of marginal groups with recognition that people who participate in their own oppression still practise agency (Khader 2012; see also Stromquist 2006). For instance, adaptive preference would examine whether an individual has adapted her academic preferences to suit under-resourced or debilitating environments. Although analysing adaptive preference is not a straightforward task, given that people may subconsciously adapt their preferences (Bridges 2006), evaluations about the equality of arrangements could be enriched by understanding how 'habit, fear, low expectations and unjust background conditions deform people's choices and even their wishes for their own lives' (Nussbaum 2000: 114; see also Nussbaum 2001; Robeyns 2010).

In my view, evidence of adaptive preference in student experiences can contribute towards an argument for structural transformation. Such evidence could challenge complacency about conditions of deprivation or vulnerability. For instance, instead of assuming that students prefer standardised testing because they do not demand change, an analysis of adaptive preference would ask whether students have ever been exposed to a different way of learning or had opportunities to experience the benefits of real alternatives (Hart 2009; see also Bridges 2006).

Well-being

The final aspect of my capability framework is well-being, which encompasses the 'rational, emotional, and social dimensions' of an individual's educational processes (Lozano *et al.* 2012: 137). The purpose of development is 'to create an enabling environment for people to enjoy long, healthy and creative lives' (ul Haq 2003: 17). Well-being is the intended outcome for each individual regardless of the bundle of resources that they contribute to their environment, so that each person is valued by virtue of their human existence. The capability approach 'takes *each person as an end*, asking not just about the total or average well-being but about the opportunities available for each person' (Nussbaum 2011: 18). Sen evaluates well-being according to an individual's achieved functionings, not happiness, choice or utility (Sen 1999; see also Khader 2012).

In my analysis, I define well-being as capability development that reflects an equitable distribution of material and symbolic resources aligned to individual needs. Well-being is achieved when the individual has the capabilities to convert distributed resources into functionings that reflect an individual's ethical commitment to herself and her social world. Whatever the income, level of education or status of an individual, the ultimate measure of her well-being is a quality of life that has achieved the capability freedoms and functionings aligned to her reasoned values, aspirations and inherent potential. In my analysis, I am interested in whether arrangements contribute to the conversion of available resources, to expand the future well-being of the individual.

According to the capability approach, well-being cannot be separated from the pursuit of justice, informed by a gradual shift within the approach from a concern about individual well-being to questions about how to arrange societies (Deneulin 2014: 46). This view of well-being is ethically individualistic in that the interest in interpersonal comparisons reflects a broader concern for the well-being of society. In this sense, an evaluation of well-being cannot be separated from questions about whether the arrangements in which students learn are enabling and just (Walker 2006).

Freire and education as freedom

In designing this framework, I have found a useful compatibility between Sen's conceptualisation of freedom and Paulo Freire's critical consciousness (1970). Both scholars ground their theories of human development and critical pedagogy as the expansion of freedom. I also found Freire's redistributive ethos aligns well with the egalitarian norms of the capability approach. These approaches recognise that institutional power involves hierarchical relationships to the detriment of people who have diminished power (Freire 1970; see also Walker in Otto & Ziegler 2013).

Freire's critical conscientisation contributes to the capability theory's focus on public deliberation as people's freedom to participate in practical reasoning (Deneulin 2014).

Freire argues that individuals who are denied access to platforms of decision-making are at risk of being assimilated into massified systems of education that preclude the development of critical-participatory consciousness: 'Any situation in which some [people] prevent others from engaging in the process of inquiry is one of violence. The means used are not important; to alienate [people] from their own decision-making is to change them into objects' (Freire 1970: 73).

Education that 'domesticates' critical thinking denies the practice of democratic values and leaves students poorly equipped to participate in the transformation of their society (Freire 1970: 34; see also MacFarlane 2012. I interrogate how higher education treads a precarious line between the provision of resources that graduates need to compete in a globalised 'knowledge economy', without such arrangements regressing into assimilation that leaves the individual with a highly specialised, yet uncritical knowledge (Freire 1970). This framework uses the capability approach to ask critical questions about participatory freedom for each student as 'a basis for assessing equality of opportunity, rather than simply access to resources or equality of outcomes' (Tikly & Barrett 2011: 7).

Resisting the banking system

I also apply Freire's critique of the banking system, defined as information that the student passively receives, memorises and reproduces (Freire 1970). As an alternative, the capability analysis investigates whether pedagogical conditions cultivate practical reason (Nussbaum 2011). My critique of the banking system shifts the focus to 'processes of learning and personal development taking place within educational institutions and elsewhere rather than on the more traditional focus on outcome measures' (Hart 2009: 396). Moreover, equal participation is framed as an approach to learning that offers critical engagement with knowledge (McLean *et al.* 2013: 65; Walker 2006). The banking system risks stifling the development of intellectual autonomy and critical consciousness. Its invisibility often leaves the individual with constrained access to knowledge (Freire 1970). A solution to epistemological access would therefore require both technical solutions to student learning, while also interrogating whether the knowledge on offer enables students to recognise how uncritical education misframes 'cognition as a neutral process that takes place in a vacuum' (Kincheloe 2008: 32). These systemic arrangements alienate students with 'a narrow academic focus, drill and recitation, little student choice of activities and materials, large group as opposed to small group instruction, truncated exploration of contextual knowledge, and emphasis on convergent questions with short correct answers' (Kincheloe 2008: 48). When the banking system normalises uncritical arrangements, it is more difficult for students to recognise and resist the barriers to capability development (Kincheloe 2008). When students' access to powerful knowledge is constrained, they may also be less able to resist the biases that 'lie deep within the very structure of the educational system's processes of transmission and acquisition and their social assumptions' (McLean *et al.* 2013: 53). This creates 'more subtle aspects of higher education pedagogical cultures [which] may themselves be creating conditions which make it difficult, or even impossible, for some students to learn' (Haggis 2006: 521).

At the same time, both the capability approach and critical pedagogy suggest that student–lecturer relationships require a participatory approach. Freire's view is that a dialogue is the only way to resolve the teacher–student binary and to enable relations that resist and destabilise unjust institutional arrangements (Freire 1970). Students who are vulnerable to unequal participation struggle to negotiate university environments where meritocracy and the unfamiliar hierarchies between professors, lecturers and students deny struggling students access to the support they need to participate. The capability for affiliation and Freire's emphasis on resolving the teacher–student duality suggest that relationships are resources that enable students to convert educational resources into valued functionings. In later chapters, I illustrate how affiliation between lecturers and students is one of the most important arrangements that enable students to convert education into equal participation (Crosbie 2013; Fraser 2000; Freire 1970; Nussbaum 2010; Wood & Deprez 2012; Walker 2006).

In making the distinction between capability and competence in higher education, 'freedom is education's core value [while] participation and dialogue are central teaching methodologies that cannot be reduced to a mere strategy for achieving an outcome' (Lozano *et al.* 2012: 138; Walker 2003). This reiterates Sen's point that people must not be 'passive recipients' of development interventions, but should play an active role in shaping these and the content and values embedded in development programmes (Sen 1999: 53). The focus on freedom supports the aims of social justice rather than 'technical interest [that] does not consider properly practical or emancipatory interest' (Lozano *et al.* 2012: 141). A capability-inspired pedagogy evaluates the fairness of actual teaching and learning arrangements (Walker 2003). Participatory teaching methods include principles such as equity, diversity, empathy, tolerance and solidarity (Lozano *et al.* 2012: 144), which are more conducive to transformative education as the 'power to reflect, calculate, analyse, draw conclusions and see beyond the immediate environment' (Stromquist 2006: 149).

Finally, Freire's pedagogy aligns with the human development concern with education for socially just ends. This means that graduates who have had access to opportunities to practise democracy in the classroom should become conscientised to the arrangements that shape their learning while becoming critically informed about widening global inequalities (Freire 1970; Walker & McLean 2013). Critical education towards the ends of a public good, freedom and social transformation would necessitate graduates with critical literacies, knowledge and technical competency, who are able to convert these resources into socially just ends (Boni & Walker 2013). In this way, education can be a social product that expands individual freedom while making educational arrangements more enabling for future student cohorts (Sen 1999; see also Gasper 2013).

Fraser and the capability approach

I used Nancy Fraser's egalitarian theory to make the structural inequalities embedded within the post-apartheid higher education more explicit. I integrated the capabilities approach's focus on individual freedoms with Fraser's concern for redistributive justice and structural inequalities in higher education (Bozalek & Boughey 2012; Bozalek & Carolissen 2012; Burke 2012). In my research framework, Fraser's notion of participatory parity deepens the analysis of narratives in two significant ways. First, because Fraser's theory is rooted in a socialist tradition, she is explicit in her vision for an egalitarian society, and proposes a redistributive framework that disrupts structures of economic and social privilege. Fraser offers a critique of inequality in capitalist economies, with the assumption that capitalist models entrench inequality (Fraser 2013). This theory of justice is: 'part of a broader emancipatory project, in which struggles against injustices [are] necessarily linked to struggles against racism imperialism, homophobia and class domination, all of which [require] transformation of the deep structures of capitalist society' (Fraser 2009: 107).

Second, Fraser's egalitarian approach is critical of neoliberal feminism, which has been co-opted to advance the careers and aspirations of elite, educated women. While women's aspirations in leadership are important, neoliberal feminism replaces an egalitarian vision with the ideals of success, financial rewards and status for elite women, often at the expense of low-paid care and service workers on whom professional women depend (Fraser 2016b). Similarly, in higher education, the neoliberal model has given a comparatively small number of students access to higher education, and some have flourished. However, once admitted, relatively few students have sufficient resources and institutional support to participate equally in comparison with their privileged peers. I incorporated three aspects of Fraser's theory – redistribution, recognition, and representation – into the analysis of student experiences, which I discuss in more detail below.

Redistribution

Fraser's economic dimension of justice sharpens my focus on capability-informed analysis of student participation and resource redistribution. This approach is a critique of the resource maldistribution that characterises twenty-first century capitalism (Fraser 2016a; Chomsky 2017). In resistance to affirmative approaches that fail to challenge systemic inequalities, Fraser's transformative approach seeks to restructure relations of production, consumption and distribution, with the goal to 'change the social division of labour and thus the conditions of existence for everyone' (Fraser 1995: 84). Fraser's focus on power complements the capability approach's emphasis on individual agency, so that I could analyse agency alongside relations of power. This redistributive ethos is an alternative to a deficit approach that fails to address the systemic roots of unequal distribution (Sen 2009). From the capability perspective, disadvantage accumulates when working-class and precariously middle-class students face financial insecurity that erodes their freedom to participate (Wolff & de-Shalit 2007). This leaves individuals without a basic needs threshold vulnerable to exclusion, misrecognition or unequal participation. I ask whether a minimum threshold is in place to ensure that vulnerable students do not suffer capability deprivation because of resource insecurity (Sen 1999). My analysis of students' resource conversion takes into consideration 'the freedoms generated by commodities, rather than ... the commodities themselves' (Sen 1999: 74). Resource distribution is relative to the environment, so that a working-class student at an urban university must compete with middle-class peers and needs more resources to take part in the university's academic and social life.

Recognition

Second, I used Fraser's notion of recognition as distinct from identity politics, defined as follows: 'recognition could involve the wholesale transformation of societal patterns of representation, interpretation and communication in ways that would change everybody's sense of self' (Fraser 1995: 73).

Misrecognition is a systemic failure to recognise the equal worth of each individual entering the institution, which recreates injustice as 'an institutionalized pattern of cultural value that constitutes some social actors as less than full members of society' (Fraser 2000: 114). Drawing on this nuanced version of recognition, my analysis frames recognition of individual resources and agency to challenge the structural arrangements that misrecognise students who face socioeconomic constraints. Fraser's transformative approach to recognition resists 'creating stigmatized classes of vulnerable people perceived as beneficiaries of special largesse' (Fraser 1995: 85). In the analysis of student narratives, I used misrecognition to capture the tension between visible forms of exclusion – such as evidence of poverty or deprivation – and the invisible forms of exclusion, such as subtle differences in being treated or perceived as less academically capable. These implicit forms of exclusion are difficult to recognise, prove or articulate, which means that they influence participation without being given sufficient credit (Fraser 2013). As an alternative to the deficit approach, a transformative approach would advocate for an equal distribution of resources and opportunities without misframing students as deficit, or perpetuating misrecognition of academic potential. Instead of deep change, allocating special courses to disadvantaged students become problematic when special treatment results in status injury, shame and stigma (Fraser 2009).

My framework resists framing students as less worthy members by acknowledging the resources that students bring to the classroom. Fraser's theory of justice 'understands that status subordination is often linked to distributive injustice' (Fraser 2000: 119). In my analysis, this integrated focus on *resources and recognition* is critical to understanding participatory equality for students who are misrecognised, while being given a smaller share of resources. As I discussed earlier, it was also important to recognise the unique resources that students contribute to higher education.

Representation

Misrepresentation is concerned not only with the freedom for political participation, such as student leadership, for instance, but with boundaries drawn to include or exclude people in structural arrangements. Fraser defines misrepresentation as follows: 'Misrepresentation occurs when political boundaries and/or decision rules function to wrongly deny some people the possibility of participating on a par with others in social interaction – including, but not only, in political arenas (Fraser 2013: 196).

The resource constraints of poverty can exclude students from accessing a platform for academic participation or success, while social misrecognition as discussed in the section above, such as discrimination and stigma linked to poverty, can also exacerbate misrepresentation. Invisibility or a lack of presence in which individuals or groups are not included in the framing of a problem would be found for instance in the exclusions of minority groups in policy decisions, which denies their existence and makes it difficult to press justice claims (Fraser 2013; Bozalek & Boughey 2012).

Conceptual framework for narrative analysis

Drawing on the integration of the capability approach and social theory, I conceptualised participation as the following:

> A multidimensional capability that expands access to resources and opportunity freedoms to convert resources into capabilities, recognises agency and existing student capabilities, cultivates values for the public good, engages critically with knowledge, and opens up participatory platforms for deliberation to challenge inequality at all levels of the institution.

Figure 3.1 below visualises this definition through three level resource and opportunity clusters. The outer level (1) is access to the institution and to a basic resource threshold needed to participate. The middle level (2) is concerned with structural arrangements that enable and/or constrain individuals' ability to convert the available access and resources into success and participation. The centre (3) represents the capabilities and personal resources that the individual brings to the university, which the student uses to convert available resources and arrangements into participation and success. In the construction of my argument, when any one of these resource and opportunity clusters is compromised, the ability to participate equally is diminished.

For instance, an individual may have access to adequate funds for tuition, and the potential to convert academic resources into success. However, if the arrangements are not conducive to learning (e.g. crowded classrooms, inadequate number of permanent staff) or if the student is misrecognised based on race, class and gender operating with pedagogical spaces, this would erode the freedom

62 The capability approach and inequality

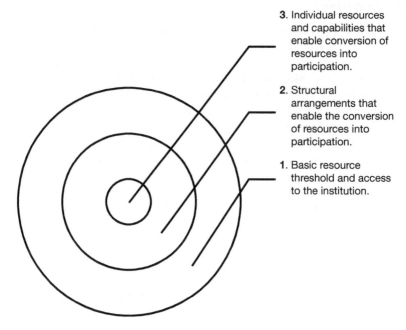

Figure 3.1 Working definition of equal participation

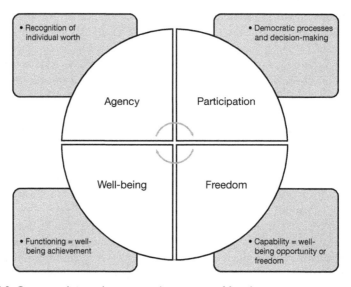

Figure 3.2 Conceptualising education as the practice of freedom

to convert available clusters into actual participation. In a different case, a student may have access to enabling structural arrangements, but a lack of tuition, or being academically unprepared for university learning might constrain her freedom to convert academic resources into participation. These levels are also interconnected in that the pedagogical arrangements – if aligned to existing student capabilities – could enable the development of underdeveloped capabilities needed for participation before the student is excluded. Figure 3.2 below summarises the principles outlined in the conceptual framework.

Inequality in the higher education system suggests that there are vastly different experiences of education, even for students from the same socio-economic status. These inequalities are influenced by the way that status, resources and opportunities are distributed across the institution. Using a multi-dimensional analysis, I theorise inequality of participation on a spectrum of freedom and equality. This means that outcomes such as test scores or degree completion are an inadequate indicator of participation, and that we need to look closely at the experiences of individual students to make sense of their freedom for participation.

References

Bauman, Z., 2009. *Does Ethics Have a Chance in a World of Consumers?* Cambridge, MA: Harvard University Press.
Boni, A., & Walker, M., 2013. *Human Development and Capabilities: Re-Imagining the University of The Twenty-First Century.* London & New York: Routledge.
Bozalek, V., 2012. Interview with Nancy Fraser. *The Social Work Practitioner-Researcher,* 24.
Bozalek, V., Boughey, C., 2012. (Mis)framing Higher Education in South Africa. *Social Policy & Administration* 46, 688–703. https://doi.org/10.1111/j.1467-9515.2012.00863.x
Bozalek, V., & Carolissen, R., 2012. The Potential of Critical Feminist Citizenship Frameworks for Citizenship and Social Justice in Higher Education. *Perspectives in Education* 30, 9–18.
Bridges, D., 2006. Adaptive Preference, Justice and Identity in the Context of Widening Participation in Higher Education. *Ethics and Education* 1, 15–28. https://doi.org/10.1080/17449640600584946
Catlaks, G., 2013. Hidden Privatization and Its Impact on Public Education. In Otto, H.-U., & Ziegler, H. (Eds), *Enhancing Capabilities: The Role of Social Institutions.* Opladen: Barbara Budrich Publishers.
Cederström, C., & Spicer, A., 2015. *The Wellness Syndrome.* Malden: Polity Press.
Chomsky, N., & Polychroniou, C.J., 2017. *Optimism over Despair: On Capitalism, Empire, and Social Change.* Chicago, IL: Haymarket Books.Christie, H., Munro, M., & Wager, F., 2005. Day Students' in Higher Education: Widening Access Students and Successful Transitions to University Life. *International Studies in Sociology of Education* 15, 3–29.
Crocker, D.A., 2008. *Ethics of Global Development: Agency, Capability and Deliberative Democracy.* Cambridge: Cambridge University Press.
Crocker, D.A., & Robeyns, I., 2010. Capability and Agency. In Morris, C. (Ed.), *Amartya Sen.* Cambridge: Cambridge University Press.

Crosbie, V., 2013. Capabilities and a Pedagogy for Global Identities. In Boni, A., & Walker, M. (Eds), *Human Development and Capabilities: Re-Imagining the University of the Twenty-First Century*. London and New York: Routledge.

Deneulin, S., 2014. *Wellbeing, Justice and Development Ethics*. London and New York: Routledge.

Deneulin, S., & Shanani, L., 2010. *An Introduction to the Human Development and Capability Approach: Freedom and Agency*. IDRC.

Flores-Crespo, P., 2007. Situating Education in the Human Capabilities Approach. In Unterhalter, E. & Walker, R.W. (Eds), *Amartya Sen's Capability Approach and Social Justice in Education*. New York: Palgrave Macmillan.

Fraser, N., 1995. From Redistribution to Recognition? Dilemmas of Justice in a 'Post-Socialist' Age. *New Left Review* 1(212), 68–93.

Fraser, N., 2000. Rethinking Recognition. *New Left Review*, 107.

Fraser, N., 2009. *Scales of Justice: Reimagining Political Space in a Globalizing World*. New York: Columbia University Press.

Fraser, N., 2013. *Fortunes of Feminism: From State-Managed Capitalism to Neoliberal Crisis*. New York: Verso Books.

Fraser, N., 2016a. Clinton Embodies a Neoliberal Kind of Feminism which Mostly Benefits Privileged Women. *ctxt*, 20 April 2016. https://ctxt.es/es/20160420/Politica/5538/fraser-feminism-Hillary-Clinton-neoliberal-feminism-redistribution-recognition-representation.htm

Fraser, N., 2016b. Contradictions of Capital and Care. *New Left Review*, II 99–117.

Freire, P., 1970. *Pedagogy of the Oppressed*. London: Penguin Books.

Gandin, L.A., & Apple, M.W., 2002. Can Education Challenge Neo-Liberalism? The Citizen School and the Struggle for Democracy in Porto Alegre, Brazil. *Social Justice* 29, 26.

Gasper, D., 2013. Education and Capabilities for a Global 'Great Transition'. In Boni, A., Walker, M. (Eds), *Human Development and Capabilities: Re-Imagining the University of the Twenty-First Century*. London and New York: Routledge.

Giroux, H.A., 2013. Public Intellectuals against the Neoliberal University. 29 October, 2013. *Truthout*. www.truth-out.org/opinion/item/19654-public-intellectuals-against-the-neoliberal-university

Haggis, T., 2006. Pedagogies for Diversity: Retaining Critical Challenge Amidst Fears of 'Dumbing Down'. *Studies in Higher Education* 31, 521–535. https://doi.org/10.1080/03075070600922709

Hart, C.S., 2009. Quo Vadis? The Capability Space and New Directions for the Philosophy of Educational Research. *Studies in Philosophy and Education* 28(5), 391–402.

Hart, C.S., 2012. *Aspirations, Education and Social Justice: Applying Sen and Bourdieu*. London: Bloomsbury.

Khader, S.J., 2012. Must Theorising about Adaptive Preferences Deny Women's Agency? *Journal of Applied Philosophy* 29, 302–317. https://doi.org/10.1111/j.1468-5930.2012.00575.x

Kincheloe, J.L., 2008. *Knowledge and Critical Pedagogy: An Introduction*. Montreal: Springer.

Leach, J., & Moon, R.E., 2008. *The Power of Pedagogy*. New York: SAGE Publications.

Lozano, J.F., Boni, A., Peris, J., & Hueso, A., 2012. Competencies in Higher Education: A Critical Analysis from the Capabilities Approach. *Journal of Philosophy of Education* 46, 132–147. https://doi.org/10.1111/j.1467-9752.2011.00839.x

Macfarlane, B., 2012. Re-framing Student Academic Freedom: A Capability Perspective. *Higher Education* 63, 719–732.
Marginson, S., 2011. Equity, Status and Freedom: A Note on Higher Education. *Cambridge Journal of Education* 41, 23–36.
McLean, M., Abbas, A., & Ashwin, P., 2013. University Knowledge, Human Development and Pedagogic Rights. In Boni, A., & Walker, M. (Eds), *Human Development and Capabilities: Re-Imagining the University of the Twenty-First Century*. London and New York: Routledge.
Nussbaum, M.C., 2001. *Women and Human Development: The Capabilities Approach, The Seeley Lectures*. Cambridge: Cambridge University Press.
Nussbaum, M.C., 2011. *Creating Capabilities*. Cambridge, MA: Harvard University Press.
Otto, H.-U., Ziegler, H. (Eds), 2013. *Enhancing Capabilities: The Role of Social Institutions*. Opladen: Barbara Budrich Publishers.
Pick, S., & Sirkin, J., 2010. *Breaking the Poverty Cycle: The Human Basis for Sustainable Development*, 1st edn. Oxford: Oxford University Press.
Pym, J., & Kapp, R., 2013. Harnessing Agency: Towards a Learning Model for Undergraduate Students. *Studies in Higher Education* 38, 272–284. https://doi.org/10.1080/03075079.2011.582096
Robeyns, I., 2006. The Capability Approach in Practice. *The Journal of Political Philosophy* 14, 351–376.
Robeyns, I., 2010. Gender and the Metric of Justice. In Brighouse, H., & Robeyns, I. (Eds), *Measuring Justice: Primary Goods and Capabilities*. Cambridge: Cambridge University Press.
Robeyns, I., 2016. Having Too Much (SSRN Scholarly Paper No. ID 2736094). Social Science Research Network, Rochester, New York.
Sen, A., 1992. *Inequality Reexamined*. Oxford: Oxford University Press.
Sen, A., 1999. *Development as Freedom*. Oxford: Oxford University Press.
Sen, A., 2009. *The Idea of Justice*. London: Penguin Books.
Stromquist, N.P., 1990. Gender Inequality in Education: Accounting for Women's Subordination. *British Journal of Sociology of Education* 11, 137–153. https://doi.org/10.1080/0142569900110202
Tamim, T., 2013. Higher Education, Languages, and the Persistence of Inequitable Structures for Working-Class Women in Pakistan. *Gender and Education* 25, 155–169. https://doi.org/10.1080/09540253.2012.752793
Tikly, L., & Barrett, A.M., 2011. Social Justice, Capabilities and the Quality of Education in Low Income Countries. *International Journal of Higher Education* 31, 3–14.
ul Haq, M., 2003. The Birth of the Human Development Index. In Fukuda-Parr, S., Kuma, S. (Eds), *Readings in Human Development*. Oxford: Oxford University Press, pp. 17–34.
Unterhalter, E., 2003. Inequality, Capabilities and Poverty in Four African Countries: Girls' Voice, Schooling, and Strategies for Institutional Change. *Cambridge Journal of Education* 42, 307–325.
Unterhalter, E., 2010. *Global Inequalities and Higher Education: Whose Interests are You Serving?* New York, NY: Palgrave Macmillan.
Vally, S., & Motala, E., 2014. *Education, Economy & Society*. Unisa Press, Pretoria.
Walker, M., 2003. Framing Social Justice in Education: What Does the 'Capabilities' Approach Offer? *British Journal of Educational Studies* 51, 168–187. https://doi.org/10.2307/3122419

Walker, M., 2005. Amartya Sen's Capability Approach and Education. *Educational Action Research* 13.
Walker, M., 2006. *Higher Education Pedagogies: A Capabilities Approach.* Berkshire: Open University Press.
Walker, M., 2008a. A human Capabilities Framework for Evaluating Student Learning. *Teaching in Higher Education* 13, 477–487.
Walker, M., 2008b. Widening Participation; Widening Capability. *London Review of Education* 6, 267–279. https://doi.org/10.1080/14748460802489397
Walker, M., 2012. Universities and a Human Development Ethics: A Capabilities Approach to Curriculum. *European Journal of Education* 47, 448–461. https://doi.org/10.1111/j.1465-3435.2012.01537.x
Walker, M., & Fongwa, S., 2017. *Universities, Employability and Human Development.* New York, NY: Springer.
Walker, M., & McLean, M., 2013. *Professional Education, Capabilities and the Public Good: The Role of Universities in Promoting Human Development*, 1st edn. London and New York:Routledge.
Walker, M., & Wilson-Strydom, M., 2016. *Socially Just Pedagogies, Capabilities and Quality in Higher Education: Global Perspectives.* New York: Springer.
Wilson-Strydom, M., 2015. *University Access and Success: Capabilities, Diversity and Social Justice.* London and New York: Routledge.
Wolff, J., & de-Shalit, A., 2007. *Disadvantage.* Oxford: Oxford University Press.
Wood, D., & Deprez, L.S., 2012. Teaching for Human Well-being: Curricular Implications for the Capability Approach. *Journal of Human Development and Capabilities* 13, 471–493. https://doi.org/10.1080/19452829.2012.679651

Chapter 4

Introducing student narratives

What do student narratives reveal about structural inequalities in higher education? Because the aim of the project was to understand how undergraduate students experience inequality in higher education, I used narrative methods to amplify student voices, to investigate the power relations between researcher and participants, and to interrogate the unequal distribution of opportunities in higher education (Mertens 2008). Student narratives informed a nuanced approach to injustice that examined individual lives within the context of economic, social and political forces that shaped freedoms and aspirations in complex ways. The first section of the chapter briefly outlines the narrative methods used in the project inequality in higher education. In the second section, I track students' experiences of schooling before they enter university.

Listening to student experiences

Listening to student voices as 'authorities about their own experiences' (Rogers 1993: 150) offered an 'insider' perspective into the interplay of social, economic and academic challenges that create subtle and invisible forms of exclusion (Brown 2009). Student narratives were constructed using a process of participatory research that aims to make research 'more rational and reasonable, more productive and sustainable, and more just and inclusive' (Kemmis, McTaggart, & Nixon 2013: 2–3). During interviews and in the process of creating students' digital narratives, we explored structural and individual conversion factors that enabled and constrained the freedom for equal participation. The participatory project resisted a deficit approach to working-class, Black and/or first-generation students (Mertens 2008; Smith-Maddox & Solórzano 2002). Students' examples of agency and resistance also challenged a reductionist oppressor–oppressed dichotomy, and suggest that power hierarchies are fluid and invisible between groups and institutions (Fraser 2009).

While sharing their experiences during interviews, students created digital narratives, which are short multimedia productions in which participants create a narrative about their lives (Lambert 2013; Robin 2008). Using this platform, students constructed their experiences in relation to peers who faced similar and different challenges. The project created a shared platform that students could use to relate to the challenges of being an undergraduate student at university, while gaining insight into the resources and agency that they used to negotiate and conquer such challenges. The project was also designed to cultivate participatory solutions to structural inequality and highlighted student agency in resistance to a deficit approach (Lozano *et al.* 2012; Josselson & Lieblich 1995). Experiences shared during interviews and focus groups deepened my understanding of structural possibilities and constraints. Participants reported that these platforms enhanced their freedom 'to reflect, calculate, analyse, draw conclusions and see beyond the immediate environment ... to analyse their realities and subsequently to devise means to transform their lives' (Stromquist 2006: 149). Narratives created mutual spaces where students could make sense of knowledge about the social, educational and political contexts that shape freedom for participation (Richardson 1997; Cousin 2009; Bathmaker & Harnett 2010).

Relational methodology was used to challenge the researcher-researched hierarchy, which enabled a deeper understanding of how university structures, cultures and relationships limit equal access to academic opportunities, and also deny, silence and erase student experiences of violence, discrimination and othering. Interviews were unstructured to allow student experiences to emerge, while focus groups offered participants the opportunity to share their biographies with the rest of the group, allowing time to comment and reflect on the narratives. Because the project stretched over three years, I was able to compare students' digital narratives with their interview narratives (Marshall & Case 2010). I was engaging with in-depth biographical material in the narratives while analysing interview data, which enriched the analysis of student experiences before entry into university and the equality of participation they reported during interviews and the digital narrative production. Using the digital narratives, I investigated themes around capabilities and functionings for higher education, which deepened my understanding of structural and individual conversion factors that influence the freedom to participate (Stein 2008).

Introducing the participants

Participatory research offered insight into student experiences that deepened over time. These platforms created opportunities to challenge and to reconstruct hierarchical research and pedagogical relationships. The production process enabled significant pedagogical and transformative opportunities as a result of the longitudinal research process. The biographical insights and analysis would not have been possible without the 'thick description' of experiences provided by the digital narratives (Kress 2011). From a capability perspective, individual voice is diminished when institutions do not create platforms for all actors to contribute to conversations about values, freedoms and agency. Since the

Table 4.1 Participant biographical information

Pseudonym/home language/race/sex/age	High school	Degree
Aziza Tswana, black female, 25	State urban	BA Social Sciences (Extended)
Clarice English and Afrikaans, Coloured female, 22	Private urban	BA Social Sciences (Extended)
Condorrera Sesotho, black female, 29	Township	BA Humanities (Extended)
Dante Sesotho, black male, 22 (Extended)	State urban	EMS, changed to BA
Kea IsiXhosa, black female, 21	Township	BA Social Sciences (Extended)
Naledi Sesotho and Tswana, black female, 21	Township	Economic and Management Sciences, changed to BA Social Sciences (Extended)
Techniques Sesotho, black male, 21	Township	BA Social Sciences (Extended), changed to BA Humanities
Thuli Sesotho and English, black female, 22	State urban	BA Law, changed to Law

capability approach is interested in lives that people have reason to value, a relational, voice-based approach offered a fertile way to investigate individual experiences. Focusing on student voice also enabled detailed accounts of structural injustice. This meant that while some participants blamed themselves for unequal participation, their narratives revealed how structural arrangements created an environment that made success difficult or almost impossible. Table 4.1 below gives a brief biographical overview of the research participants.

Student experiences at school

This section sets the backdrop for individual students' participation at university by mapping their experiences of school, at home and in the community. My aim is to explore how structural conditions at school, in the family and the community enable and constrain the conversion of resources into capabilities for equal participation. By separating student experiences before university from experiences at university, I show how the distribution of resources and recognition enables and constrains the capability development needed to participate equally in higher education.

In the first half of this section, the analysis of student experiences frames school, the home and the community as social structures that enable and/or constrain an individual's freedom to access resources, convert resources into capabilities and achieve well-being (Hart 2012). These experiences also illustrate how students use agency to convert scarce resources into capabilities by resisting structural barriers. It was important to understand the school context in order to make sense of student experiences in higher education (Wilson-Strydom 2015).

At the beginning of the project, I explored how structural conditions at school, in the family and the community enabled and constrained students' conversion of resources into capabilities for equal participation. Student experiences are organised into two evaluative sites – education and aspirations – (see Table 4.2) that I use to analyse how resources and recognition are distributed and converted into capabilities. I stress the importance of individual agency in converting resources and argue that, despite structural inequalities, some participants are able to convert scarce resources and support provided by families to aspire to and access higher education.

Inequality and South African schooling

As an introduction to participant experiences of schooling, I give an overview of the challenges facing the South African public school system, in order to contextualise the findings and analysis in the chapter, and to set the scene for students' opportunities for equal participation at university. Although a nuanced discussion of the complex issues related to schooling is beyond the scope of this book, it is important to outline the realities of an education system in crisis, which have been widely researched and documented (Bloch 2009; Chisholm

Table 4.2 Organisation of analytical codes

Evaluative sites	Structural conversion factors	Agency	Freedoms
Education	• Access to resources • Learner identity development • Aspirational development • Language as educational capital	Agency as: • deliberative reasoning • creative production • resistance/subversion • compliance/assimilation	Agency freedom Opportunity freedoms
Aspirations	• Access to resources • The role of women • The role of school • The role of family/community • The role of work		Capabilities

2004; Jansen & Blank 2014; Fleisch 2008; Taylor 2008; Van der Berg 2008; Wilson-Strydom 2015).

University entrants graduate from South African's notorious two-school system, in which many public schools are severely under-resourced, staffed with poorly qualified teachers, and ranked as detrimental to the well-being of both students and teachers. The point is not to blame the school system, but to ask what can be done for the many students who will enter the system before public schooling improves. These systemic problems with infrastructure and human capacity will take decades to solve. In 2011, the Department of Basic Education reported that 79 per cent of state schools in South Africa have no libraries (Paton-Ash & Wilmot 2011). This means that young people spend their formative years in an environment where neither their school, their home nor their community can offer access to the most fundamental educational resources.

In a nutshell, South Africa's present-day public school system[1] reflects the uneven distribution of resources and infrastructure created by three and a half centuries of colonial exploitation, and the social engineering of the apartheid regime, where education was used to reproduce oppressive and race-based ideologies (Bloch 2009; Fataar 2012). Apartheid era (1948–1994) education policies ensured that schools for Black, Coloured and Indian populations were severely under-resourced, while their administration was stratified according to racial classification (Christie, Butler, & Potterton 2007).

Despite a number of major structural overhauls since 1994, the current system reflects these inequalities. A small number of schools – most of which were previously reserved for the white population – are well-resourced and offer relatively good quality education. The remaining majority of schools are 'Black schools in relatively poor socio-economic circumstances [which are] often under-resourced in terms of laboratories, computers, sports fields and opportunities for extra-curricular activities' (Christie *et al.* 2007: 4; see also Bloch 2009; Fataar 2012). With between 60–80 per cent of South African schools that could be identified as dysfunctional, this creates an extremely concerning gap in the quality of education for the majority of learners in the system (Bloch 2009). This 'high cost, high participation, low quality system' (Taylor 2008: 4) shows evidence of 'massive disparities in performance between schools . . . to a large extent structured by a history of poverty and deprivation, with African schools overwhelmingly represented in the poor performing category' (Taylor 2008: 3; see also Van der Berg 2001).

Another concern, directly related to the first research question, is whether conditions at schools are conducive to the conversion of available resources into educational outcomes (Van der Berg 2008: 145). Despite the introduction of a school quintile system, which is an intervention aimed at allocating more resources per pupil to poorer schools, this has been criticised for failing to address the complex mobility patterns of South African learners. For instance, many students from poorer communities travel to schools in higher quintile areas, which means they do not necessarily benefit from this investment in resources. At the same time, only a small minority of students have access to schools that have the ability to set higher fees, offer a rich variety of extracurricular activities, employ more teachers and resourced libraries and other teaching and learning infrastructure (Taylor 2008).

A related area of national concern has been South Africa's persistently low performance in regional and international tests in strategic areas such as numeracy, literacy and science, given the fact that South Africa is outperformed by poorer African countries (Taylor 2008: 2; see also Van der Berg 2008: 2). This suggests that unequal resource distribution is not the only factor responsible for the failures of the education system. Another significant constraint to creating a robust, functional school system has been dramatic and disruptive changes to the school curriculum. For instance, the introduction of outcomes-based education, introduced without well-trained teachers, led to a neglect of disciplinary content that exacerbated the gap in academic quality at poorly resourced schools (Wilson-Strydom 2015).

Therefore, in addition to resource maldistribution, the public school system faces serious logistical, administrative and management barriers. For this reason, the management of schools has been scrutinised to investigate the structural cause of dysfunctional schools (Bloch 2009). This foregrounds for instance the professionalism of teachers and school management structures in creating or inhibiting environments that are conducive or detrimental to teaching and learning (Taylor 2008: 4). Other concerns include teacher absenteeism and low teacher motivation and morale, exacerbated by the low status, remuneration and training opportunities of the teaching profession in South Africa (Bloch 2009; Wilson-Strydom 2015). One critical evaluation summarises these issues as 'a culture of complacency and low expectation [that] permeates the entire South African system, including those schools which were privileged under apartheid' (Taylor 2008: 2).

There are also deep-seated problems created by persistent social inequalities, such as school violence, sexual exploitation of learners, race-based discrimination, and poverty. A report commissioned to investigate functional state schools in the middle quintiles confirmed the finding in the 1961 Coleman report, that even though schools cannot compensate for broader social failures of inequality, poverty and violence, the freedom to attend a functional school makes a significant difference in the lives of vulnerable young people (Christie *et al.* 2007: 20).

Within the context of this landscape, participant voices illustrate how experiences at school are shaped by structural arrangements across the intersectionality of socioeconomic class, gender and race. Their experiences confirm that 'while South Africa has improved access to schooling, it has not provided access to quality schooling for the majority of the population', even though the minority receiving quality education now represents a more diverse mix of population groups (Christie *et al.* 2007: 28).

Resources and recognition at school

Keeping in mind the realities of the school system discussed above, I now turn to participant experiences of schooling. While taking into account the serious consequences of under-resourced schools and community environments in which the students had to learn, the analysis also draws attention to evidence of individual agency with narratives, as a way to resist a deficit approach to students from disadvantaged backgrounds. I also focus on agency to argue that student participation at university is also not necessarily a reflection of existing ability or potential, but in many cases the consequences of the corrosive effect of unequal distribution of resources and recognition at home and in the institution, such as the harsh conditions within schools discussed above (Leibowitz 2011; Boughey 2007). I also hope to demonstrate how unequal conditions at school and in the community make it difficult for some students to participate equally in higher education, to gain recognition as valued members of the institution and to participate in decision-making processes. Importantly, the analysis is guided by students who frame themselves as agentic actors within their experiences of school and university, while remaining realistic about the barriers that they face in participating in higher education.

I now turn to the eight student narratives, which will be discussed in terms of resources and opportunities available to the individual student. The aim of this section is to understand how students negotiated resource constraints at school, and how they used agency to reach university despite structural inequality. By listening to student experiences, I also wanted to find out how structural arrangements at school were complicated by unequal access to resources and recognition, and how these arrangements enabled and constrained participants' conversion of resources into participation later in their academic trajectories. My analysis intends to balance a structural critique of unjust conditions with recommendations for transformative action without either pathologising students educated in unjust conditions or romanticising their aspirations and struggle to access and participate in higher education. As much as the dysfunctional system continues to exclude and marginalise millions of South African children and adolescents, there is a danger of imposing a deficit discourse onto individual people because of systemic failures. So while I stress the importance of redressing structural inequality in the provision of resources, opportunities and infrastructure, I have also been influenced by research that suggests that despite disabling circumstances and structural injustice, adverse conditions can cultivate capabilities in resistance to inequality (Marshall & Case 2010).

In Aziza's narrative, school emerged as an important site where she was able to access resources for future participation at university. She explained her uncle's decision to send her and two male cousins to a well-resourced primary school:

> *I am one of the few in the family that is privileged enough to have gone to a 'white' school. That opportunity kind of also put pressure on me, 'cos the cousin*

> *that I was always with was in the normal Black school. . . . For me it, how can I put it, it shaped the way I look at things, the way I view things, the way I view my intelligence as well, and work, work in general, books. And my view of the world [INT 1].*

Being recognised as a relative who is 'worthy' of the scarce resources needed to send children in the extended family to a better school increased Aziza's status in the community. In contrast, the academic and personal development enabled by these resources was not available to her cousins who attended a township school. The status and worth inscribed onto this selection is material and symbolic: Aziza was able to convert resources at school into valued academic and social functionings, while also developing recognition as a person who is capable of academic achievement and who holds a privileged position within her family and community. Having physical access to a well-resourced, formerly 'white' school means that Aziza escaped both the stigma of a township school and the material reality of poorly resourced facilities and fewer qualified and motivated teachers. She explained that these early experiences of a well-resourced environment:

> *helped me focus in a sense . . . I also think it helped broaden my horizon more than the Black schools, 'cos the Black school was initially just school, homework and everything else [INT 1].*

Aziza explained that there was fierce competition for limited space at elite urban high schools; however, when she did not gain entry into the well-resourced girls' school of her choice, she was forced her to attend a high school that was not aligned with her educational aspirations. Aziza described her entry into a 'Coloured mixed school' as an unsettling adjustment that negatively affected her experience of education:

> *First I didn't wanna be there, I totally . . . I just felt like, this is not where I am supposed to be. I hate this school . . . because I came from this high standard of learning and we had sports and we all these things that . . . shaped the way I behaved. . . . And this school had nothing [INT 1].*

In contrast to her experience at her primary school, Aziza was then forced to adjust to a 'very, very different' academic standard, which she experienced as teachers who lacked the will or the passion to teach:

> *[I]t was because they had to teach. It was because they had to. There was never really a teacher who stood out for me in my first year while I was there [INT 1].*

Aziza struggled to adjust to a student culture defined by prevalent ill-discipline and disengagement with learning, so she isolated herself to maintain academic focus:

Introducing student narratives 75

> *I valued learning and I wanted to learn. [The other learners] were 'just' [accented slang suggests passivity and laziness]. And I didn't like that. And I ended up being more alone. I wouldn't say a teacher's pet, but I did my work and I asked questions. I'm a person who loves asking questions [INT 1].*

Within an enabling primary school environment, Aziza had developed confidence in her ability to convert her intelligence into reasoned judgments. She also used her agency to convert her aunt's advice into aspirations for an independent life and made a conscious decision to abandon substance abuse to prioritise her education. Although she was demoralised by the dramatic shift in educational quality and teacher engagement at her high school, Aziza used this reasoning ability in a constraining environment to isolate herself and resist assimilation into a culture of mediocre disengagement modelled by peers at school.

Condorrera attended a township school in an informal settlement. Her family is a single-parent household where her mother's limited income provided the basic needs for her siblings and unemployed and disabled adults in the extended family. She described the school as a strict environment that lacked the educational resources available to develop capabilities. For example, a science experiment performed at her school failed because of inadequate laboratory equipment, while the same experiment performed during a field trip to an elite girls' school was performed successfully by a teacher who had access to proper laboratory facilities. This experience sharpened the contrast between her education and the opportunities available to privileged peers:

> *Because [the pupils] took it as [the teacher] didn't know what she was doing. Only to find out that lack of equipment didn't support the whole experiment to work out. So we left that school (after matric), not knowing whether they're going to improve on that or not [INT 2].*

For Condorrera, the intersection of maldistribution and misrecognition and the opportunities provided by the school compromised her freedom to convert resources into capabilities and functionings (see also Rivera 2015). Their teacher was also misrecognised as incompetent because of the lack of adequate facilities that she needed to teach:

> *Black schools and [former] Model C, they are different[2]; they were taught differently than how we are. Our background from which schools we have been to, is not easy. If you go to [elite girls' school], compare [elite girls' school] with [township state school], it's just top class. They take drama, music. We don't have that [INT 1].*

One tragic consequence of this structural injustice was a distorted belief that students value education based on their race. Condorrera's quotation below illustrates how this discourse blames individuals for not successfully pursuing education, while masking the structural root of unequal participation:

> *It's believed that most Black people do not like learning, and Coloured people. So I think white people are just fortunate. You [white] guys believe in school [INT 2].*

Despite the inequality of township schooling, Condorrera used her agency to create opportunities for employment and entry into university. However, she was reflective about the historically embedded inequality that constrained her peers' capability freedoms:

> *So I feel like they [the school system and teachers] should have done more. Most of the people who have completed high school, some of them they are not studying. They are working at Pep Store³; most of them they are taxi drivers. They were brilliant, but if some things were instilled in them, then, as young as they were, they could have done something with their lives [INT 2].*

While Condorrera is able to develop aspirations and an academic identity through opportunities after school, she is concerned that many of her peers at school were unable to exercise agency in the same way, and are trapped outside higher education in low-paying menial work or unemployment. While she managed to escape the limitations of the system, many of her classmates were not able to convert scarce resources into employment and education after school. This is significant because even though Condorrera was able to participate in higher education, her peers were failed by the public school system, which left them particularly vulnerable to growing youth unemployment and the consequences of extreme socioeconomic inequality (Vally & Motala 2014).

Techniques was also raised by a single parent, as the youngest of four siblings. His experience of the township high school was boredom and little motivation to attend school or engage with learning:

> *Before I came to varsity, I used to just go to school, just like, you just learn what you have to learn, you don't go beyond ... what you were given. ... At school I never studied [Laughs]. No, really, even my matric years, I didn't study [INT 1].*

He explained that his older siblings were not successful in pursuing higher education, which increased the pressure on him as the youngest child to obtain a degree. But his home environment did not offer resources that encouraged the capability development needed for participation at university. At school, the maldistribution of resources framed education as an obligation disconnected from his lifeworld or aspirations for employment or higher education. Techniques was demotivated by perceived instrumental logic of school, but in rebelling against the system was misrecognised by teachers as a 'naughty' student, but had disengaged to cope with a stressful home environment and his family's poverty:

> *I grew up whereby I didn't have a father ... why should [I], like, be a man, when at home there is no man. So I always did funny stuff to forget where I come from. But now, ja, I think I've changed, whereby I see myself as a better man. Not only for me, but the future. Should I have kids, they should have a father to be proud of [INT 1].*

An important agentic move was the way Techniques converted experiences of a poorly resourced, alienating school environment into critical reflexivity about social inequality more generally. Using his precarious position at a township school, Techniques developed narrative imagination that enabled him to convert experiences of maldistribution and misrecognition into an empathetic understanding of young people who are excluded from formal structures of education and employment. This other-regarding agency (Walker 2015) shaped his aspirations for transformative action once he entered university. However, these earlier educational experiences and resource constraints continued to be profoundly challenging, and Techniques was left vulnerable to exclusion throughout his academic journey.

Kea described her township school as a challenging environment that she negotiated despite extremely difficult personal circumstances. Kea was orphaned during primary school and was raised by her grandmother who supported an extended family facing unemployment and poverty. Following the death of her grandmother, she found a job as a petrol attendant and managed to pay her school fees and apply for a university bursary. The scarcity of resources in her extended family made her vulnerable and shaped her aspirations to become financially independent:

> *So my grandmother passed away in 2008. I was doing Grade 10. And from that year, I started working, actually from the day that my [grand]mother passed away, that was my first day at work. ... 'Cos when it comes to serious things that contributes towards my education, I feel that I don't want to burden my family, so much, 'cos they have done so much for me. So if I can do something for myself, then why not? [INT 1].*

Kea explained that these harsh conditions made her determined to resist the deficit view of students who attend township schools. So despite the constraining environment, Kea developed the ability to communicate fluently in English, which became a valued resource for participation at university:

> *And then in high school, I was this girl who was from ... a Black primary school ... I started speaking English, by the way. I started speaking English from Grade 4. And a lot of my friends were in white schools, so I was the only*

> one who was in a Black school. But I did not tell myself that, 'I'm not gonna not learn English just because I'm in a Black school.' I told myself, 'I'm gonna learn English, no matter how many times I make a mistake.' That's how you learn. And my primary teachers, they used to love me! [INT 1].

The scarcity of resources at home inspired Kea to pursue higher education, which she believed could help ease the poverty in her extended family. Two important parallel threads running through her narrative were an agentic resistance to unfair conditions on the one hand, while on the other hand the meritocratic discourse in which the lone individual must achieve success despite unequal arrangements and limited support. This made Kea vulnerable to possibly inaccurate judgments about her potential that ignored structural inequality:

> *I'm not clever; I'm a hard worker. And when I put my mind to something, I just make sure that I excel in it [INT 1].*

She negotiated the school environment using personal resources such as the ability to plan her future, her determination to contribute to the family income, and a highly-developed sense of responsibility shaped by early hardship and loss. She also drew on social resources like encouraging teachers who supported her efforts to learn and speak English:

> *I keep pushing. I don't get intimidated easily; that's one of my strengths. And I really am proud of that I don't let people get to me [INT 1].*

While Kea demonstrated extraordinary resilience in navigating her environment, years of stress in balancing work and school, combined with the loss of her parents and grandmother and little family support, escalated into precarious participation at university, as discussed in the next chapter.

Naledi attended a boarding school and recalled the psychological effect of relentless teasing by male peers. She described an environment where harsh treatment and punishment by teachers and management constrained her ability to convert educational resources into academic functioning. The staff at times used abusive disciplinary practices, which alienated and demoralised Naledi and her peers. Naledi also described a lack of encouragement from teachers in formulating aspirations:

> *[T]he teachers, you know, they were that awful. They told us: 'By the end of the month we will be earning, and you guys are just gonna be here and failing.' And they were saying discouraging things [INT 1].*

The lack of recognition or support from teachers was combined with pressure from Naledi's parents to pursue subjects to ensure an economics major at university, even though she was passionate about writing, journalism and literature. Naledi experienced school as an instrumental focus on assessment and performance, with few opportunities to develop critical academic capabilities:

> *I think teachers were there to teach us and leave. I don't think there were teachers who would say to us: 'Go and do it' [INT 1].*

Naledi's agency at school was constrained by structural conditions where teachers focus on the instrumental value of memorisation and study, while hierarchical teacher–student relationships produced a climate of fear, punishment and coercion. While her home community was severely impoverished, with few libraries and other opportunities for capability development, Naledi's parents encouraged her to read newspapers and books, and she converted these resources into an interest in politics and journalism. She also converted the routine imposed at school into the discipline needed for university study, and her love for reading into literacy capabilities. Yet, Naledi's freedom was ultimately constrained by her parents' insistence on her pursuing an economics degree for the sake of future employability, which compromised her capability to participate equally in higher education.

In sharp contrast to the previous narratives, Clarice's parents had enough resources to send her to a well-resourced high school. Both she and her younger sister had the freedom to choose between their local public school and the private school that Clarice chose to attend. She attributed her capability development and participation at university to the quality of education and the abundant resources available at school:

> *That's what changed my life, the school environment, the teachers ... sports. That kept me busy. 'Cos I seriously think that if I was at what we call a Coloured school, I would be exactly the same as everyone else. My sister is there right now, and she doesn't have any ambition to go to varsity, or to do well at school [INT 1].*

Besides access to excellent resources, Clarice's parents helped her to convert these educational resources into capabilities and functionings for participation. Her father played an active role in her extracurricular activities and encouraged her to study hard and to sacrifice time with friends and family to achieve university entry. She described a supportive and well-resourced family environment within the context of an impoverished neighbourhood where the majority of adults suffered chronic unemployment and substance abuse. As the outlier in this environment, Clarice was able to convert available resources into aspirations for higher education. The resources that Clarice's father and mother were able to provide – both parents have full-time employment – enabled her to attain recognition as a capable student with the potential for higher education. However, while Clarice's sister had access to the same supportive home environment, she chose to attend the poorly resourced government school. Although it was not clear why she chose to attend a different high school, Clarice explained that her sister was demotivated and influenced by peers who did not aspire to post-school education, although she was encouraged by her parents to pursue a university education after matric.

Enabling pedagogical arrangements at school also cultivated critical academic capabilities that Clarice transferred to university. While developing a love for knowledge and learning was not dependent on a well-resourced school, participants who attend such schools appear to have significantly more freedom to pursue opportunities for meaningful engagement with knowledge and learning. The classroom was an engaging space where Clarice was nurtured by teachers who were able to dedicate ample time and resources to good-quality teaching. Individual attention, supportive relationships between teachers and students, and a rigorous learning environment were valued resources that shaped her experiences of education as a positive and engaging process:

> *We were never more than 25 at all. From Grade 1. I've always been used to that. And my Grade 1 teacher, her husband taught me science. I had a bond with the two of them. They were already 70 [years old] when I left school [INT 1].*

Clarice had the freedom to choose from a wide variety of subjects, which enabled her to develop an appreciation for history. Clarice then converted her historical knowledge, enriched by trips to museums and historical sites, into the capability for critical engagement with knowledge at university. She also developed high expectations of and a critical approach to pedagogical and institutional arrangements at university, which I discuss in more detail in Chapter 6.

Thuli attended a well-resourced urban boarding school where opportunities to participate in debating, travel with the choir, and a diverse student body were converted into participation at university:

> *I really liked choir, to sing. Because we used to travel a lot. . . . And debating. It helped me improve my English a lot. It helped me to like think effectively, like in terms of critical thinking. And not always give what the question . . . I must just think way beyond. It improved my essay writings as well and finding research. Not always talking about research as what 'they' said, it's more about what you think of it [INT 1].*

These opportunities gave Thuli the freedom to travel and to network across different social groups. The school offered career guidance that Thuli supplemented with her own research into different careers. The detailed advice offered at high school was an enabling structure that helped Thuli make accurate decisions about university. Thuli used her agency as reasoned deliberation in choosing subjects that aligned with her aspiration to study law, which she was able to achieve. The diverse student body at Thuli's school was another positive resource that she converted into an appreciation for diverse cultures, another capability that was transferred to university:

> *And she [career counsellor] told us that with maths and science, we can get into anywhere, provided you have those requirements. You can study law, even if you did maths and science [INT 1].*

Even though her high school offered the freedom for capability development, teachers still misrecognised student potential. Thuli explained that while she was able to resist these negative messages because of her academic achievement and parents' encouragement to pursue higher education, many of her peers did not have the same resources and support:

> *And then you get other teachers that discourage you, that tell you, you're not gonna make it. Like if you are getting in the 50s now, they say: 'What's gonna happen in Grade 11 or your final year?' They tell you you're not gonna make it [INT 1].*

The combination of resources and recognition means that Thuli entered university with confidence in her ability to cope in a challenging environment.

Dante's experiences at school were constrained by his exclusion from a preferred well-resourced private school, since the school only accepted a small number of top-performing international students, and the struggle to adjust to an urban state school. He described the experiences of moving between a private school and an urban state school:

> *It [state school] was not that good. For the smart people who were already equipped [it was ok], but for me, I needed a lot of time. For me, the teachers didn't really care much about you. It's either you passed or you failed. It was a different environment. My grades fell; it was too much. With the private [former Model C] school you get to interact with the teachers more; they see your problems and they tell you 'This is a problem.'*
>
> *The teachers at [the well-resourced independent school] came to us sometimes at hostel. They said to us: 'Hey, are you free? Do you wanna talk about something?' They were very cool [INT 1].*

Dante's travels across different school spaces highlighted the elite resources required for access to private schools:

> *When you say private [independent] school, people think it's diverse. But it was all Black, all Black. It was not really what I wanted. I wanted to go to Saint Andrew's or Grey College in Bloemfontein. They take very few international students, and obviously they take the best international students in terms of academics and grades and mine were just average so I didn't get into that.*

> *I've had friends that went to . . . these nice private[4] [former Model C] schools . . . and they have sort of have like a thing, they have an aura. And it lasts for a very long time, because they teach them manners, and a lot of things that you don't really notice. And that's exactly what I wanted; I wanted to be groomed in that way. When you apply at Rhodes or UCT, they actually take the Saint's guy . . . more into consideration. It's not fair, but I understand. They don't know our facilities and if we'll be able to cope [INT 1].*

The arrangements that enabled and constrained Dante's agency and freedom are distinctively aligned with his middle-class identity[5] and an affluent two-career family. As another participant who is not a first-generation student, Dante's educational trajectory was strategically mapped out with the help of his parents. While other participants found a combination of limited resources and under-resourced school constraining, state schooling offered a different set of constraints for Dante's aspirations to upper middle-class identity and the 'grooming' offered by elite schools. His narrative revealed the way that Dante uses available resources to navigate the university environment even though he struggles to compete academically, compared with Naledi who is isolated off campus and does not have the same mobility. Yet despite not being a first-generation student, Dante struggled to participate academically at university and had trouble adjusting to the demands of unfamiliar academic discourses for which he was not adequately prepared.

As he transitioned between different schools, Dante used his agency to resist the lower quality education offered at an urban state school. This occurred after he was not accepted into the highly competitive and well-resourced state school of his choice. The structural arrangements offered at his state school included low teacher involvement, large classes with minimum individual attention and a system that offered high-achieving students more resources. Despite constraining structures, Dante converted extra-curricular opportunities into valued capabilities for public speaking and student leadership, which he transferred to university:

> *I was an orator, and did public speaking, for Grade 8 and Grade 9. And I won best junior male orator for 2009. And then I was also a newspaper editor for the school. I did a lot of poetry, cultural and arty stuff [INT 1].*

While Kea's, Techniques' and Condorrera's experiences of township high schools reveal a struggle against a constrained socioeconomic environment, Dante's account of schooling directed attention to the connection between school and class identity. His freedom to convert an elite school education was constrained by the rigorous selection process that admitted only a small number of international students. Dante's failure to gain entry into the school of his choice limited his agency freedom, and resulted in a transition between a less prestigious private school and a state school. His freedom to pursue a valued educational trajectory was also constrained by his perception of an 'average' academic ability, which made him more vulnerable to exclusion from valued higher education institutions. According to Dante, the unfair structure of this selection process suggested the perception that students at well-resourced schools are given an unfair advantage in accessing elite universities.

Developing aspirations

Another important aspect of participatory parity that emerged in student narratives is the development of aspirations for higher education. Nancy Fraser's principle of participatory parity brings together the distributional and social dimensions of justice to investigate the equity of structural arrangements (Fraser 2013: 11). The focus of this section is the freedom that students had to develop aspirations for university. In particular, I wanted to understand the social conditions in which resources and recognition provided by the school, family members and the community environment were converted into aspirations. I focused on status and recognition to interpret the way that students are misrecognised within structures (Fraser 2009).

Student narratives showed how aspirations are constructed in relation to available educational, material and community resources. Most participants lived in communities where the consequences of extreme socioeconomic inequalities are visible. The participants shared experiences of unemployed relatives, friends and peers who had dropped out of school, and the physical and psychological effects of unemployment. These narratives suggested constructed discourses of failure, mediocrity and low aspirations: social relations were structured around the binary of someone as either a failure or a success story. Students made comparisons between themselves and family or community members to reveal unjust arrangements where access to educational resources, social support and opportunities for capability development were highly competitive and excluded the majority of citizens from the freedom to participate in higher education.

Participants framed as 'outliers' were not immune to the systemic injustices that reproduce social, educational and economic participation. They relied on scarce resources and precarious family and community structures to provide the support they needed for entry into university. Their narratives revealed how resources enabled the development of aspirations, without necessarily offering the sustained support required for university participation. Some students developed aspirations in resistance to unjust structures within their family and community structures to pursue opportunities that might enable social mobility.

Resources and recognition at school were the first site that developed aspirations for higher education. Condorrera attributed her pursuit of work overseas to an inspiring maths teacher:

> *We had a math teacher from London. I would look at her and think, 'Wow she's a mathematician; she has money.' So I took maths, but I didn't do so well. I was very good but ... The love for schooling was built from then. She even told us about programmes that would take you overseas. And I would write it down. And then later on I applied for an au pair programme and I left for the US [INT 1].*

While inspiring her to apply for au pair work in the United States and cultivating her love for learning, this teacher also inspired Condorrera to associate mathematics with success and a stable income, in line with the education department's strong emphasis on scarce skills in STEM [science, technology, engineering and mathematics] subject areas. Condorrera was constrained by the policy-driven focus on STEM subjects because her school could not provide the resources she needed to develop capabilities for strong mathematics skills or creative writing and art-based subjects that she has reason to value. Condorrera eventually chose to focus on mathematics, but eventually accepted that her interest and talent lay with the humanities and social sciences:

> *I remember I wanted to be a mathematician because I thought, wow, maths is the only way to go [INT 1].*

While Condorrera was passionate about the arts and creative writing, her freedom to choose a career as a writer – which she explained is her first choice – was constrained by the socioeconomic pressure to support her impoverished family. This freedom was also compromised by an economy that offers few educational opportunities and precarious employment for the creative arts. She explained how her peers were similarly discouraged by the absence of resources and the pedagogical neglect of languages and the arts:

> *[T]his teacher came to us and ... addressed us about maths, science and biology, and you know, which is very good. But was only looking at those who could do well in those subjects. She forgot about those who were more creative, in terms of writing, singing, expressing themselves. And I kept wondering how come school promotes maths and science, except creativity? I loved writing [INT 1].*

Despite this constraint, Condorrera converted her aptitude for writing into a novel written during her undergraduate degree. Her aspiration for university was shaped by her experiences while working and studying overseas, where she had access to opportunities to learn Spanish and American Sign Language, which cultivated her aspiration to pursue sign language as a career:

> *I was working with autistic children. I was based in Washington but travelled between New York, New Jersey, and I've also been to Texas. It's like you see it on TV. It really changed me. When I came back, I wanted to study [INT 1].*

She did not choose her degree programme for instrumental reasons and decided to drop out of a bursary-sponsored computer engineering course because 'it was not what I wanted to do'. Instead, she converted her work experience, her experiential knowledge of South African Sign Language, and her interest in African languages into educational and career aspirations. Her narrative in Chapter 6 illustrates that this decision enabled Condorrera to participate more equally at university compared with students who were coerced into degree courses that misrecognised their academic talent and interests.

Kea valued teachers and motivational speakers at school who encouraged her to draw on her experiences of hardship at home, together with her confidence and strong verbal abilities to develop career aspirations:

> *So I felt like I can motivate those children in primary school to tell them that, 'Do not look at where you are right now, do not limit yourself.' And my teacher used to say that I should be a motivational speaker.... 'Cos I've been through most of the challenges that most people my age have never been through.*
>
> *There were motivational speakers every now and then, people that encouraged learners to work hard [INT 1].*

The fact that Kea's mother was killed during political protest action, as part of the struggle against the oppressive apartheid regime, shaped Kea's aspiration to become a female business leader who empowers Black women to discover their potential. Kea converted this loss into an aspirational trajectory that was evident throughout her university experience. This personal aspiration extended to Kea's dream to empower women in her community who are vulnerable to social and economic exclusion.

Aziza also experienced enabling arrangements for aspirational development at school when a career guidance counsellor tried to help Aziza connect her existing capabilities to a specific career trajectory:

> *'Cos this other guidance counsellor in high school [said], 'Your voice and your bubbliness, go into radio. You talk a lot!' So I was like, mmm, radio ...? But radio, you need to be doing something to get in, you can't just jump into radio. That's when I looked at the courses that [the university] has, and I thought marketing [INT 1].*

Clarice described how her aspirations shaped the knowledge she encountered in high school history class:

> *I think the first time in history class when I read his 'I have a dream' speech; I think that's when my life changed. That's one of the speeches that I remember a lot about. Where he says, 'I have a dream', it stuck with me, and made me wonder what my dream was, what I want to achieve. And I think I've drawn a comparison, not that you can really compare because our lives are different.*

> *Not like changing the world or something, but it kind of makes you wonder what you want to do [INT 1].*

She had access to both the knowledge and educational and social structures in which to convert this knowledge into the capability for critical literacy.

School and identity

Students identified school background as being the distinction between a more prepared self and the others who are excluded. This was the case for all students who had attended well-resourced schools, though only one student had an uninterrupted school career at a well-resourced school. It is clear that students had an intimate knowledge of schooling, and understood the important role that school plays in offering academic and social capitals. In contrast to the students who had attended good schools, four students had attended rural and township schools, which they described as poorly resourced, constraining and even abusive environments. While schooling was described as a privilege by the four students who had attended urban schools, the other students described their resilience despite the conditions at school, and framed their identity formation in resistance to the limitations in their school and community environments. Whereas the more privileged cohort imaged that schooling had offered a relatively solid bridge to higher education, the second group experienced schooling as something that had to be overcome in order to succeed in higher education, with specific reference to quality of teaching, relationships with teachers, quality of infrastructure, and career guidance.

Family resources and aspirations

Student narratives show that school is neither the only nor the primary site where aspirations are developed. Instead, family and community are influential in developing and directing individual aspirations. For students from working-class families and communities, this foregrounds the interrelated issue of access to *resources*, and how access to resources shapes aspirations.

Naledi experienced the role of family in creating aspirations as intense pressure to pursue a career that would earn her a stable income. The difficulty for Naledi was that she was drawn to a career in political journalism, which her parents were reluctant to support because of their own beliefs, the discourse around employability, skills and higher education, and the reality of living in poverty:

> [W]hen I chose ... accounting, I think it was to please my parents. 'Cos they were like, 'Choose a career that you gonna get a job after.' But I was like 'People, I don't want to do accounting!' They'd be like, 'Are you going to get a job after doing this degree [media studies and journalism]?'

> *He's [Naledi's father] always emphasising the fact that 'Oh we are dying, we are dying, you have to have an income.' Yoh! That's a lot of pressure [INT 1].*

The lack of ownership or a sense of importance in what Naledi would be achieving through this degree constrained her freedom; education was framed as a means to a financial end, which limited her freedom to choose a degree aligned with her aspirations. Unlike other participants, Naledi did not have the freedom to take a gap year after school to make a different decision about her options.

Techniques explained that he did not aspire to higher education during school, and was encouraged by his uncle to attend university. Both a lack of resources and recognition constrained his ability to aspire to higher education, and the capabilities[6] he needed to prepare himself for university study:

> *Maybe I thought I couldn't do it. . . . But, uh, I don't know. Ja, I never took into consideration to say, that one day I'll go to varsity and study further. For me, it was always, after matric, go look for a job, do something [INT 1].*

When his uncle encouraged him to attend university, Techniques uses his agency to prepare for this transition by reading books and newspapers in preparation for a different academic environment.

Aziza entered university with the support of a network of women in her family who guided her towards aspirations for higher education. During the turbulence of adolescence, a close relationship with a supportive aunt cultivated aspirations for the expanded independence that university education could offer:

> *'You know Aziza, I understand the stage you're going through . . . but imagine you having your own car, your own house. Having to go on holiday, having to do all things without the pressure of someone else telling you what to do.' She just put that image in my mind of mmm, that's the kind of life I do want. And from that day again, got back to my books, studied [INT 1].*

Aziza relates how her father, who offered limited support and care throughout her childhood and adolescence, abandoned her after a move to Gauteng, which resulted in an unplanned pregnancy:

> *During that time, for me, that was the most difficult year of my life . . . I had to get myself up amongst strangers, amongst people who really didn't care whether I went to school or not. And the worst thing that my dad was like 30 minutes away. He didn't check up on me. There was a time I didn't speak to my dad for almost a year because of what happened. I was like really, really mad. And he got mad at me for getting pregnant. What did you expect? I mean [this was] the jungle [city in Gauteng]. I mean how else am I supposed to? I actually [did] well under the circumstances. I went to school every day.*

> *I ended up . . . my dad couldn't pay my flat, my mom couldn't keep up with school and she was paying my school fees and the only thing he was responsible for was me, my food and my flat. And he couldn't even keep that. . . . So I didn't know where to go. So I ended up moving in with my son's father [INT 1].*

Following the move to the city, Aziza was isolated from the enabling structure of female support at home, which as an unsupervised minor left her vulnerable within a risky social environment. At the intersection of gendered vulnerability and socioeconomic scarcity, Aziza's freedom to make a reasoned choice was severely compromised when she was forced to choose between homelessness and accommodation with an older male partner.

Aziza explains that after the birth of her son, her aspirations were shaped by the necessity of finishing school, and providing for him financially. This responsibility was intensified by an extended family that relied on an educated, first-born family member to provide financial support:

> *There was a time in high school . . . I was just feeling heavy. And when I sat down and I was thinking a lot, the whole thing came: I'm the first born in my family, and I got a son, my mom has a child, my brother, my dad has always been, what can I say, a half dad, he's never really contributed to my success, in a way like my dad was there for me. So in a way, this pressure of saying, if I don't succeed now, what's gonna happen? I'm the only person who could help me, my son. It felt like the whole world was on my shoulders [INT 1].*

Despite these early challenges, Aziza's supportive network of relatives and mentors offered career guidance in the gap years between matriculation and university, and she converted their advice and encouragement into aspirations for higher education that aligned with her work experience, career interests and school subjects. Like Condorrera, Aziza also worked and studied for a few years after school, which gave her time to pursue a number of bursaries for post-school education before she began university. It is evident throughout her narrative that the knowledge and resources offered by these experiences expanded her capabilities to participate at university.

Although material resources in her family were severely limited, Condorrera was inspired to value education because of the transformation that education brought to their lives after her mother completed her high school qualification:

> *We were told back home that school is important and the only way to make it is through school. And I saw that when my mother went to school, then our lives started to change. So which was, it gave me confidence to say 'oh well, if I go to school, chances are I'm not going to live below the poverty line, like I grew up' [INT 2].*

Condorrera described how her mother struggled to afford basic needs and education for three children while earning a minimum wage. Yet her mother's resilience also cultivated her aspirations to respond to urgent needs within her extended family. Condorrera's aspirations and career choices were shaped by her concern for her deaf cousin, who she described as vulnerable to exclusion because of his disability, exacerbated by unemployment, violence and poverty, and the difficulty of accessing legal and medical services. Condorrera's intimate knowledge of the consequences of disability and poverty inspired her to qualify as a sign language expert:

> *And then one day my grandmother was saying, someone should take this as a profession. 'Cos who's going to interpret for him when he's in court? 'Cos we very poor; we cannot afford an interpreter. ... So who is going to explain to the doctor? [INT 2].*

Unlike participants who were pressured into choosing degrees associated with better employment prospects, Condorrera's reasoned decision to study sign language aligns with the four conditions of agency identified by Crocker and Robeyns (2010). First, she played an active role in pursuing and completing this degree course; she was reflexive about how her knowledge of sign language will impact positively on the lives of her family and on the deaf community, and she had chosen this degree after a process of deliberation of its value and function.

Yet Condorrera was one of the only members of her community who is privileged enough to access this level of agency in pursuing aspirations that she has developed through a process of reasoned deliberation. A recurring thread in her narrative was the consequences of poverty and unemployment, where structural conditions deny access to the services and resources that enable capability development. Although the picture she paints of youth aspirations in North America was idealistic, the point is that the severity of inequality in South Africa is eroding the aspirations of a large proportion of South African youth:

> *Those people there [in the United States], they follow their dream. If they want to do music, they study music. If it's acting, then go to Hollywood. They do something about their dreams. They don't just sit at the corner and wonder what would it be like if they were there [INT 1].*

Kea's experiences of poverty and vulnerability shaped her aspirations to secure resources that enabled her to attend university. The scarcity of resources inspired her to convert education into financial support:

> *But I did manage to get a bursary. 'Cos if I sit at home, who's gonna pay for my fees? My family don't have money to take me to varsity, so I need to make sure that I pass well and I get a bursary. And I had this thing, mentality of 'I am going to go to varsity'. I even told my friends ... that I'm going to go to varsity [INT 1].*

Her family's precarious situation meant that Kea was reliant on external funding to participate, which was the main source of the pressure that led to her eventual collapse at university. While her agency and determination are evident in her educational trajectory, the pressure of pursuing these goals with limited financial and social support compromised her freedom for equal participation:

> *I had this idea of like trying to better my community. I wanted something that could make them see how important bettering them self is. Like how they should stop having this mentality of, 'I failed. There is nothing I can do.' If ever you failed in the road of education, can't you try something else? Can't you find your skill, your thing that ... makes you better, that makes you, like, you. Because many Black women do not see themselves as being leaders or bringing changes in other Black women's lives [INT 1].*

Kea's experiences confirmed that economic maldistribution leaves many Black women in South Africa vulnerable to gender, class and race-based injustices. Her aspirations remained connected to the empowerment of Black women throughout her degree, and she converted available resources into opportunities at university to prepare herself to achieve this aspiration, which I discuss in more detail in subsequent chapters.

Thuli's aspirations were shaped by violence and abuse experienced at home, where she experienced how gendered inequality, money, power and exploitation are connected. Even though Thuli had greater access to finances than some other participants, the abusive situation at home shaped her aspirations for independence:

> *Things at home weren't very nice. My dad is like the breadwinner, he always has been. He's one of those people with a lot of money and, ja, he treats people like dogs. You have to beg him for everything. I saw how my mom is always stranded for him; whenever my mom needs something, she always has to comply with whatever my dad does. And I was like 'no, I don't wanna live like this'. And yes, being all independent on myself [INT 1].*

Within this constraining environment, Thuli used her agency to find employment while finishing school.

Another site where aspirations were developed is through work experiences during high school and gap years before entry into university. Clarice was encouraged to save for her registration fee before deciding on a degree, although it was assumed that she would attend university. Unlike other participants, Clarice was not dependent on a bursary to attend university. Clarice had worked at her godmother's catering company, which she identified as a valuable opportunity to gain work and life experience:

> *[I]t's made me realise ... that there's more to life ... but I think it matured me in the sense that, I can personally say that I grew up, my parents gave me*

> *everything, and I had to save and pay my registration fee. . . . As a child you don't really realise everything your parents give you and that you take for granted. . . . You kind of have to plan first. It's not just, 'I'm getting my money', 'cos you have to plan for the 'what ifs' [INT 1].*

Although Clarice's parents had moved into the middle class, they live in a relatively poor community close to her extended family where the effects of unemployment and poverty are visible. Clarice described how her aspirations were shaped by her concern for the girls and women in her community whose lives and opportunities are constrained by unemployment, violence and exploitation:

> *I don't want to put a race card on it, but just the sense for us, like I explained in my journal, the 'matchbox' living, for us as Coloured people. Just to kind of make my story that there is more to life than pay cheque to pay cheque. Especially for women, 'cos I think that's where women find their independence or their sense of empowerment.*
>
> *If I could change most of my neighbours or my friends who I grew up with, if I could change their minds, it would at least be a start [INT 1].*

Because of her family's relative affluence, Clarice's aspirations are not directed towards providing financially for her family. She therefore had more freedom than other participants to use time, energy and resources to pursue valued goals instead of meeting basic needs such as food and transport.

Another significant theme throughout the student narratives is the development of aspirations *in isolation* from the people at school or in the community. In some cases, the separation from community members also correlates with the development of academic identity, while entry into higher education creates a barrier between friend and relatives in the community. Aziza's mother controlled her interaction with community members, which Aziza explained as a way to create a routine aligned to the values of her elite primary school:

> *I didn't have friends at all in the location [township]. She just felt they are not in par [emphatic tone] where I am, so she just felt that they will influence me again in a bad way [INT 1].*

Condorrera's separation from the community during high school was because of her mother's fear of her daughter being at risk of pregnancy. She limited Condorrera's movements to school, church and home. Although Condorrera did not have many friends, she claimed that this isolation was a good thing that kept her focused on her school work. Clarice also explained that she had no friends at home because most of the young women her age had children, and so she felt that they had nothing in common.

Techniques explained that when he returned home for university holidays, his friends viewed him with suspicion, and would accuse him of being 'different' and speaking a 'different' type of English. He explained that it was difficult to prove his belonging to his community while he was making the transition to becoming a university student. Similarly, Kea explained that some school friends and neighbours at home were jealous of the opportunity she had to attend university, which damaged her relationship with them and informed her decision to avoid visiting friends during the holidays.

Summary of themes

The aim of the chapter was to demonstrate how educational and social structures enable and constrain individual agency and freedom. An analysis of student experiences across two evaluative sites, which were schooling and aspirational development, illustrates how conversion factors, agency and freedom emerge at the sites of education and aspirational development in student experiences. The analysis showed how participants used agency within structural arrangements to negotiate different conditions of schooling, while relying on resources at home and school to develop aspirations for higher education, and how structural constraints played a significant role in shaping educational trajectories. Student narratives highlighted agency within constraining structures while not down-playing the systemic conditions that compromised students' equal access to resources and opportunities for equal participation. While each participant brought resources to university that enabled the negotiation of pedagogical and institutional structures, such as work experience, knowledge from earlier studies, the ability to learn and work under harsh conditions and aspirations for the public good, some participants entered higher education with significantly fewer capabilities aligned with the demands of higher education structural arrangements. In particular, the secondary school system perpetuated an unequal distribution of educational resources based on the level of tuition that parents can afford, with some exceptions in the case of low-fee private schools (Case 2013; see also Wilson-Strydom 2014: 60–61).

The struggle to meet basic needs compromised aspirations for broader community concerns. This constraint was complicated by the tension between individual aspirations that demanded resources, and the ethical commitment to share resources with family members. Socioeconomic inequality, in combination with constraining school environments, narrowed the capability freedoms available to students to choose from a range of alternatives. Although students used their agency to pursue opportunities, these were constrained by structural injustices that limited the freedom that they had to pursue real alternatives. Despite these constraints, the evaluation of freedom and agency above suggests that each student achieved the capability for entry into higher education.

Notes

1 Schools are organised into quintiles (1–5), which across institutional data acts as a rough proxy for socioeconomic class. Across the education system, socioeconomic status and poverty are correlated with lower scores, such as the 2003 and 2015 TIMSS scores (see TIMSS 2015), in which the highest percentage of students performing under the minimum level of competence were from no-fee paying schools (quintiles 1–3).
2 'Model C schools are quasi-government schools that are administered and largely funded by parents and alumni bodies. The schools receive government subsidy and fall under the jurisdiction of the provincial education department. In most cases these schools are those that, under apartheid, served white children only. The term Model C is no longer used officially and it has thus become commonplace to refer to these schools as ex-Model C schools' (Wilson-Strydom 2012: 62).
3 Local, low-cost retail store.
4 Neither of these schools is private, and Dante's inaccurate assumption is informed by the fact that they are considerably better resourced than townships schools, due in part to some schools' ability to employ more and better qualified teachers. In this case, his perception about private schooling is informed by the resources and status rather than by the school classification, and speaks to the gap in provision between poorly resourced and understaffed state schools and schools whose middle-class and elite students provide a more stable resource base to ensure quality provision.
5 While neither Dante nor Naledi are first-generation students, their experiences have been included in the analysis to illustrate that structural conversion factors that constrain equal participation are not limited to working-class or first-generation students.
6 Wilson-Strydom's pragmatic capabilities list for the transition to university includes the following seven capabilities: practical reason; knowledge and imagination; learning disposition; social relations and social networks; respect, dignity and recognition; emotional health; and language competence and confidence (Wilson-Strydom 2015: 115).

References

Bathmaker, A.-M., & Harnett, P. (Eds), 2010. *Exploring Learning, Identity and Power through Life History and Narrative Research*. London and New York: Routledge.

Bloch, G., 2009. *The Toxic Mix: What's Wrong with South Africa's Schools and How To Fix It*. Cape Town: Tafelberg.

Boughey, C., 2007. Marrying Equity and Efficiency: The Need for Third Generation Academic Development. *Perspectives in Education* 25, 1–11.

Brown, R.N., 2009. *Black Girlhood Celebration: Toward a Hip-hop Feminist Pedagogy*. New York: Peter Lang.Calitz, T., 2018. Starting with Intersectionality: A Decolonising Approach to Entanglements of Gender, Race, Class and Language in Higher Education. In *Starting with Gender: Concept and Methodology in International Higher Education Research*, Routledge Critical Studies in Gender and Sexuality in Education. London and New York: Routledge.

Case, J.M., 2013. *Researching Student Learning in Higher Education: A Social Realist Approach*. London and New York: Routledge.

Chisholm, L., 2004. *Changing Class. Education and Social Change in Post-Apartheid South Africa*. Pretoria: Human Sciences Research Council Press.

Christie, P., Butler, D., & Potterton, M., 2007. *Schools that Work: Report to the Minister of Education of the Ministerial Committee on Schools that Work.* Department of Education, Pretoria.

Cousin, G., 2009. *Researching Learning in Higher Education: An Introduction to Contemporary Methods and Approaches.* New York and London: Routledge.

Crocker, D.A., & Robeyns, I., 2010. Capability and Agency. In Morris, C. (Ed.), *Amartya Sen.* Cambridge: Cambridge University Press.

Fataar, A., 2012. Pedagogical Justice and Student Engagement in South African Schooling: Working with the Cultural Capital of Disadvantaged Students. *Perspectives in Education* 30, 52–63.

Fleisch, B., 2008. *Primary Education in Crisis: Why South African Schoolchildren Underachieve in Reading and Mathematics.* Pretoria: Juta and Company.

Fraser, N., 2009. Feminism, Capitalism and the Cunning of History. *New Left Review* 56, 97–117.

Fraser, N., 2013. *Fortunes of Feminism: From State-Managed Capitalism to Neoliberal Crisis.* New York, NY: Verso Books.

Hart, C.S., 2012. *Aspirations, Education and Social Justice: Applying Sen and Bourdieu.* London: Bloomsbury.

Jansen, J.D., & Blank, M., 2014. *How to Fix South Africa's Schools: Lessons from Schools that Work.* Johannesburg: Bookstorm.

Josselson, R., & Lieblich, A., 1995. *Interpreting Experience: The Narrative Study of Lives.* California: SAGE Publications.

Kemmis, S., McTaggart, R., & Nixon, R., 2013. *The Action Research Planner: Doing Critical Participatory Action Research.* New York, NY: Springer.

Kress, T.M., 2011. Inside the 'Thick Wrapper' of Critical Pedagogy and Research. *International Journal of Qualitative Studies in Education* 24, 261–266. https://doi.org/10.1080/09518398.2011.569768

Lambert, J., 2013. *Digital Storytelling: Capturing Lives, Creating Community.* New York and London: Routledge.

Leibowitz, B., 2011. Academic Literacy as a Graduate Attribute: Implications for Thinking about 'Curriculum'. In Bitzer, E., & Botha, N. (Eds), *Curriculum Inquiry in South African Higher Education: Some Scholarly Affirmations and Challenges.* SUN MeDIA Stellenbosch, Stellenbosch, pp. 221–236.

Lozano, J.F., Boni, A., Peris, J., & Hueso, A., 2012. Competencies in Higher Education: A Critical Analysis from the Capabilities Approach. *Journal of Philosophy of Education* 46.

Marshall, D., & Case, J., 2010. Rethinking 'Disadvantage' in Higher Education: A Paradigmatic Case Study Using Narrative Analysis. *Studies in Higher Education* 35, 491–504. https://doi.org/10.1080/03075070903518386

Mertens, D.M., 2008. *Transformative Research and Evaluation.* New York, NY: Guilford Press.

Paton-Ash, M., & Wilmot, D., 2015. Issues and Challenges Facing School Libraries in Selected Primary Schools in Gauteng Province, South Africa. *South African Journal of Education* 35, 1–10.

Reddy, V., Visser, M., Winnaar, L., Arends, F., Juan, A., Prinsloo, C., & Isdale, K., 2016. TIMSS 2015 Highlights of Mathematics and Science Achievement of Grade 9 South African Learners. Department of Basic Education.

Richardson, L., 1997. *Fields of Play: Constructing an Academic Life.* New Brunswick, NJ: Rutgers University Press.

Rivera, L.A., 2015. *Pedigree: How Elite Students Get Elite Jobs.* Princeton, NJ: Princeton University Press.

Robin, B.R., 2008. Digital Storytelling: A Powerful Technology Tool for the 21st Century Classroom. *Theory into Practice* 47, 220–228. https://doi.org/10.1080/00405840802153916

Rogers, A., 1993. Voice, Play, and a Practice of Ordinary Courage in Girls' and Women's Lives. *Harvard Educational Review* 63, 265–296.

Smith-Maddox, R., & Solórzano, D.G., 2002. Using Critical Race Theory, Paulo Freire's Problem-Posing Method, and Case Study Research to Confront Race and Racism in Education. *Qualitative Inquiry* 8, 66–84. https://doi.org/10.1177/107780040200800105

Stein, P., 2008. *Multimodal Pedagogies in Diverse Classrooms: Representation, Rights and Resources.* London and New York: Routledge.

Stromquist, N.P., 2006. Gender, Education and the Possibility of Transformative Knowledge. *Compare: A Journal of Comparative and International Education* 36, 145–161. https://doi.org/10.1080/03057920600741131

Taylor, N., 2008. What's Wrong with South African Schools? In JET Education Services. Presented at the What's Working in School Development?

Van der Berg, S., 2008. How Effective are Poor Schools? Poverty and Educational Outcomes in South Africa. *Studies in Educational Evaluation* 145–154.

Wilson-Strydom, M., 2012. Using the Nbts to Inform Institutional Understandings of 'Under-Preparedness': Implications for Admissions Criteria. *South African Journal of Higher Education* 26, 136–151.

Wilson-Strydom, M., 2014. Confronting Contradiction: Diversity Experiences at School and University. *Perspectives in Education* 32(4), 56–73.

Wilson-Strydom, M., 2015. *University Access and Success: Capabilities, Diversity and Social Justice.* London and New York: Routledge.

Chapter 5

Structural constraints to participation

As an introduction to undergraduate engagement at a South African university, the previous chapter explored students' experiences at school. Based on a close reading of students' interview data and an analysis of their digital narratives, this chapter focuses on pedagogical and institutional conditions at the university that constrained students' freedom to participate. I analyse student narratives to understand how students engaged across diverse sites at the university, including classrooms, residences, administrative and academic staff, and the institutional cultures and practices of the university. How did university structures and institutional cultures influence students' freedom to engage with knowledge, to build meaningful connections and to cultivate belonging? Instead of assuming individual weaknesses or failure, my analysis of student participation begins with the assumption that resource and opportunity scarcity could play an important role in limiting students' freedom for participation.

Student narratives showed how inequalities emerge from unevenly distributed resources, recognition, knowledge and power. Sustained opportunities to convert available resources into capabilities and functionings were scarce, unreliable and inaccessible. In many instances, students experienced escalating accumulation of stress without access to sufficient resources and sustained support to help them navigate their studies. In some cases, pedagogic structures designed to empower students seemed to do the opposite by reducing agency and diminishing some students' voice and self-confidence. Students shared their experiences of how university structures eroded their freedom to participate. I organised these *negative conversion factors* into five categories, which include: individualising failure, uncritical engagement with knowledge, lack of participation in decision-making, alienation from lecturers, and misrecognition. While every student had a unique experience of participation, all narratives reflect these five factors to some extent.

Individualising failure

The first aspect of unequal participation was located at the intersection of socioeconomic disadvantage and low academic performance as students adjusted to university life. Participants who struggled to access basic resources such as food and textbooks while making the transition to university were particularly vulnerable to a deficit discourse. From this perspective, failure, disengagement and low academic achievement were framed as personal failures, lack of ability or disengagement. In her comment below, Condorrera was reflexive about the pressure of being a university student despite poverty at home:

> *It depends on background. Some students are here to do better, to benefit themselves, and maybe they know that back home they are the breadwinners. They have a whole burden to look after [INT 2].*

In contrast to Condorrera's balanced view as a mature student, younger students tended to blame themselves for their failures, which they expressed as self-doubt, anxiety and fear. Across narratives, a discourse of individualised failure downplayed the role of structural constraints, so that instead of criticising unjust structures, students were more likely to describe their academic achievements as a reflection of their inherent academic ability.

Kea's narrative is an example of this internalised deficit discourse. Kea entered university as a first-generation student dependent on financial aid and placed on a bridging degree programme. During her first year, the pressure of residence living, adjusting to an urban environment and the academic demands of her degree course resulted in significant physical health problems, as she explains below:

> *My first year wasn't that good. Actually, it was terrible. I collapsed in three months. In two months I was admitted [to] hospital three times. I had fits. After that, I collapsed in class during a tutorial and they called an ambulance. They told me it was stress because I was putting so much pressure on myself. So I was admitted at a psychiatric complex for a month. Last year was also a hectic year for me. Failing during my first year was so much tension on me that I even had two operations last year in less than six months [INT 1].*

Although Kea recovered sufficiently from these early setbacks to continue her studies, she had limited access to academic and psychosocial support that could help her adjust to university life. At the same time, her family's poverty limited the resources that Kea needed to access services that could improve her health and help her cope with the academic stress. Because support structures did not explicitly take into account how Kea's access to resources and participation were interconnected, her health crises were private problems for which she had to find privately-funded solutions, as reiterated throughout her narrative:

> *But then again, I feel like I can't keep on being so weak. Because I'm not a weak person. I'm not a weak person. I've never been a weak person [INT 1].*

Instead of citing conditions that constrained her freedom to access knowledge, Kea framed her academic failure as individual weaknesses that could be overcome with a simple combination of determination and hard work:

> *Every year, first semester, I have to fail a module or two. And I'm not proud of it. I'm not going to say I'm blaming my family or blaming everyone who's in my life, no. I'm blaming myself, and this year I'm working past it [INT 1].*

Kea explained that in order to escape the shame of being a 'weak' person meant succeeding without putting pressure on her family or her boyfriend. Kea's admirable determination to take responsibility for her own academic success is complicated by the fact that she did not have access to the same resources and privileges as the middle-class peers with whom she was competing (Wilson-Strydom & Walker 2015).

Because Kea was a first-generation student, her family's support was constrained by scarce financial resources. The resources needed to cope as a university student were not only material, but included the guidance of people who understood the demands of the institution, who had access to strategic networks, and who could give insider information about the challenges of university life (Reay 1998; Sayer 2005; Skeggs 2004; Walker 2008; Hart 2012). In Kea's experience, it was difficult to navigate university life without integrated support:

> *I'm not going to blame my family for it. Because my family is like that. They are not too involved. They don't ask you, how are your studies? They'll just ask you if you are ok. And then I'll say, I'm fine. I don't want to stress them [INT 1].*

Because Kea occupied a relatively privileged position in her family as a university student, instead of receiving support, she was expected to begin supporting her relatives. In her second year, Kea shared her bursary with a younger cousin to help her attend university, which decreased the resources Kea needed for basic living costs (see also Mngomezulu, Dhunpath, & Munro 2017). This material scarcity exacerbated the pressure on her to retain her bursary, without which she would be unable to continue her studies:

> *Because if I fail one module, I'm gonna be required to add another year. I can't afford it. So now I'm feeling if I don't sleep that much, it'll be worth it. I know it's gonna drain me, and I still have problems within me that I need to sort out. And at some point during my first year I felt like dropping out. But then by the grace of God I didn't. I just felt like it. But then again I thought to myself if I drop out, what's my second option? [INT 1].*

At a structural level, Kea was trying to access higher education as an individual who must succeed against all odds, but with very limited resources and support. Because she lived in a campus student residence, she enjoyed some social support from peers, yet her degree programme seemed to offer relatively limited opportunities or resources that enabled Kea's academic participation (Pym &

Kapp 2013). Instead, resource scarcity diminished her experience of learning as a struggle to study and pass tests, assignments and exams. Although Kea used her agency to navigate academic and social pressures, she had limited freedom to engage deeply with learning, since much of her time and energy was spent trying to juggle competing demands.

Techniques also relied on a state bursary and identified the fear of failure as his greatest challenge at university. Similar to Kea, his narrative framed failure as an individual weakness that would disappoint relatives who had invested in his education:

> *[M]y biggest fear, and I always tell everyone I engage [with]... my biggest fear is failing. Not failing literally* [e.g. a test or exam], *but failing like failing ... failing the people who have invested a lot in me, and who believe I can become something better. So I think that's one of my toughest and difficult things that I'm still trying to overcome. Every day when I wake up, that's the first thing I have to think: am I really going to finish this race? [INT 1].*

Techniques' freedom to participate was constrained by poverty and complicated by family members who were uninformed about the challenges of university. Although he identified structural failures in other aspects of the university system, he did not connect these failures to his own academic struggle and was also determined to find personal solutions to academic and social problems:

> *I'm the first in the family to come to varsity. So it's a bit difficult because they don't understand. When I tell my mother I'm struggling with one of my modules, she'll say, 'Just study hard.' But I am studying, but I'm still struggling [INT 1].*

At the same time, Techniques had to navigate financial scarcity and pedagogical conditions that compromised his ability to convert academic resources into participation:

> *I was speaking to my sister and she asked me how I am doing. I told her I need money for a textbook, because my bursary didn't pay all my tuition fees. So I can't go to admin and get credit to buy the textbook. So she said she will make a plan. But now she asked me, why don't I copy the textbook from someone? And then I told her, how can I copy it if I don't have money? [INT 1].*

Instead of university being a space in which he could develop academic capabilities, Techniques explained how escalating stress about money for textbooks, accommodation and transport limited his freedom to engage with knowledge and to become integrated into the university culture. Compared with privileged peers, Techniques did not have sustained opportunities to convert available resources and support into academic capabilities. Similar to Kea's experience, his participation in learning was focused on coping strategies and on passing tests and exams, which eroded the time, energy and resources, and sustained opportunities needed to critically engage with knowledge or to develop an academic orientation.

Academic failure emerged as a barrier to equal participation for Naledi during her first two years of university. She described how her family was disappointed when she was forced to change her degree from Economic and Management Sciences to the Humanities. In Naledi's experience, being unable to pass her subjects was described mostly as an individual failure. She explained how financial pressure to contribute to her family income did not give her the opportunity to take a gap year to decide what to study. As a consequence, Naledi had no choice but to study accounting because her parents associated a degree in finance services with guaranteed and stable employment, although this choice contradicted her own career aspirations (Archer & Hutchings 2000; Vally & Motala 2014). The pressure underlying of this career choice diminished Naledi's ownership of her studies and career aspirations, which are crucial conditions for the individual expansion of agency (Drydyk 2008; Crocker & Robeyns 2010).

Naledi described how making the transition to university was a major challenge for which she did not have adequate resources or support:

> *During my studies in 2011 here I'm struggling. I have to admit it, and I can't continue with this . . . I would always be studying and studying, the next thing you write a test and fail. And I'd think I don't want to do this anymore. I was stressing about this module, did I study enough? [INT 1].*

Naledi's participation was compromised by the lack of choice in pursuing a valued goal, while pedagogical conditions did not enable her to convert available resources into equal participation. Although she interpreted this failure as a personal weakness, there was little evidence in her narrative of resources and structures that enabled her to negotiate access to a deeper engagement with disciplinary knowledge. Under these conditions, her experience of learning was limited to an attempt to pass tests and exams, without the time, energy or freedom to develop critical academic capabilities.

Even though her family's financial situation was not as precarious as Kea's or Techniques', scarce financial resources also constrained Naledi's freedom to participate. She lived in cheaper accommodation far from the university, and relied on public transport to access campus. The distance from campus alienated her from academic and social support structures, and made her more vulnerable to exclusion. She only travelled to campus some days, and struggled to stay focused on her academic work with distractions at home like housemates' friends, social media and television. Aziza, who also lived off-campus, similarly reported that travelling time and the lack of finances to afford regular trips to campus contributed to decreased participation in campus life. Some students reported being mugged when walking home after class, which made them reluctant to attend evening lectures.

Aziza identified being a first-generation student as a constraint on her ability to participate equally. In her experience, lack of family support was a significant constraint:

> *When it comes to university, I think a lot of us Black people don't know what it entails, 'cos a lot of our parents have not been here. So when you come here you kind of feel lost. And with the day-by-day experience, you ask: 'Am I learning something, am I gaining something?' I do have that fear that I might not make it [INT 2].*

Aziza's experience of university suggested limited resources or support to develop academic capabilities. In the quotation above, she described the expectation that students need to cope on their own without knowing where to seek support. At the same time, there was evidence that lecturers misrecognised students' need for opportunities that facilitated the transition from school, as she describes below:

> *So I think again some lecturers don't understand that we coming from a community who don't know what it entails for us. As much as we have learned from high school, our high school is substandard, we all know that. And it's not up to scratch. And we do study in a different way [INT 2].*

Fear of failure was closely related to the self-doubt that students expressed in their ability to participate academically, which was complicated by an environment that misrecognised students' academic potential. For Aziza, this was expressed as doubt in her own ability to perform well, despite evidence that she was in the process of developing academic capabilities:

> *I would always read my article again and be like, did I really write that? [Laughs] I would just check my marks again – is this me sometimes? I just doubt myself a lot. But I go like, when I look back I can do this hey, if I can write this then, hey, there must be something in here that's working, right? [INT 1].*

Similar to other student experiences, structural constraints perpetuated an individualised view of failure and underachievement, leaving the individual vulnerable to anxiety, low self-esteem and less confidence to engage academically.

Despite having access to relatively more financial resources, the precarious status of being a first-generation student means that, for Clarice, the pressure to prove her ability was constrained by an instrumental view of success as the ability to pass standardised assessment:

> *I failed one module last year, but I can't say I didn't put everything in. But I'm still disappointed in myself [INT 3].*

As a relatively privileged student who attended well-resourced schools for a part of his high school career, Dante also struggled to adjust to the academic demands of his accounting course, and later changed to a social sciences degree. He interpreted this academic failure as a reflection of the state school that he attended, which did not prepare him for the demands of university study.

The first cluster of conversion factors was centred around a discourse of individual effort and failure, with the onus on the individual to find personal solutions to structural problems even when structural support seemed to be inadequate or absent (Bauman 2009). Throughout the narratives, students were critical of institutional arrangements in these aspects of student life that related more directly to political engagement, but then reverted back to self-blame when describing their academic failures. Embedded beliefs about race, academic ability and quality of schooling emerged as important themes for students who had internalised a deficit approach cultivated at school and deepened by real or perceived unsupportive arrangements at university. At the same time, individual academic failure was connected to pedagogical and social arrangements that framed learning as the ability to pass tests and exams, while constraining student freedom to develop critical academic capabilities.

Uncritical engagement with knowledge

Another cluster of structural conversion factors that emerged in narratives was related to pedagogical arrangements that failed to create critical engagement with knowledge. In the analysis, these arrangements reflect the resource constraints faced by higher education institutions, which is detrimental to the quality of teaching and learning. These structural concerns were evident, for example, in crowded undergraduate classrooms with too few qualified lecturers and tutors. When students struggled to meet assessment requirements with limited access to resources and support, they reported that academic support programmes offered low-quality arrangements that were misaligned with the demands of their mainstream courses, which also points to inadequate resource investment, departmental support and the infrastructure needed to embed these programmes into faculties (Leibowitz & Bozalek 2015; Boughey 2010). Even though students valued teaching and learning that could enable them to become engaged and critical students, they explained how some academic support programmes were more likely to teach them how to summarise and regurgitate information for assessment, or to learn decontextualised, generic skills that they viewed as less important to access complex disciplinary knowledge (Hockings Cooke, & Bowl 2007). Students described few opportunities where discipline-specific ways of thinking, writing and reading were made explicit to students (Kapp & Bangeni 2009; Leibowitz 2004). At the same time, uncritical access to information was frequently associated with pedagogic distance between students and lecturers, which further decreased the availability of 'structured opportunities for students to learn how to learn in a university setting' (CHE 2010: 104; see also Wingate 2007).

Clarice explained how facilitation sessions for students on the bridging degree programme misrecognised her ability to participate as a valued member of the institution, and therefore compromised the freedom to convert academic resources into meaningful engagement with knowledge. Instead of having access to tutorials, the perception of the poor quality of academic support programmes was a structural conversion factor that constrained her freedom for equal participation:

> *I'm in the extended [bridging] programme. So for every module I have to go to the facilitation sessions. The tutorials are for the mainstream people. The facilitation sessions are basically where you're telling me that I'm stupid. I feel so stupid in those classes. I listen and my brain switches off after they make me feel like I'm stupid [INT 2].*

As discussed earlier, the danger of differentiated provision – mainstream students attend regular tutorials while bridging degree students attend separate sessions – is that low expectations and a deficit discourse are perpetuated for 'underprepared' students (Leibowitz & Bozalek 2015; Boughey 2010). This division of students according to ability created an experience stigma while devaluing the important academic resources offered by these sessions (Hlalele 2010).

Students who resisted separation according to real or perceived ability highlighted the status injury associated with being separated from peers on the mainstream. Clarice's experience of being forced to attend sessions that she found patronising and misaligned to the demands of her mainstream modules also decreased her motivation to participate, and diminished the perceived value of academic support programmes resources on offer:

> *Although it obviously helps those people who are struggling to connect life skills with academic literacy skills, so for them it will be the summarising of content. But for me, personally I feel like I don't need to be there. But now you have to attend 80 per cent of the lectures otherwise I don't qualify to write exams, even if I have an average of 80 per cent. So I just go to class to go sign my name. I'm so tired. I'm frustrated. The people in the mainstream tutorials sessions get more information, whereas you're limiting me to this page, summarise this chapter, or this paragraph, highlight the important words. I think, really now? So I just sit there for the hour. I'm so mad [INT 2].*

She described a facilitation session designed to teach students the skills that she associated with rote learning, framing academic success as the ability to absorb, summarise and reproduce the contents of the curriculum during summative assessment. Although Clarice valued opportunities for rigorous engagement with knowledge, the academic support programmes on the bridging degree programme offered the opposite:

> *That's why I say it's low expectations. Basically in life skills and in academic literacy you're still spoon-feeding me. You're giving me a worksheet like I used to get in high school: fill in the blanks, or match this column with that column. And I'm just sitting there thinking, how is this going to help me remember the work that I have to study for the test? [INT 2].*

Throughout the narratives, I found examples of students assimilated into uncritical academic practices demanded by a banking system (Freire 1970). Students explained that they approached university study with the memorisation techniques they had learned at school. Because summative assessment are important indicators of success or failure, getting to know 'what the lecturer wants' and the scope for the test or examination emerged as more important than a deep or sustained engagement with knowledge across disciplines. Aziza describes the cycle of memorisation and testing in her experience of higher education:

> *Some of us cram and by the time we write exams, we don't know jack shit. When we are done writing, ask us anything about the book and we would say uhhhhh ... [Mimics thinking]. I remember that chapter but most of the time we are cramming. We won't actually be studying [INT 2].*

Although Condorrera was reflexive about different lecturers' pedagogical approaches, she was strategic about meeting lecturer expectations and held a more nuanced view of compliance to assessment instructions as the measure of academic success. Her ability to master these academic expectations helped her navigate the university:

> *Because you must adhere to instructions, otherwise you're going to get it wrong. The topic is about marriage and how marriage fails. And that's what the lecturer expects and that's what they want to see in the essay. If you don't do that, then you're not going to get it right [INT 2].*

Other students commented on the lack of control to challenge academic arrangements because of fear of punishment or not being taken seriously. Despite feeling disillusioned by the instrumentalism of rote learning, students who occupied a precarious position at the institution could not afford to risk exclusion by challenging these arrangements. The power imbalance seemed to compromise some students' freedom to access alternatives or to use reasoned deliberation to influence conditions not conducive to learning (Sen 1999: 4).

For this reason, students like Kea and Techniques, who both struggled to pass enough modules to retain their bursaries, were also strategic in approaching university study as learning how to pass tests and examinations. Despite imperfect conditions, both students invested in their academic work so that they were not excluded from university. Under the pressure of poverty, narratives suggest that there are limited opportunities to cultivate a critical approach to learning.

As participants discussed in the previous chapter, opportunities to develop critical capabilities at school were eroded by impoverished material conditions, poor teaching practices and curricula that had not prepared them to engage with a critical approach to education, which means that students' vocabulary with which to demand an alternative was constrained (Bozalek & Boughey 2012). When confronted by the uncritical arrangements in developmental modules that Clarice described above, some students did not have the capabilities to recognise, let alone resist, arrangements that perpetuated uncritical ways of learning. In my analysis, these are remediable institutional failures and not merely a reflection of students' ability to develop critical academic capabilities.

A focus on rote learning distorted opportunities to develop critical academic capabilities. Clarice identified history as her favourite subject at school and was disappointed by the narrow approach taken at university to develop 'critical thinking'. The module she describes below was an interdisciplinary module designed to teach critical thinking across the undergraduate student cohort:

It teaches you to think 'critically', but in the way they want you to think. Everything that the unit says, that's what you have to do. It's not critical thinking as what actually happened in our past. The questions they ask you are specific to what and how they wanted you to think. That's why I feel like it's just doing the right thing in the wrong way [INT 3].

In the comment below, Clarice contrasted her experience of small classes and individual attention at high school with pedagogical arrangements at university and connected the lecture-and-leave approach to students' regurgitated learning and assessment practices:

When lecturers wonder why we've only studied to get our degrees and we've learned nothing else it's because they don't share their knowledge with us either. They've been through the whole process. But if you have the whole perception 'let me just lecture and leave', I'm gonna have the whole perception, let me just listen to you, do what I have to do, pass, and I'll leave too. Then my study method would be, study study, or cram, do it the night before, get 50 per cent, I don't care. If lecturers start breaking that gap, I think students will start thinking more critically. And the fact that most of the content you have to study, you have to study in a parrot form. It has to be like it is in the textbook. And if it's not like it is in the textbook, I'm going to lose those five or six marks [INT 2].

In the situation above, a rote learning approach to teaching constrained Clarice's freedom to engage critically with knowledge. Although she was frustrated by assessment that required her to regurgitate information, she did not have the opportunity to access an alternative way of learning and therefore adapted her preference to progress through the system.

While there was evidence that selective courses like law and medicine develop valued capabilities using intensive pedagogical support structures, student narratives suggested that under conditions of massification, oversubscribed degree courses risk unevenly distributed resources and opportunities. In these courses, crowded classrooms and high lecturer–student ratios were not conducive to converting academic resources into the capability for practical reasoning and other valued capabilities. Naledi attributed the absence of sustained mentorship as a conversion factor that made it difficult to enter a new academic discourse:

> *Lecturers, I think they were there to teach us then leave. Then we'd have practicals and there'd be a single person for the practicals. And we'd always have to wait for the question, so it was a bit discouraging [INT 1].*

Students had to work independently to access knowledge, while the academic mentorship reserved for selection courses was not available to the majority of students, who struggled to create meaningful connections with abstract theory without sustained guidance from lecturers. As mentioned earlier, this discipline-specific engagement was crucial to make the discourses and rules of academic participation explicit, and to avoid leaving students overwhelmed, demoralised and alienated.

Another conversion factor was the low quality of academic support programmes presented by staff unfamiliar with the disciplinary discourses and who resorted to generic skill development (Boughey 2010). While Techniques struggled to articulate why he did not engage with an academic support module: 'There's just something about [the module] when you get here, it's not nice,' Clarice offered a more detailed analysis of her experience of the constraining pedagogical environment:

> *I know it's class and it's not supposed to be that fun, but you at least supposed to look forward to coming to class, and to learning something. But you walk out of there, and you're like, today we learned about teenagers, or today we learned about this, and that's it. You don't go home, like I'd never open my textbook unless I had to study for a test. I never touched it again. I'll never go back and think 'wow, that topic was so fascinating'. 'Cos [the lecturer] would never bring extra information, 'Guys I found this article!' I felt more like I was in a box. I wasn't being me in [this module] ever. I never spoke in class because there was nothing for me to say. It was that bad [INT 3].*

Other students expressed ambivalence about developmental modules, with some believing they are unchallenging yet important, while others were unclear about the value of these modules, which Clarice summarised as her experience of constrained freedom to cultivate critical capabilities:

> *I think most students were scarred by [the developmental module] last year, so they think you're just going to do the same thing [in the second year of the*

module]. I know, potential wise, I think most people can write better. I think it's because of how we started varsity, after a while you just want to do this to leave [INT 2].

In other cases, these modules were perceived as 'too easy' and did not develop the capabilities that students needed to access knowledge. For example, Condorrera did not find either her academic literacy modules challenging or relevant to her course. Because academic literacy has been identified as a fundamental area of student underpreparedness (Leibowitz 2011; CHE 2010), there should be cause for concern when literacy interventions at university are reported by 'underprepared' students as unchallenging, 'like high school English' and 'too easy'. It is also worrying when students find ways to avoid potentially important developmental modules: a number of students postponed these modules until their final year because of negative reports from peers, which defeats the purpose of modules designed to develop crucial literacy, numeracy and other capabilities in the early stages of bridging degree programmes.

Students who are not given sustained opportunities to cultivate capabilities for practical reasoning, who are crammed into large classes, who are not taught by qualified lecturers and tutors, and who are not explicitly taught to read, write and think beyond assessment rubrics will be less likely to develop the intellectual freedom, curiosity and imagination needed for equal participation. In this sense, higher education treads a precarious line between the provision of resources that graduates need to compete in a globalised knowledge economy, without education regressing into assimilation that leaves the individual with a watered-down experience of higher education.

Lack of participation in decision-making

The third cluster of structural conversion factors was decision-making processes about both pedagogical and institutional arrangements. Even though the political function of the SRC (student representative council) has been diminished, student leaders still contributed to decision-making, even when their function was symbolic. This means that the entry point into consultation is generally at an advanced state of decision-making, which creates a thin version of student representation (Crocker & Robeyns 2010; Kosko 2013). However, very few students reach leadership positions and many students are uninformed about policies that influence their participation. Some participants expressed disillusionment with student leadership, and most agreed that student voices were not taken seriously in decision-making. The broader student population therefore has a limited role in determining or influencing decision-making, although the recent student protests have introduced a significant wave of student-led activism around tuition fee increases. Even though students had reasonable and justified opinions about the process of their education and the choice that influenced their engagement with knowledge, some students' experiences indicated that they did not enjoy the freedom to contribute to conditions that would have enhanced their participation (Sen 2004).

The evidence in this section suggests that misrecognition of student potential and an overemphasis on students' measurable academic performance creates a vicious cycle of exclusion from decision-making platforms, as a form of misrepresentation (Fraser 2013). Since 'one thing which is not for choosing is the condition under which the choices are made' (Bauman 2013: 23), unequal opportunities for decision-making are misinterpreted as disengagement, lack of interest and apathy. However, participants explained that structural conditions played a significant role in constraining their freedom to pursue leadership and other strategic student positions, such as the fear of academic failure (Fraser 2009; Bozalek & Boughey 2012).

Arrangements that silence student voices and that do not allow for decision-making limit the freedom to convert resources into participation. Clarice and other students who expressed discontent with these developmental modules felt powerless to influence or transform arrangements; it was accepted that if you were 'unlucky' to be allocated a disengaging facilitator, then you could either accept it or try to change classes, which was almost impossible given the problem of timetable clashes:

> *When I got to [developmental module] I was like, what is this? And why am I doing this? It was more frustration, and now I understand why. I don't think they explained why you're doing what you're doing. They just give this thing to you, and tell you to do it because you're in the extended [bridging] programme, or because you need to do it [INT 3].*

Across all narratives, students shared limited freedom to change the environment or contribute towards a more negotiated approach to learning. Since teaching and learning arrangements were frequently perceived as an extension of an uncritical high school culture, some students experienced lecturers as powerful members of the academic hierarchy, who could at best be resisted by skipping class or complaining of unfair treatment to peers and friends (Bloch 2009). This hierarchy, entrenched in South Africa's authoritarian social structures, means that the provision of education is being framed increasingly as a commodity, which creates an uncritical approach to learning that could risk silencing critique and hollowing out the critical traditions of higher education. Participants described their experiences as reminders of school culture and felt patronised by lecturers who insisted that 'we stick the label on the left hand of the book like at school' because it forced them to be complicit in reproducing a culture of low expectations, as Clarice explained.

The contradiction of a university that retains practices such as compulsory attendance, while forgetting that the 'services' a university provides to its adult 'clients' are not free, and therefore the client should arguably be free to decide whether class attendance is worth her time (Marginson 2011). For example, Clarice was deeply unhappy about being forced to register and buy expensive textbooks for a compulsory computer literacy module although she was already proficient. From a capability perspective, the needs of the individual must be taken into account when prescribing resources, and then the individual must still be consulted in a deliberative process about the value and nature of this provision (Feldman & Gellert 2006).

In Kea's experience, the lack of resources described in the previous section meant that she abandoned her aspirations for student leadership:

> *I don't think I can manage to become an SRC member whereas I can't manage my studies and SRC it's gonna to be too much work for me. I have to focus on my studies [INT 1].*

She explained that her dependence on a bursary and her academic struggles made her vulnerable to academic exclusion, and so she could not risk participating in demanding leadership without financial stability and social support.

Because of the requirements of the official and selection-based leadership structures, students on bridging programmes had an unfair disadvantage and were more vulnerable to exclusion from leadership structures without appropriate alternatives that are open to students who do not meet these requirements. Although Dante aspired to student leadership, students require an appropriate bundle of resources and capabilities, to which Dante did not have access:

> *I would have loved to balance my varsity life better. I had to take an extra year. I knew I wanted to be on the RC [residence committee] and the SRC. But things changed because academics become like your money for everything. So any form of leadership, you needed a 60 average. Which was not good, because I was always average in the 50s. From first year you must have at least 60 per cent. I only had 58. So I wish I had concentrated more on my work rather than on extramural activities [INT 1].*

Dante framed his aspiration for leadership into the broader reality of an academic environment where the ability to convert resources into capabilities and functionings enable the 'competitive edge' for future employment:

> *For me, what was important was experience at varsity, your marks don't count that much, just pass and get a degree. But the thing is things are getting very competitive. Everyone has a degree, what sets you apart? [INT 1].*

Aziza and Clarice also aspired to leadership, but felt that it was not even worth trying to access the leadership trajectory, because some programmes were not open to students on bridging degree programmes. Aziza also reported being excluded because of her age, and because they did not have the leadership, sport

110 Structural constraints to participation

and cultural achievements at school that the university required for entry into these relatively elite programmes.

Lack of consultation was not limited to opportunities for student leadership. Another pattern emerging across student narratives is the absence of decision-making in pedagogical arrangements, which decreased the incentive to attend lectures and engage with knowledge. Techniques found developmental modules beneficial in developing valued functionings at university, but the lack of opportunities to negotiate conditions was experienced as coercive:

> *I think the only problem is the approach that they placed the whole modules and stuff... It's a nice module but I don't know. There's just that something that makes you not want to go to class... And they are too much. Like they force the module on you. If you don't attend, if you don't participate, if you don't do this, you gonna fail. So you end up just going because you, you have to go... It shouldn't be like, you have to do this, even though you don't want to [INT 2].*

It seemed that the problem with making attendance compulsory for academic support programmes is that the purpose of these modules was not explained to students. As discussed in the previous section, there was also misalignment between these courses and the mainstream work required by students. But given the lack of participatory processes or consultation of students, these modules were perceived as additive and irrelevant courses. For this reason, Techniques did not experience the pedagogical arrangements as valuable or enabling. The experience of coercion is complicated by low-quality conditions, crowded classrooms, inexperienced tutors and uncritical forms of teaching, as Clarice describes below about the same module:

> *That's why [they] are pushing the module. [They] want us to think critically, but it's no use preaching it to the students. No one listens in that class, and everyone sits on their phones. So I read a book, and got kicked out. It's so boring you don't know what to do [INT 2].*

The module that Clarice describes above is a potentially valuable resource with high operational costs to the university. But when lack of consultation about pedagogical arrangements constrains students' ability to benefit, this is a waste of resources and reproduces the inequality that it tries to address by offering additional resources to academically 'vulnerable' students. If these resources are to have a measurable impact on students' ability to become equal academic participants, then it would be crucial to ensure that students understand the purpose of these modules and that the pedagogical arrangements are sufficiently enabling so that these resources can be converted into critical capabilities and functionings, as Kea explains below:

> *Like I said, if the teachers don't show the worth in what you are studying . . . you do not see it, you really do not see it. You don't kind of want to do what you were supposed to you. You know you're supposed to do it, but kind of like, oh gosh, this thing. And you get frustrated, you don't go beyond and seeing the bigger picture in what you studying [INT 2].*

The absence of consultation points to an interesting contradiction in pedagogical arrangements: while autonomy, independent learning and the development of 'critical thinking' are pervasive learning outcomes and policy goals, students described often have very little agency in choosing their degree course, contributing to course content or participating in decisions that influence the structure of the curriculum. Hierarchical pedagogical structures where students exert little control or decision-making, and depend on a lecturer to outline the purpose of learning, thus alienate students from the process of learning.

A lack of participatory freedom was also evident in the structure of the bridging degree programme. The lack of flexibility built into the programme meant that Clarice's academic needs were not taken into account when allocating academic resources:

> *I just feel like when I get to university, can you first assess me, and figure out do I want to do this? Do I need to do this? Because they just put everyone in this bubble: you guys on the extended [bridging] programme – just do this. Because I feel like I would have benefitted more if I had taken English or another language than academic literacy.*
>
> *I know it's hard when you think that there are so many students on this campus but I feel like if you can motivate or back up why you want to, and if they see that at the end of the year you can or you can't, then you can go back to your method [INT 2].*

This raises an important distinction between a 'one size fits all' approach that does not align to individual academic needs and a flexible approach that takes diverse capabilities into account (Pym 2013; CHE 2013). In this case, increased agency and ownership in the design of her degree programme could have been more enabling for Clarice.

For Techniques, a lack of agency also extended to choices about his degree course. Because he entered the university with a lower entry score, the assumption was that he was not able to cope with his choice of degree, which forced him into another discipline which he did not value:

> *I'm not trying to criticise, but I don't think [this] is an institution where you can do what you want. . . . They give you what they think is what you want. Like, I told you, when I came here, I wanted to study something in economics. And then they told me, no, my points are low, so I should study social sciences.*

> *Why don't they refer me to an extended [bridging] programme of economics, [instead of] giving me something new? [INT 2].*

The systemic constraints that decreased his agency to pursue a valued goal became a structural conversion factor that eroded his ability to engage with knowledge.

Another critique from students is that ineffective consultation processes between university management and students create anger and resentment, which not only decreases the freedom to choose between alternatives but also diminishes students' ownership of the process of decision-making, as Kea expresses below:

> *So now we thinking that every time he wants to change something, maybe the vice chancellor or the board, they change it without consulting students. . . . I have a problem with them not consulting with students. I feel that this university makes decisions for us, and then we just implement them [INT 2].*

In describing a peer mentor, Kea identified that she valued this student's freedom to challenge unjust structures, although Kea did not have the same opportunity to do this:

> *And she's not scared to challenge the varsity, the directors, the leaders here; she's not scared to challenge them. She feels like she has that capability of challenging her superiors [INT 1].*

Students described an experience of pedagogical structures that are uncritically assimilated or resisted by students, depending on their position in the institution, thereby compromising the freedom to participate. Students who negotiate uncritical learning arrangements to pass and 'get it over with' also decreased the critical capabilities needed to position students as emerging members of an academic community. Unequal participation translates into decreased epistemological access, which is exacerbated by the absence of exposure to conditions that these structures ought to provide.

Student experiences also suggest that decreased agency in one area of participation translates into decreased agency in another area. According to Crocker and Robeyns (2010), as soon as one aspect of agency is compromised, then other dimensions are also diminished. The pattern emerging across student experiences of pedagogical arrangements is that when attendance or participation is explicitly forced by threat of exclusion or failure their 'reasoned agency', which Dréze and Sen (2002: 258) define as 'the freedom and power to question and reassess the prevailing norms and values', also decreases. The compliant mode of learning into which students are socialised by schooling structures is reproduced within higher education, compromising the development of critical capabilities needed for equal participation. Freire imagines a critical education in which people 'perceive themselves in a dialectical relationship with their social reality' so that people can transform this reality (1973: 34), while the capability approach positions education as a valued process that expands individual freedom.

Alienation from lecturers

The fourth cluster of conversion factors is related to the uneven distribution of staff time, energy and commitment to students' need to connect meaningfully to knowledge, given the range of teaching, research and administrative demands that lecturers have to negotiate. According to participant responses, this maldistribution created alienation and prevented students from converting educational resources into the capability for equal participation. Students identified different degrees of alienation across institutional and pedagogical arrangements, particularly in relation to lecturers and tutors. A significant aspect of alienation was student experiences of some lecturers who did not enable students to develop a critical approach to learning. In some cases, supportive lecturers spent their time helping students reach assessment standards. For this reason, most participants defined a good tutor or lecturer as someone who helped students achieve better results for tests and examinations, while there was little evidence of interactions with staff that enabled critical academic capabilities.

The analysis was focused on understanding whether the pedagogical distance between lecturers and students could be constraining students' freedom to convert available resources into academic participation. Condorrera was the only participant who believed that lecturers offered sufficient resources to help students participate:

Lecturers assume that we're adults, so we know what we're supposed to be doing here. It's not the same as high school. You're not here to baby us. So I think you are restricted from some of the things that you should be doing. If lecturers go to class, they go prepared to give class. But the students' underpreparedness is the one thing that is causing them not to perform and not to attend classes. If they don't understand, they don't go for consultation hours. Not taking an extra mile to do something about that particular subject. It's causing us not to do well. And maybe when we see another student passing, some of them will wonder why are they doing well? But they are attending class, they research, they make time, they go for consultation hours, they attend tutorials. I believe the university is doing enough. You provide tutorials; we're doing this extended [bridging] programme. It's something to help us get somewhere. But it's up to us to do something about that [INT 2].

Condorrera's comment above outlined the distinction between resources that are available and the conditions required to convert these resources into actual capabilities and functionings. In contrast to the other participants, she is a mature student who accumulated valuable resources while studying, working and travelling overseas before university entry, which she converted into the confidence to access support structures and develop supportive relationships with lecturers. At the same time, she was registered on a relatively small selective course where she received sustained individual guidance and mentorship from lecturers and tutors for the duration of her degree. She also brought significant life and work experience to the institution, which made her confident in approaching lecturers and demanding fair treatment by her department. Because she is confident in her approach to learning, she attracted the interest of lecturers, which increased her confidence in seeking guidance and pursuing her career aspirations. Given these enabling conversion factors, she was able to convert available structures and resources into equal participation despite an impoverished background and under-resourced schooling. To some extent, these fertile capabilities (Nussbaum 2011) also helped Condorrera mitigate the constraints of poor-quality courses and underprepared lecturers, since she had access to enabling alternatives.

However, less experienced participants did not have access to these pre-university opportunities, and therefore did not have the same freedom to convert available resources into capabilities and functionings, or to navigate poor-quality pedagogical arrangements as successfully as Condorrera managed to do. Clarice explained that alienation from lecturers in large classes, combined with lecturers' lack of availability, or poor relationships between lecturers and students, decreased her freedom for academic participation:

> *I don't think I was struggling per se with something that was different. It was more lack of interest. Yes, it's a big class, but at least make your consultation hours longer. You can't have two [consultation] periods of two hours per week and you have 800 students. And you don't give your email address so people can ask you questions, and after the test there's no memo [INT 3].*

The interest in history and politics that emerged in her digital narrative, cultivated by a well-resourced school environment, was misrecognised where uncritical ways of thinking and reproduction constrained her efforts to participate as an equal member of the university. During the course of her degree, Clarice became increasingly less engaged in her studies, eventually claiming that '50 per cent is enough'.

Closely related to an equal distribution of faculty time was participants' need for relational affiliation with lecturers (Walker 2006: 95). Student experiences showed that affiliation with lecturers expanded their freedom to participate and made learning more accessible and meaningful, as Clarice explained:

> *Are they really listening to me? Are they paying attention? Because in my very first class for [a mainstream module] last year, we were about a thousand students. The lecturer said, she doesn't care, you're just a student number to her. If we don't want to be here we can leave. And they don't encourage you to come to them, so you're never going to come to them [INT 2].*

These conditions limited their freedom to convert resources into participation that eroded Naledi's motivation to approach her lecturers for assistance, as she describes below:

> *I think it's a dog-eat-dog environment there. I don't think one feels part of the department. I don't think so. I think it's lecturer teaching, then they move to another class [INT 3].*

In the examples above, pedagogical arrangements excluded students who had not yet developed the resources to navigate the academic environment, or who were vulnerable to exclusion because their confidence to challenge these unfair conditions has been compromised. Naledi did not enter the university with the confidence to engage with academic knowledge in a way that she found meaningful. Therefore, she did not have the freedom to convert assistance from lecturers and tutors into equal participation, and struggled on her own with a compromised degree of participation. Although she was agentic in her independent approach to learning, this was not a fair distribution of resources, especially for a student who lived off campus and had limited personal resources for other forms of participation that could compensate for unengaged lecturers. At the same time, this alienation contributed to the perception of being excluded from the university, which compromised the ability to form an identity as a valued member of the institution (Tinto 2014).

In making the transition to university, Kea explains below how she was also alienated by arrangements that offered 'no support' in contrast to the teachers at school who pushed students to learn:

> *It's just lecturer, lecturer, talk, after that, test. If you fail that, you fail it. I'm not going to lose my salary at the end of the month. It's just like that. So I felt here was a bitter world . . . people were bitter. So I didn't like varsity that much. I didn't feel like I was in an environment where I was welcome [INT 1].*

Clarice was discouraged by her experience of a lecturer who did not offer many opportunities to engage students in dialogue:

> *Our [. . .] lecturer never cared. She never asked questions so we never answered her. She was just there. Gosh, I just sat in the class, can this just end? That was my attitude towards it. And I'm not saying I regret it, but it was just wasting my time. She never offered to help or asked if we were OK. After class she just packed her bags and left [INT 3].*

Clarice's critique of her lecturer points to an accumulative lack of interest and engagement that created a systemic cycle of disengagement where less engaged students were unlikely to attract lecturer support and investment. Yet without enabling structural conditions, students were less likely to become engaged enough to attract this support. Given the resource constraints faced by support structures, it is understandable that lecturers had to make judicious decisions about investing time and energy in student development and were less likely to commit time to students who appeared to have little interest in learning, who were failing, and who did not show initiative in pursuing engagement with knowledge. For this reason, my analysis suggests that students who had fewer good quality opportunities for critical alliances with teachers and other authority figures at school or at home adapted their expectations for affiliation and were therefore less prepared to initiate engagement with lecturers. I also suggest that most participants had less confidence than Clarice or Condorrera to initiate contact with lecturers. These experiences may suggest that students misunderstood the value of affiliation for academic engagement and success, and therefore failed to pursue available opportunities to communicate with lecturers, which maintained the unequal distribution of lecturer affiliation.

Misrecognition

The final cluster of structural conversion factors was related to the misrecognition of students' academic ability and resources. This misrecognition created the assumption of student deficit that contributed towards low expectations and decreased engagement. In the analysis below, students found it difficult to resist misrecognition because stereotypes of deficit potential and ability were coupled with resource constraints that made it almost impossible to challenge faculty beliefs about student potential. Students described pedagogical interactions where a deficit approach, combined with weak or non-existent relationships with staff, de-contextualised content, and poor-quality teaching practices constrained their freedom to develop capabilities that could challenge deficit beliefs. For instance, Dante described this situation as 'wanting to run with the big horses but being held back to learn grammar rules I had been taught at school'. Students' passive resistance to alienating and misaligned developmental modules also fuelled an uncritical crisis discourse around student illiteracy that failed to take into account the range of social and personal factors that detach working-class students from traditional academic and textual practices (Leibowitz 2011). Students described experiences of assumptions about academic ability based on achievement in academic support programmes in which students were not invested, thereby misframing student disengagement as poor performance, illiteracy or underpreparedness.

Students identified misrecognition within pedagogical arrangements that limited their freedom to participate equally. On a spectrum of exclusion, these incidents ranged from verbal discrimination to implicit forms of silencing and marginalisation. For working-class students in particular, misrecognition acted as a corrosive disadvantage that intersected with socioeconomic injustices that decreased student freedom to participate (Wolff & de-Shalit 2007). Kea described an incident where she was confronted with pedagogical arrangements that misrecognised her existing capabilities based on her lecturer's judgment of potential, race and class.

> The [developmental module lecturer] would write 'Where did you pick this from? Where the hell did you get this?! Who wrote this?! Where did you uplift [copy] this?! Whose words are these?! Are those your words?!' It's like we're not capable of writing such [an essay]. If ever something sounds intelligent, or it sounds like it makes sense, it's not yours. Because if ever she reads your essay, and she looks at you, and how you speak in class, she's like, 'That person can't write this essay.' Because we wrote our essay at home instead of writing it in class, so that's why she didn't believe us. I almost got crushed emotionally [Group members agreeing] [FG 2].

Another aspect of misrecognition occurred when students were not taken seriously or listened to within hierarchical relationships between lecturers and students, which was complicated in particular by the race and class distinctions between Black working-class students and white middle-class lecturers. Condorrera recalls an incident where she felt misrecognised as a student who does not belong at the institution because of poverty and the struggle to adapt to university:

> [T]he lecturer said, one of the doctors . . . 'Some of you when I'm sitting here, I can see that you have a lot of problems. Hence, you cannot even perform well.' Then I said: 'No, how come you're saying you see problems? You are supposed to see beyond that. If you can make it to this point, whether we have problems or not, hungry or not, it means we are willing to do something about our lives, regardless of what. It means we are able to put aside any problems that we have, to make it here. But if you can still see that [the problems], it means now we're not going to achieve what we came here for.' So, that has always been my question about, what do they see in us? Because that's what he saw in us [INT 2].

The lecturer identified socioeconomic barriers to participation without acknowledging the potential that students have to resist these barriers and, more importantly, to provide the institutional and pedagogical support that would ensure that socioeconomically vulnerable students are able to participate alongside privileged peers. This form of status injury reflected patterns of institutional value that could frame working-class students as less likely to succeed and reach equal participation (Fraser 2009).

There was also evidence that maldistribution was exacerbated by pedagogical practices that ignored or devalued existing student capabilities, instead of focusing on capabilities that students are in the process of developing. Condorrera's concern with lecturers' perception of students was that misrecognition eroded the capability for belonging that could enhance participation and deepen student motivation. In her experience, the freedom to feel connected to academic mentors helped her navigate resource deprivation. However, in her experience this freedom was thinly spread amongst peers who had less freedom to resist the damaging effects of misrecognition, as she describes below:

> *The lecturer once said to us, 'I don't think one of you is going to get 35 per cent out of that test. It is so complicated that I don't think even one of you is going to make it.' Wow ... That's low expectations.*
>
> *But for me, I wouldn't see it as him discouraging us. I want to study hard. Because it's in a way of saying, 'It's so complex, that if you're not going to be prepared, you're not going to do it; you're not going to make it.' But other students, they'll never go back. So lecturers should watch their approach they bring to students. It can make or break them [INT 2].*

Condorrera was also critical of lecturers who failed to prepare students for assessment, while dangling success as an unattainable goal, instead of helping students access the resources they need to meet academic requirements:

> *Our lecturer said, 'Well, you're going to write this test and I don't feel that one of you is going to pass. I don't see even one of you getting five per cent for this test.' So when we left this class, this guy said, 'I didn't like the comment he made. It means he doesn't have confidence in us.' So he should have actually told us what to do to nail the test. But in fact, he didn't. And if you see a person is getting 50 per cent, or a 60, at least that is something that they can still improve. So it's not like we were failing. And the test that he was referring to, none of us failed that test. It's just that the passing rate was not what he expected. But had he told us what he wanted, and how he prefers us to answer his questions, maybe we could have done better [INT 2].*

A pedagogical environment that draws on the misrecognition of student ability to maintain students' fear of failure could be discouraging to students who already feel vulnerable to failure. As Condorrera pointed out, there would have been more value in preparing students to access the unfamiliar discourses required for academic achievement rather than producing fear of failure in less-prepared students (Kapp & Bangeni 2009; Paxton 2007).

Another aspect of misrecognition was evident in Kea's example of peers who mocked her attempts to engage with a lecturer in the classroom. This misrecognition created a double bind in which asking questions was an important tool that could increase her participation, while the fear of being mocked silenced students like Naledi and Techniques who had less confidence than Kea to resist derogatory treatment:

> *The thing about students [is] they don't want to ask. Immediately they regard me as the one whose is always asking questions, 'You [are] boring!' If the lecturer is asking, 'Do you understand?', and you raise your hand, they'll say, 'Ahhhhhh, booooo!' You are regarded as the 'boring' one in class. But then at*

the end of the day, you are helping them. You want to understand more, so you are helping them in a way. Some people get discouraged because when they ask a question in class, people just do whatever and say silly things in class [INT 2].

This vulnerability also constrained Thuli's participation, whose well-resourced school had made her confident in her ability to access knowledge:

Because [when] I am in one of those big classes, like 700 people, and I am shy. Whenever I put a hand up, people just look at you and I can be very insecure and I can stutter. Oh my gosh! What do I say? Is this relevant? Is it stupid? [INT 1].

Even before entering the institution, students described their fear of failure embedded within perceptions about university that excluded students who are not recognised as suited to university. Aziza explained that she feared university because she was told, 'It's so theoretical, and am I gonna cope with this studying? Am I gonna cope, am I gonna make it?'

Some students experienced lecturers and professors who maintained this hierarchy by reminding undergraduates of their position within the institution. Condorrera described classroom engagement with a lecturer who foregrounded misrecognition as differentiated status:

There's this other lecturer who once said to us: 'You see I'm a doctor and I don't associate with people who aren't doctors.' And then I raised my eyebrows and said, 'What do you mean?' And then he said, 'Well, I cannot go out with people like you and then sit in a restaurant. It's not going to look good for those who know me.' And then another student said, 'Do you belittle students who are not as educated as you are? Do you think that they are ripping something out of you, because you are a doctor and they are not?' And then his response was: 'You see people who are not educated, who are not doctors, they don't have the same mindset as us doctors.' So that could be one of the things that could be discouraging to a student, if students are discouraged [INT 2].

While Condorrera was confident enough to challenge her lecturer, other participants were intimidated by this hierarchy, which worked by using racial stereotypes about intelligence and ability, but also class-based distinctions about accent, school and community of origin, and family position to decrease the freedom to participate, as reflected in her comment below:

It's believed that most Black people do not like learning, and Coloured people. So I think white people are just fortunate. You guys believe in school. You go to school. For me, it has always been the case. This high school that I went to, most of the teachers they were white and we were Black students [INT 2].

At a structural level, it remains difficult to challenge the assumption of academic superiority based on race or class when it is perceived that lecturers and students in programmes with more stringent admission requirements reflect the inequality of the school system, as Condorrera explained below:

I think most white students are medical students; they get into law. Let me tell you something. In my department, language practice, I get taught only by white people and they teach me about my language, how to apply my own language [INT 1].

Another consequence of misrecognition was lecturers who expressed low confidence (Walker 2006: 94) in students' capability to participate, which made students afraid to contribute in class for fear of being humiliated and misrecognised as incapable of learning, as Aziza explained:

I always asked the question and the lecturer would explain. And then afterwards, students would come and ask me to explain to them. And I would tell them, but you can ask the lecturer a question. You know, there is no stupid question. If you don't understand something, you don't [INT 2].

While she had negotiated the system using her confidence to ask questions in class, students like Naledi and Techniques were intimidated by peers who 'make remarks' and mocked students who asked questions. A pattern emerging across the narratives is that students from township schools who spoke with a recognisable accent[1] were treated derisively when they spoke up in class, thereby misrecognising students who are not judged to be articulate enough to contribute to academic discussions. This meant that a small group of students dominated discussions while less confident students did not have the freedom to develop the capability for voice, as Naledi described:

When you get to varsity there's 300 students in a class. So it's difficult to ask questions; don't know how to ask a question. I don't know some of the people, some people are making remarks, so we are afraid of asking questions, and people are doubting themselves [INT 1].

The language issue was complicated by its association with intelligence and academic status, with 'rural' English accents perceived as less intelligent, forcing students to change their accent, as Kea explained:

When it comes to English, I think people want to teach themselves how to build your voice to be something else when you are speaking, instead of using your original voice [INT 2].

In concluding this chapter, I want to emphasise the fact that discriminatory treatment of students in pedagogical spaces was a reflection of broader social inequality. These systemic barriers preclude the autonomy of students who imagine the university as a transformed space, and misrecognise students as agents who play a role in social cohesion on campus (CHE 2010). In her experiences at residence, Kea reported that racial discrimination imposed by hierarchical decision-making deepens social divides along both race and class:

> *And if there is a mentality with white people in one corridor, and Black people in another corridor with labelled corridors, where this corridor is called 'city of class' or 'corridor of class' and the other corridor is called 'corridor of ghetto students', or kasi.*[2] *It's saying Black people should go that way, white people should go that way. And really? Is that really life? Is that really the generation that we want to transfer to our kids? [INT 1].*

Second, an important step towards countering the stigma of developmental modules like academic literacy is to recognise, as Naledi commented below, that most students enter university unfamiliar with the discourses, practices and capabilities associated with university study. Extending the provision of critical capabilities such as the multimodal literacies required by engagement with twenty-first century knowledge systems could level out the student hierarchy, and challenge the deficit stigma fuelling the misframed 'illiteracy' discourse:

> *I think academic literacy is for all students. Because when they have it for specific students the feeling is that they are much better than you. Because with physics and accounting and economics – what about the language they are actually using to learn those things? [INT 3].*

The difficulty of receiving educational resources that are misaligned with the development of capabilities that students need for equal participation is alienating students from pedagogical environments which could cultivate such capabilities (Pym & Kapp 2013: 273).

Transformation and structural constraints

This chapter explored students' experiences of pedagogical and institutional arrangements that constrained their freedom to participate as equal members of the university. Unequal participation was intensified by academic structures, distribution of resources, historical patterns of race, class, language, ethnic and gender-based discrimination and exclusion. I interpret constraining arrangements as evidence of the ongoing work of transformation needed at South African universities. Student narratives suggest important contributions to the everyday project of transforming higher education pedagogy, curricula and cultures. While students explained some constraining arrangements as logistical failures, my reading finds that stereotypes about race, ethnicity, class, language and gender are found in student experiences. Although students referred to race or class, they were mostly tentative in their critique of the institution and hesitant to suggest just arrangements, and discriminatory treatment was sometimes accepted as an inevitable power imbalance between students and staff. In some cases, students were apologetic about including race in their narratives, and reflected a post-racial discourse in which unfair treatment by white lecturers was interpreted as well-meaning 'encouragement'.

Students were also particularly vulnerable to unequal participation when they faced a cluster of socioeconomic scarcity and structural challenges, which made it difficult to find alternative pathways to participation. Students facing resource scarcity were more likely to experience pedagogical arrangements that decreased agency and compromised epistemo-logical access.

Structural conditions that decreased agency directed student effort away from activities that could expand capability development through meaningful engagement with knowledge. The primary example of this was learning as an uncritical assimilation of content for standardised testing. This was particularly evident in academic support programmes that taught generic 'study skills' and were misaligned with the epistemological demands of mainstream modules (Leibowitz & Bozalek 2015). Students described fragmented and devalued programmes (Walton, Bowman, & Osman 2015). Alienation created by developmental modules had a negative effect on critical participation and created apathy towards learning and mistrust of the institution and its structures. In making the trade-offs for academic survival, some students adopted an instrumental approach to their education, with a focus on passing tests, gaining minimum scores for progressing to the next level, and finding as many short-cuts as possible, such as using friends' notes or memorising summaries. While these coping strategies are important evidence of agency, these trade-offs had a negative effect on students' motivation, autonomy and enthusiasm about learning, and they seemed more likely to experience the university as boring, oppressive and restrictive. Students using 'short cuts' signalled low engagement, thereby deepening stigma and low expectations associated with poor students from under-resourced schools (Rivera 2015).

In addition to teaching and learning environments, academic engagement was compromised by accumulative disadvantage such as weak family support, poverty and insecure living arrangements. These intersecting factors distracted students from academic engagement because they were forced to spend time and energy worrying about finances and negotiating alternatives (see also Wilson-Strydom 2016). Across narratives, I found instances where instead of time to focus on reading, engaging with academic staff and peers, or participating in lectures, students spent time finding ways to buy textbooks or to photocopy notes, reporting and replacing stolen goods, travelling long distances to campus, standing in queues at state hospitals, working part-time, and taking care of family members. For this reason, students with limited financial resources and social support had less time to obtain the high academic scores needed as evidence to attract academic support, bursaries and even future employment opportunities (Rivera 2015). While this juggling shows how students harness their agency to tackle challenges, it also confirms that socioeconomic inequality erodes the freedom for equal participation.

Because of resource scarcity, students spend time managing trade-offs between basic needs and the pressure to compete with middle-class and elite peers who were more likely to afford goods and services that signal class position and status. Discretionary spending and consumption were themes that emerged during interviews and focus groups: access to technology such as laptops, tablets, smartphone upgrades and airtime, and to clothing, cosmetics and toiletries, were important themes for students who had managed to access basic needs. Money for entertainment was important to maintain social connections and to cultivate belonging within peer groups, both for residence and off campus students (Kaus 2016). Access to resources enabled students to acquire goods and services that contributed to their sense of worth, esteem and belonging, and that strengthened their status as emerging as middle class, within the confines of an institution where their disadvantage is relative to the wealth and resource status of middle class and elite peers.

Unequally distributed opportunities limited engagement with institutional support, affiliation and networks on campus, opportunity to access student leadership, aspirations for work and study, and the freedom to plan a valued life. Due to financial insecurity, students had limited or in some cases no access to enriching extracurricular activities, which required time and resources that students are more likely to spend doing casual work or catching up with their academics. As Kea explained, social activities carried a higher risk for students with lower family income and less academic preparation for university. While privileged peers had the financial and academic safety nets that acted as a buffer during the turbulent transition from school to higher education, for working-class students, the stakes were much higher, with fewer resources to alienate personal crises. I found much evidence of anxiety in the balancing of the tightrope between socialising and academic investment. While socialising and extracurricular activities are part of the university experience of many students, for individuals with limited resources, these opportunities were luxuries that they could not afford in terms of time invested.

In order to facilitate transformation within pedagogical and institutional structures, it is important to understand the alienation and complexity underlying the participation at university. An in-depth understanding of constraining factors could inform the design of pedagogy, curricula and other institutional spaces that are able to better mitigate exclusion and patterns of unequal participation more effectively to enable more students to convert educational resources into capabilities and functionings. While the arrangements described in this chapter paint a relatively bleak picture of teaching and learning and other institutional conditions, this is not the complete picture, which is why the next chapter presents enabling conditions at the institution that were conducive to learning.

Notes

1 This refers to the distinction between a 'proper' English accent associated with middle-class schooling and some urban environments, compared with accents associated with township schooling, rural geography and working-class identities.
2 Word to describe an information settlement.

References

Archer, L., & Hutchings, M., 2000. 'Bettering Yourself?' Discourses of Risk, Cost and Benefit in Ethnically Diverse, Young Working-Class Non-Participants' Constructions of Higher Education. *British Journal of Sociology of Education* 21(4), 555–574.
Bauman, Z., 2009. *Does Ethics Have a Chance in a World of Consumers?* Cambridge, MA: Harvard University Press.
Bauman, Z., 2013. *The Individualized Society.* New York, NY: John Wiley & Sons.
Bloch, G., 2009. *The Toxic Mix: What's Wrong with South Africa's Schools and How to Fix It.* Cape Town: Tafelberg.
Boughey, C., 2010. Understanding Teaching and Learning at Foundation Level: A 'Critical' Imperative? In *January 2009 Rhodes University Foundation Seminar.*
Bozalek, V., & Boughey, C., 2012. (Mis)framing Higher Education in South Africa. *Social Policy & Administration* 46(6), 688–703. https://doi.org/10.1111/j.1467-9515.2012.00863.x
CHE, 2010. *Access and Throughput in South African Higher Education: Three Case Studies. Higher Education Monitor.* Pretoria: Council on Higher Education. www.che.ac.za/sites/default/files/publications/Higher_Education_Monitor_9.pdf.
CHE, 2013. *A Proposal for Undergraduate Curriculum Reform in South Africa: The Case for a Flexible Curriculum Structure.* Council on Higher Education, Pretoria, South Africa. www.che.ac.za/sites/default/files/publications/Full_Report.pdf
Crocker, D.A., & Robeyns, I., 2010. Capability and Agency. In Morris, C. (Ed.), *Amartya Sen.* Cambridge: Cambridge University Press.
Drèze, J., & Sen, A., 2015. *An Uncertain Glory: India and its Contradictions.* Princeton, NJ: Princeton University Press.
Drydyk, J., 2008. How to Distinguish Empowerment from Agency. Paper presented at the 5th annual conference of the HDCA, New Delhi, India.
Feldman, S., & Gellert, P., 2006. The Seductive Quality of Central Human Capabilities: Sociological Insights into Nussbaum and Sen's Disagreement. *Economy and Society* 35, 423–452. https://doi.org/10.1080/03085140600845008
Fraser, N., 2009. *Scales of Justice: Reimagining Political Space in a Globalizing World.* New York, NY: Columbia University Press.
Fraser, N., 2013. *Fortunes of Feminism: From State-Managed Capitalism to Neoliberal Crisis.* New York, NY: Verso Books.
Freire, P., 1970. *Pedagogy of the Oppressed.* New York, NY: Penguin Books.
Freire, P., 1973. *Education for Critical Consciousness.* London: Bloomsbury.
Hart, C.S., 2012. *Aspirations, Education and Social Justice: Applying Sen and Bourdieu.* London: A&C Black.

Hlalele, D.J., 2010. Do Learning Skills Acquired in the University Access Programme Enhance Participation in Academic Practice? *South African Journal of Higher Education* 24(1), 98–110.

Hockings, C., Cooke, S., & Bowl, M., 2007. 'Academic Engagement' within a Widening Participation Context – A 3D Analysis. *Teaching in Higher Education* 12(5/6), 721–733.

Kapp, R., & Bangeni, B., 2009. Positioning (in) the Discipline: Undergraduate Students' Negotiations of Disciplinary Discourses. *Teaching in Higher Education* 14, 587–596. https://doi.org/10.1080/13562510903314988

Kaus, W., 2013. Conspicuous Consumption and 'Race': Evidence from South Africa. *Journal of Development Economics* 100, 63–73. https://doi.org/10.1016/j.jdeveco.2012.07.004

Kosko, S.J., 2013. Agency Vulnerability, Participation, and the Self-determination of Indigenous Peoples. *Journal of Global Ethics* 9(3), 293–310.

Leibowitz, B., 2004. Becoming Academically Literate in South Africa: Lessons from Student Accounts for Policymakers and Educators. *Language and Education* 18(1), 35–52.

Leibowitz, B., 2011. Academic Literacy as a Graduate Attribute: Implications for Thinking about 'Curriculum'. In Bitzer, E., & Botha (Eds), *Curriculum Inquiry in South African Higher Education: Some Scholarly Affirmations and Challenges*. Stellenbosch: SUN MeDIA Stellenbosch, pp. 221–236.

Leibowitz, B., & Bozalek, V., 2015. Foundation Provision – A Social Justice Perspective: Part 1: Leading Article. *South African Journal of Higher Education* 29(1), 8–25.

Marginson, S., 2011. Equity, Status and Freedom: A Note on Higher Education. *Cambridge Journal of Education* 41(1), 23–36.

Mngomezulu, S., Dhunpath, R., & Munro, N., 2017. Does Financial Assistance Undermine Academic Success? Experiences of 'At Risk' Students in a South African University. *Journal of Education* 68, 131–148.

Nussbaum, M.C., 2011. *Creating Capabilities*. Cambridge, MA: Harvard University Press.

Paxton, M., 2007. Students' Interim Literacies as a Dynamic Resource for Teaching and Transformation. *Southern African Linguistics and Applied Language Studies* 25, 45–55. https://doi.org/10.2989/16073610709486445

Pym, J., 2013. From Fixing to Possibility: Changing a Learning Model for Undergraduate Students. *South African Journal of Higher Education* 27(2), 353–367.

Pym, J., & Kapp, R., 2013. Harnessing Agency: Towards a Learning Model for Undergraduate Students. *Studies in Higher Education* 38(2), 272–284.

Reay, D., 1998. 'Always Knowing' and 'Never Being Sure': Familial And Institutional Habituses and Higher Education Choice. *Journal of Education Policy* 13(4), 519–529.

Rivera, L.A., 2015. *Pedigree: How Elite Students Get Elite Jobs*. Princeton, NJ: Princeton University Press.

Sayer, A., 2005. *The Moral Significance of Class*. Cambridge: Cambridge University Press.

Sen, A., 1999. *Development as Freedom*. Oxford: Oxford University Press.

Sen, A., 2004. Elements of a Theory of Human Rights. *Philosophy and Public Affairs* 32(4), 315–356.

Skeggs, B., 2004. Exchange, Value and Affect: Bourdieu and 'The Self'. *The Sociological Review* 52, 75–95.

Tinto, V., 2014. Access without Support is Not Opportunity. *Community College Week* 26, 4–4.

Vally, S., & Motala, E., 2014. *Education, Economy & Society*. Pretoria: Unisa Press.

Walker, M., 2006. *Higher Education Pedagogies: A Capabilities Approach*. Berkshire: Open University Press.
2006
Walker, M., 2008. Widening Participation; Widening Capability. *London Review of Education* 6(3), 267–279.
Walton, E., Bowman, B., & Osman, R., 2015. Promoting Access to Higher Education in an Unequal Society: Part 2 – Leading Article. *South African Journal of Higher Education* 29(1), 8–25.
Wilson-Strydom, M., 2015. *University Access and Success: Capabilities, Diversity and Social Justice*. London and New York: Routledge.
Wilson-Strydom, M., & Walker, M., 2015. A Capabilities-Friendly Conceptualisation of Flourishing in and through Education. *Journal of Moral Education* 44(3), 310–324.
Wingate, U., 2007. A Framework for Transition: Supporting 'Learning to Learn' in Higher Education. *Higher Education Quarterly* 61(3), 391–405.
Wolff, J., & de-Shalit, A., 2007. *Disadvantage*. Oxford: Oxford University Press.

Chapter 6

Student agency in higher education

I now examine how students used their agency to navigate the resource constraints and structural arrangements described in the previous chapter. The focus of this chapter is student experiences of converting resources into capabilities and functionings for equal participation. This chapter attempts to capture the enabling factors that contribute towards equal participation. I also track how student agency, resistance and resilience and worked against personal and structural constraints.

Student narratives show the complexity of arrangements that fostered participation despite limitations. I also foreground student agency and suggest that we pay attention to how undergraduate students negotiate personal and institutional challenges. The chapter is organised using five clusters of conversion factors that were found to increase participation: affiliation with lecturers; affiliation with peers; the platform for voice; access to information; and recognition of capabilities.

Enabling affiliation with lecturers

Students identified lecturer affiliation as a conversion factor that enabled them to convert resources into participation (Pym, Goodman, & Patsika 2011; Pym & Kapp 2013). For some students, alliances with lecturers helped them engage more deeply with learning. In this section, participants describe interactions with faculty members who were not limited by student–lecturer hierarchy even though opportunities for mentorship were reported to be relatively scarce and unevenly distributed across academic programmes. In the narratives, participants encouraged at school to recognise the value of mentorship pursued affiliation with lecturers. Drawing on her positive experience with teachers at a well-resourced school, Clarice pursued affiliation with supportive lecturers, as she explains below:

> I like theory. And when I understand it because [the lecturer] explained it properly, I actually remember it. After the exam I went to [the lecturer's] office, and she asked: 'How did you write?' And I [said]: 'So cool!' I had my exam paper in my hand, and I had highlighted and scribbled in pencil. And she

looked at it and said: 'Wow, you actually used the Vodacom [mobile network] example to explain!' [I replied]: 'But you said it in class. Why was I going to break my brain and come up with my own?' And she [replied]: 'Wow, you actually listen' [INT 3].

The interaction described above was a resource that Clarice converted into meaningful participation with knowledge. Another positive functioning was being recognised and acknowledged for her effort as a capable student, which Clarice valued within an institutional context where there were limited opportunities for engagement between lecturers and undergraduate students. In contrast to the classroom environments identified in the previous chapter, this example of affiliation expanded Clarice's freedom to convert available resources into valued functionings. Clarice also valued an opportunity to be recognised as capable by her lecturer, which expanded her engagement with knowledge.

However, in her approach to affiliation I also identified barriers to cultivating critical academic capabilities. In the example above, Clarice framed academic achievement as the ability to reproduce the lecturer's example given in class, instead of critical processes and interpretation to construct her own example. Clarice explained that being connected to a lecturer helped her to understand what she was doing 'wrong':

I'm forever there [at her office]; that's just me. I want to know. I need to know where I'm going wrong. She knows me now [INT 3].

Instead of cultivating an independent approach to learning, Clarice became dependent on guidance from the lecturer to show her the 'right' way to learn. In the previous chapter, Clarice had emphasised how her academic support modules were misaligned to the demands of her degree course, whereas in this instance her uncritical dependence on a supportive lecturer was a substitute for the absence of critical engagement with knowledge.

Condorrera believed that the confidence to seek affiliation outside the classroom distinguished successful students from those who struggled to engage:

I think this university [has] a platform [where] underprivileged students can go and get help... like developmental modules. Now there's that Centre for Teaching and Learning, the Writing Centre which is really good. So I think they are trying, they are doing something. I don't think that Centre [academic writing centre] existed before. . . . But it's up to us to seek that help [INT 2].

While Condorrera's approach to converting available opportunities and resources into participation helped her to achieve academic success and to make the transition into postgraduate study, there was less evidence that other participants had been able to convert these support structures into academic participation. In the other narratives, it was evident that access to these resources was not linear or evenly spread across student experiences. As discussed in the previous chapter, Condorrera registered for a specialised degree course that enabled her to connect academically with her lecturers, tutors and peers while she also used her knowledge of institutional cultures, acquired through travel and study abroad, to network with staff members affiliated with these programmes. Her description of a supportive faculty reflected intellectual engagement amongst peers more than the lecturer–student hierarchy in younger student narratives:

> *I only took these developmental modules from my third year with [lecturer], who also taught me linguistics. I've always known him, so it was not difficult to get academic literacy from him. I know his style of teaching and what to expect. However, academic literacy is not a very difficult module; it was an easy ride. I got a distinction for it [INT 2].*

It is significant that Condorrera postponed the bridging degree programme's requirement of two years of literacy modules in the first and second year. She found an administrative loophole and only registered for these modules in her third and final year. By her third year, Condorrera was familiar with the practices and discourses of the academic environment, and experienced the course as an 'easy' experience. Unlike Techniques who was anxious about the writing requirements of the literacy course, or Clarice who was frustrated by the perceived irrelevance of the content, Condorrera's familiarity with the requirements of essay writing meant that she converted the opportunity into affiliation with her lecturer, intellectual development and appreciation for learning:

> *One lecturer from the sign language department would explain something so you absorb it. Only [lecturer's name] can do that. She's just a friend. I compare lecturers; the approach depends on the type of module. I don't want to be too judgemental. Some modules are too complex compared to the others ... so in terms of complexity, I have to take extra effort to understand [INT 2].*

The experience above suggests that Condorrera converted affiliation with supportive lecturers in her department to the capability for navigating academic challenges. Once she had access to staff members who made knowledge accessible, she had the confidence to critique different teaching styles instead of projecting a deficit belief onto her ability to learn. In contrast to Techniques' confusion about lecturer expectations, Condorrera was confident about navigating different academic terrain, while creating opportunities for resource conversion and recognition outside of formal pedagogical interactions. Condorrera was also the only participant who reported predominantly enabling conditions for learning. Other students did not know about or had not used resources like the university's writing centre. Most courses in their degree programmes served as electives for thousands of students, which meant that overcrowding and alienation from lecturers was the norm (Hockings, Cooke, & Bowl 2007). These interpersonal comparisons are indicative of important differences in structural arrangements that resulted in unequal opportunity freedoms for individual students.

An important aspiration that emerged from student experiences was the need for conditions that could enable participation. Students constructed these aspirations after being exposed to lecturers who created affiliation, despite resource constraints, as illustrated by Kea below:

> *The lecturer was never standing still in class! She knew some of the students personally; that made us connect a little more to her. . . . I liked the fact that she was more of a presentation person. She walks around and talks to people. She laughs; she makes jokes. If ever you get something that is practical, you not going to forget it. . . . She spoke about marketing products which makes it easier for students to write about it. It makes it easier for students to interact, and to ask questions [INT 2].*

It was concerning that Kea could only identify a couple of instances where a lecturer facilitated access to content. Yet while the lecturer engaged student attention using games and sweets, which helped Kea to memorise content for assessment, some may be skeptical about arrangements where students are 'treated as either clients or as restless children in need of high-energy entertainment' (Giroux 2013) enabled critical participation. Tracking Kea's approach to learning during her narrative suggests that these interactions with popular lecturers did not develop the critical capabilities and limited her academic engagement to reproducing information for assessment.

Although the outcome of pedagogical affiliation appeared to be largely instrumental, Kea framed her lecturer's ability to connect to students as an arrangement that could expand a sense of belonging as a crucial part of redistributing recognition (Fraser 2009):

> *Because if lecturers are teaching a lot of students they must find a connection. For instance, if the lecturer talks about her personal experience or maybe something that is very similar [to student experience], then the students feel more connected to their lecturer because she is being open [INT 2].*

Naledi also described a lecturer who transformed a disengaged classroom with her performative style:

> *[T]his other time, [a soft-spoken lecturer] had a substitute just for a day, and the class was active. And the class asked, 'Are you the new lecturer?' And we felt: Yeah! Could it be more active, more loud, more examples? [INT 3].*

While participants valued lecturers with the ability to capture students' attention, the relationship between resource distribution, recognition, quality of teaching and the ability to entertain students was unclear. Although lecturers who 'perform' may expand students' interest in the subject, it is unclear whether the ability to entertain students cultivated capabilities required for equal participation such as analytical thinking and critical literacies. A lecturer's ability to create opportunities for students to convert information into critical capabilities and functionings depends more on discipline-specific strategies to make invisible discourses more explicit and abstract knowledge accessible (Kapp & Bangeni 2005; Hockings et al. 2007).

Condorrera offered a more nuanced critique of pedagogical arrangements, while also highlighting the conceptual shift towards teaching as a service offered to paying clients:

> *So if you go to class with somebody who is passionate about what they are doing, it's not the same as going to class and getting a service from a lecturer who is not as passionate about what they are doing. Maybe they are doing it as a substitute or they know it, or they can do it, or they are just specialised in it. But they are not just passionate about it [INT 2].*

In Aziza's experience, the role of lecturers should be to connect learning with skills and knowledge beyond the classroom, which she had had the freedom to develop in an academic literacy course:

> *But if lecturers could make you see beyond just words and grammar. . . . But students don't see literacy as something that is very important and something you are going to use until you die [INT 2].*

Another aspect of affiliation identified across narratives was students' need for an *ethics of care* between students and lecturers (Tronto 2010; Pym et al. 2011). In Techniques' experience, the participatory climate of our academic literacy classroom helped him to mediate the isolation and confusion he described in Chapter 5:

> *You are able to relate with students more . . . you are more involved in the personal lives of your students. That's why we find your class so interesting [INT 3].*

Given the limited resources with which many first-generation students enter the institution, material and symbolic resources that enable them to cope with stress are unevenly distributed, making students dependent on campus-based support structures. In response, an ethics of care developed by a lecturer–student alliance seemed to alleviate the alienation that disconnect students from support structures outside their immediate families. Given the intensity of identity work at university where students must develop the qualities associated with being a university student (Pym & Kapp 2013; Pym et al. 2011), lecturer affiliation emerged as a conversion factor that enabled both access to knowledge and individual development. Yet, as mentioned earlier, an ethics of care cannot act as a substitute for arrangements that facilitate critical access to knowledge; rather, belonging and engagement with knowledge must be developed simultaneously. While this approach could be an important way to begin challenging hierarchies that alienate students from knowledge, it would require a more equitable distribution of resources because it is time and labour intensive, and requires both financial resources and commitment from faculty.

In Clarice's experience, the power imbalance between lecturers and students was complicated by misrecognition of students who valued being recognised as autonomous individuals. She suggested that lecturers should consider that:

> *I'm teaching adults now. How do I engage? How was I at varsity? What did I want to do? What didn't I want to do? [INT 2].*

Because of the different social position occupied by many lecturers, this may limit the cultivation of narrative imagination about the struggles of first-generation students from impoverished communities (Leibowitz 2009). At the same time, a massified university system makes it difficult for lecturers to invest time and energy into academically vulnerable students. Although in policy, commitments to social justice are embedded into institutional mandates (DHET 2013), translating this policy into enabling pedagogical arrangements is more complicated (Walton, Bowman & Osman 2015). For example, part-time contract lecturers on development programmes have limited opportunities for research, which could decrease staff's incentive to extend their teaching function beyond minimum requirements (Boughey 2010). The skills discourse embedded in academic support programmes also shifts the focus from critical capability development to short-term remediation of student 'problems' (Leibowitz 2011). This is an institutional challenge that requires a sustainable approach so that reliable freedoms, opportunities and resources are made available to the most vulnerable students.

Enabling affiliation with peers

Peer affiliation emerged as another set of conversion factors that enabled students to convert academic resources into participation. In contrast to students who have access to residence life, Naledi was a commuter student vulnerable to academic and social exclusion. She described the isolation of living as a commuter and being unable to make friends:

> *I remember in all of my classes besides your academic literacy course, I didn't talk to anyone after my friend left the university. So I would just go to lectures, then go back home. But in this class I started talking to people [INT 3].*

The research project offered sustained opportunities for peer affiliation, which alleviated Naledi's isolation and broadened her participation beyond the classroom. This opportunity to participate in the research project expanded her social engagement with peers, which in her experience acted as a fertile functioning. Naledi also converted affiliation into empathy when her academic struggles were recognised in the experiences of peers:

I've learned a lot about other people. Like for me, [university] was ... get a degree, and go and do something. Like for other people, it's actually ... understanding [their] different ... history and backgrounds [and that] other people have been through a tough time like myself [INT 3].

Another aspect of this fertile functioning enhanced Naledi's capability for critical reasoning. Even though she was frustrated by the lecture-and-leave approach, informal interaction with peers on the research team enabled her to construct a more critical approach to planning her life:

I've learned being able to be open and not accepting everything and saying – being able to say no, this is what I want to do, [being] open minded to other things, and learning about other people's experiences [INT 3].

The opportunity to work reflexively with her educational trajectory also helped Naledi realise the emotional and academic impact of bullying, and she was able to acknowledge her resilience despite these constraints (Gachago et al. 2014):

Reflecting back, just thinking about the whole high school thing, I had to reflect and think ... those things [being bullied and teased] had an impact in how I ... chose my [studies]. ... How could people be so cruel? 'Cos not a lot of people talk about [bullying]. ... It had an impact in how you learn and how I'll be a [...] student [INT 3].

Naledi explained how the pedagogical arrangements of the research project enabled her to make important connections between her experiences at school and her initial struggle to succeed at university. As she explained in the second year of the research project, she shifted her focus from wanting to obtain a degree to realising the opportunities for capability development at the institution:

[T]he university has contributed much for me, to be able to reason differently from someone who is sitting at home. I have more ambition; I just wanna go big and not just sit at home and limit myself ... if I was at home, I was just going to think, let me just work somewhere. Now at varsity there's a lot of opportunities. I can go and study abroad or I can do something about my situation in terms of having kids, and think, I'm at varsity now. Let me just

wait [before having children] and do something that I'm passionate about [INT 2].

Techniques similarly reported that peer affiliation created an opportunity where he could develop capabilities with the support of research participants:

Like for me, this group has motivated me a lot. I'm able to gain ideas, and do things I never thought I'd be able to do. So it has done a lot for me. So I think it depends on what type of person you are, and the type of environment you associate yourself around. Because people have an influence on who you become; especially your friends [INT 3].

Peer affiliation expanded Techniques' agency for pursuing capabilities and functionings, such as the opportunity to make friends who enhanced his academic participation. Academic pressure and the fear of failure directed his energy and time towards study, leaving limited resources for valued peer connections.

Peer affiliation also enabled Techniques to develop valued capabilities aligned with his aspiration for community development projects:

[P]ublic speaking ... though I'm not a fan, and I don't see myself [as a public speaker]. But ... you gain confidence as time goes, depending on the type of people you have around you. Whether it's people who are going to press you down or people who motivate you.

[At university] you get the opportunity to mingle around different people. ... You get the opportunity to find your strengths and weaknesses as a person, as you grow, as you develop. You see where you lack and where you are most comfortable in. So it helps in self-definition of who you are [INT 3].

In the extract above, it is evident that Techniques had the freedom to challenge inherent beliefs about his ability to learn. The research process expanded his critical thinking to incorporate his ideas about democratic education into the design of a community project:

Isn't that the whole aim behind education? So you become educated and then you educate other people? [INT 3].

Peer affiliation is aligned to his aspiration to convert educational resources into outcomes that benefit people in the broader community. Affiliation with peers expanded Techniques' aspirations, which in time also enhanced the development of capabilities such as confidence and an independent approach to learning.

Thuli also converted peer affiliation into an opportunity for individual development:

[What helps me learn is] my ability to share what I have with other people. There are people who struggle to understand certain work. I share what I've

learned with them, and I also learn something from them. You get to test your knowledge of something. Whenever I have an essay or assignment, when I'm chilling with my housemates, I always ask them, then some of them elaborate on their different views [INT 1].

Access to an international student residence was a valued resource that Thuli converted into a platform to exchange knowledge with peers. Thuli valued peer affiliation because of the freedom to transfer knowledge using informal tutoring in a mutually beneficial exchange of knowledge.

Peer affiliation enhanced academic engagement for Clarice despite the structural constraint of large classes. Her freedom to develop academic capabilities was expanded in a small group environment where integration of interdisciplinary learning is encouraged:

When you're in a group of 20 with a [module] facilitator, you speak about something and it goes off that topic. I engage and get to know people from the medical faculty. So that's nice [INT 2].

Kea described the conversion of peer affiliation with a member of the SRC into well-being achievement. Kea converted achieved well-being into future aspirations for socially just engagement:

I feel like there is a lot I can give. That's why I like associating myself with [student leader] because she inspires me. She teaches me so much more. I even told her: I value your presence in my life. I've been through so much, [and] you're not this perfect person, but you're a human being that I can learn from. You inspire me as a human being, as a Black woman [INT 1].

Affiliation with a mentor enabled Kea to convert the traumatic pre-university experiences of losing her parents and living in poverty, and the difficult transition to university into functioning as an engaged student. In particular, Kea valued the ability to convert these traumatic experiences into functioning as a student leader in her residence:

Because many Black women do not see themselves as being leaders or bringing changes in other Black women's lives. But [the mentor] being the person that [she is], having a personality that is similar to mine, makes me see that I can go somewhere with my life. I can go somewhere in life. I feel like I'm growing ... every day and I can now see that I can associate with people that contribute to my life [INT 1].

Other participants reported valuing a small-group pedagogical environment because it enabled a critical dialogue between peers from different racial and ethnic groups, which challenged students' embedded beliefs about race and language.

A pattern emerging across student experiences is that opportunities for individual and small group engagement enabled the development of valued academic and personal capabilities.

For first-generation students adjusting to the demands of the institution, the opportunity to share and make sense of experiences with peers emerged as a valued opportunity that helped negotiate an alienating environment, as Aziza explained:

> *So what I mean is for us to have begun this journey, there was a level of no awkwardness ... that's when we would actually be able to be comfortable enough to open up to each other, or even to open up to you. That's what I mean with the voice and platform. 'Cos when you have a voice ... you have a platform where you can be listened to [FG 4].*

Clarice reflected on the value of the research group in transcending superficial engagement with peers and in personal benefits to academic participation:

> *This has made me work harder in a sense, to push myself and to try and engage with my lecturers even though they have 800 students in their class [INT 2].*

She made this comment in an interview following a focus group where students revealed the psychological consequences of their university experience:

> *Like the group we are – it's just made me respect everyone more ... we just learned so much about people and their lives. People might seem happy but you don't really know what's going on [INT 2].*

Research participants shared experiences of fear and anxiety, depression, worry and loneliness compounding the pressure of being a first-generation student.

Creating platforms for student voice

The third cluster of enabling conversion factors was pedagogical arrangements where students could develop an independent and critical voice (Brooman, Darwent & Pimor 2014; Burke 2008; Cook-Sather 2006; Nkoane 2010; Paxton 2012; Seale *et al.* 2015; Sellar & Gale 2011). This opportunity seemed to be quite thinly spread across the narratives and only a few references were made to the freedom to cultivate student voice. Nevertheless, the capability for voice was an important way to resist the passivity of the banking system and to disrupt deficit beliefs about first-generation students, as Aziza describes below:

> *Before we actually write our writing assignments, we've been discussing it in class. Then ... ideas are coming ... you're using Kea's words, you're using*

[classmate's] words, you're using your own words, you're using your own planning in class. And you [think] but Kea said something, or [classmate] said something! Oh, let me research about that! [INT 2].

In this way, the platform for voice enabled her to convert academic resources into engagement with knowledge. The capability for knowledge was also enhanced as Aziza collaboratively engaged with ideas that developed her ability to practise discipline-specific academic writing:

That kind of insight to put yourself in there like a big melting pot. And you'll be able to find your voice and see the skill that you're acquiring could be beneficial. Because I think that's what academic literacy has shown me. That now I have actually got my voice. I'm thinking now [INT 2].

Aziza valued the freedom to develop critical thinking and to navigate different disciplinary codes while incorporating valuable experiential knowledge. Kea similarly converted resources in the academic literacy module into the capability for voice:

I loved my class from the first day I was in the class. Because everyone spoke in class, everyone was interacting, so I felt part of an intelligent group of people who are very knowledgeable in terms of what they know [and] what they are talking about. So that inspired me to be part of the group, instead of me being Kea and me showing people how much I know. I listen, I interact, we argue about something and then at the end of the day, we come out having something that is worth more than billions [INT 2].

Kea valued the freedom for group interaction, and its corresponding development of confidence, belonging and access to knowledge, and the opportunity to play an agentic role in her education, which included the freedom to develop as an interdependent individual who is capable of listening to other voices (Pym & Kapp 2013). Another functioning was the recognition of herself as a valued member of a student community, in contrast to her earlier experiences of misrecognition described in Chapter 5. These arrangements suggested evidence of the freedom to co-construct knowledge instead of passively absorbing information (Freire 1970; Gee 2005).

Clarice also valued the freedom to develop her academic voice in an academic literacy module that acknowledged the divergent voices and identities that students brought to the classroom:

I walked in and [thought]: I like this class. And then I started speaking. And I never stopped speaking; that's me! I also want to feel part of class, and you are interested. Oh my gosh! You actually listen to what I'm saying [INT 3].

The narratives provide evidence that creating platforms for student voice was an important conversion factor that enabled students to convert educational resources into engagement with knowledge, although these opportunities were rarely identified in student narratives.

Distributing access to knowledge

The next set of conversion factors was access to strategic knowledge that students could convert into capabilities and functionings. Keeping in mind the influence of rote learning identified in the previous chapter, these experiences illustrate tentative alternatives to uncritical reproduction of information.

In contrast to her critique of first-year academic support programmes, Clarice's experience of her subject major aligned to content that inspired her to read and expand her engagement with knowledge:

> *It might sound silly – I'm studying communications. Everyone communicates. But it's so much deeper. It's just talking, but there's communication within cultures, and within cultures there's differences. It's this whole cool thing that I've studied. It's so wow! I did intercultural communication, and then organisational communication, and they also have conflicts in organisations. And you can actually see it [in the practicals], and it's like ah! That's cool! [INT 3].*

I noticed that this subject was taught by the lecturer with whom Clarice cultivated a critical alliance. At the same time, Clarice described specific career aspirations for becoming a communication specialist, which suggested an important connection between aspirations and engagement with knowledge. Another important aspect of participation is that the course offered 'practical' [tutorial] sessions with small-group engagement and continuous assessment. Her parents were also able to buy her a laptop, which enhanced her ability to develop technical capabilities associated with learning.

However, the pedagogical approach in these modules did not encourage Clarice to question information. There is little evidence of a wide range of opportunities to learn about and access alternatives, in particular opportunities that reflect a socially just approach to being a graduate. For this reason, the freedom for critical capability development appeared to be limited by a constrained pedagogical environment where resources are constrained. Equal participation was not possible when only a small part of academic engagement was supportive and resourced, and when the overall approach to learning mirrors the banking system. An administrative error held Clarice back for a year to complete outstanding electives, which separated her from peers and lecturers in her communication science network in the crucial third year of the course, while extending her bachelor's degree to six years.

Techniques' access to knowledge was mediated by his aspirations for community engagement aligned with his interest in issues of political power and exploitation. Once he changed his degree to political science, he was able to convert information into meaningful engagement with knowledge. However, because Techniques' potential was misrecognised by lecturers, his freedom to convert formal content was limited, and he found informal learning with peers more conducive to developing critical capabilities, which he described in the extract below:

> *And when it comes to politics, you learn how the whole system works: the different functions of government, and how politicians [and] the global arena tend [to] exploit other people. The funny thing about the system is that people who are most affected are the ones who don't know. And that's basically the truth. Because when you sit at home you don't read newspapers, you don't follow the news. People in the higher positions tend to take decisions for you, because you don't know [INT 1].*

Techniques did not have the freedom to develop affiliation with lecturers in the 'dog-eat-dog' environment described by Naledi. Inspired by his aspiration to contribute towards social change, he gleaned critical knowledge from his major and occasionally from other modules:

> *[The module] although it's boring, but it helped a lot. We spoke about economics and inflation and how it affects the country. We did something on climate change, where we spoke on different projects that are being done in South Africa. We learned about a lot of things that we never thought happened. Though you see them on TV you never take them into consideration [INT 3].*

Although the module above offered an uncritical approach, Techniques converted the information into a critical interpretation of the economy using his own experience of socioeconomic marginalisation and his interest in unequal distribution of opportunities. It was also significant that although he had not been exposed to enabling conditions at school, Techniques recognised the passive reception cultivated by the institution's banking system:

> *You go to a lecture, just sit there and listen to a lecture and then we leave. That's too formal. Why not make it interesting? Why not ... try to involve the students in what [you're] doing? So it's not a matter of facilitator coming and facilitating and telling you this is what, and then you have to answer questions, but more on you telling them what do you think you have learned, and your peers helping you answering the questions [INT 3].*

The institutional limitation for Techniques was that he was unable to convert his passion for social change into functionings. He reiterated these commitments during the project, and became increasingly articulate about the shape of his aspirations. But his time and energy were directed to the struggle to conform to the banking system and lecturer expectations to pass enough modules to retain his bursary. By his third year, decreased resources forced him to move from accommodation, in walking distance from campus to a remote neighbourhood where he could stay with a relative, making transport to campus difficult. These academic and socioeconomic pressures were barriers to opportunities outside the curriculum to develop and implement his aspirations for social change. The selection criteria for opportunities for capability development such as volunteering and mentorship programmes excluded Techniques, who was forced to direct all available resources to preventing his academic exclusion.

Aziza used her agency to navigate decontextualised content by focusing on the development of marketable skills:

> *I think even though they disregard academic literacy but it does truly help if you just look beyond the grammar and the work that you have to do, and see it as a skill that you're learning. That's what I always try to do in every module. Even though it can be a drag, but I see it ... could be connected to something in ... find the value ... even though the lecturer is boring ... find the value in what you are doing so even if you tried your best, you tone down your own negative voice [INT 2].*

In trying to compensate for the poor quality of teaching and misalignment of content, Aziza reverted to an uncritical 'skills' discourse. But justifying disabling arrangements with the hope that they prepare students with skills needed for employment is an inadequate response since it shifts sole responsibility to the individual while downplaying structural failures (Vally & Motala 2014). Her attempt to engage despite unjust pedagogical arrangements did not address deeper questions about the critical capabilities that university spaces could be offering to students, although it does give evidence of her agency in negotiating these restraints.

Aziza's overall experience of knowledge offered in her degree was the cram-and-exam approach she described earlier. Juggling parenting responsibilities at home also meant that Aziza was excluded from opportunities for critical capability development. By her final year, there was limited evidence of a critical approach to knowledge as she was forced to adapt to the pervasive rote learning in order to retain her bursary.

In Condorrera's experience, her status as a mature student enhanced her freedom to engage meaningfully with knowledge:

> *I think because of I'm fourth year now and I'm older, I pick up a lot of things. You can go to the same class with first years. They are not the same as ... the older students. They come here to ... explore. So they don't really listen to what*

the lecturer is saying. . . . They just want to go to class [to] get it over and done with. Some of them are here just to get a degree to maybe have something to fall back on. So they are not really paying attention to that. But I think the older students in class . . . are very critical; they listen, they pay attention. They digest what the lecturer has said when they get home [INT 2].

However, the quotation above speaks to an instrumental approach evident in the responses of younger participants, which is exacerbated by structural limitations. It also suggests that some pedagogical arrangements offer poor quality education with few opportunities to develop critical engagement with knowledge. Yet the ideal version of a student who engages meaningfully with knowledge is difficult to achieve when students enter the institution with diverse resource bundles, within the context of an insufficiently resourced higher education system. Condorrera is able to negotiate knowledge using the rich bundle of resources and capabilities developed before university. Just arrangements would enable more students the opportunity to convert information into knowledge despite different resources constraints:

I believe everybody who is here . . . can read and write. But we have to have interest for reading and writing. . . . Being interested in what you do . . . . It has to come from the course itself. Listening to the lecturers, doing what is expected, and seeing that you are going somewhere with this. . . . Students [who] are more interested in class . . . never miss a class [INT 2].

While previously Condorrera emphasised that the individual should take responsibility for her own participation, she shifted her focus to the role of pedagogical conditions, although she still framed participation as meeting lecturer expectations. Even though she was critical of unfair treatment by lecturers, she did not have real freedom to challenge her experience of academic constraints.

Kea described the value of a developmental module that enabled her to convert knowledge from our academic literacy module where the arrangements had been designed to help students synthesise relevant information from different academic sources:

Academic literacy actually helps us to improve some of the skills. You put . . . people with the same disciplines or ones that are related [into] a group. So that helped me to implement that in other modules. I used the knowledge that they have and I used the information I got from my textbook, and made it one. So that helped me as an individual to communicate . . . especially this year [INT 2].

The conversion of pedagogical arrangements into knowledge was enabled by a combination of structural and personal conversion factors.

Recognising student capabilities

The final cluster of conversion factors recognised student capabilities and resources (Leibowitz 2011). Students reported instances both in classrooms and in our research project that offered platforms for students to convert individual resources and capabilities into deeper participation.

Techniques brought a cluster of capabilities and resources to the informal research space created by our project. These capabilities included a commitment to challenging social inequality, curiosity about the structure of political and economic systems, and experiential knowledge about alienated young people in his community:

> *But now I've realised that it's only when you engage yourself, when you read, when you research, then you will know the basis of living. . . . Because if you know how the system works, how language works, and how people interact, you tend to know the basis of living. You are one step [ahead] in that . . . at least now I know, not my purpose, but the purpose of life as a whole [INT 1].*

Because opportunities for critical engagement with knowledge are thinly spread in the formal curriculum, Techniques converted interaction with peers into opportunities to resist the misrecognition of an unjust school system:

> *Because with varsity you learn how to become yourself, independent, and you acquire skills that you were unable to acquire when you were at school. You see yourself [as someone who] could sit down and study [INT 1].*

A crucial part of his capability development involved navigating his school history; university enabled Techniques to identify areas of development that he valued and that had been left 'under-developed' by the school system. Techniques used his agency to claim the recognition of himself as, in his words, a 'work in progress' who developed the freedom to challenge the stigmatising labels attached to his former inability to learn. He converted resources and opportunities into valued functionings as a university student capable of independent and critical thinking.

Techniques' narrative suggests that he was able to resist the banking system. As the research project deepened over time, he used this informal pedagogical space to convert knowledge and aspirations for community-based projects into critical consciousness. This capability then enabled him to act on the belief that 'every individual person plays a role in the transformation of a community':

> *We should try to relate to different people. It's the same that if you want to change . . . a group of gangsters; if you go there . . . and if you wanna to speak English, do you think they are going to take you seriously? Definitely not. So you need to go to their level and speak their language. . . . So I think that's one way*

of doing it. Speaking the language of the youth. Get something that you know the youth loves and they enjoy. . . . It should be something informal. Because people are tired of formal things [INT 3].

In the quotation above, Techniques' experience of being alienated by learning arrangements that are 'too formal' is applied to vulnerable groups who are excluded from higher education. He experienced these 'formal' teacher-centred arrangements as alienating:

Because people who are back home, who are not in higher [education] institutions, they see education as, not a waste of time, but as an unfair object of society. Because not everyone is able to come to varsity and not everyone who has a degree is able to obtain a job [INT 3].

During the research process, Technique navigated the conflict between the value of education as an instrumental good and a social good, and grappled with conflict between the value of education and the inequality that the education system perpetuates, created by his experiential knowledge about the effect of social inequality on the lives of family and peers in his community:

What is life? Is life just living and dying and doing nothing? Or is life to transform and create or reproduce what we already have? How do we produce if we keep asking for things and not creating them for ourselves? And I think that is the most important message that we need to convey to the youth especially. Because we are the future leaders, so if we don't have that mind-set to say, we want to make a difference, I believe our country is going to a downfall. So those are the types of messages we need to send out. So how do we change that type of mind-set? [INT 3].

In later stages of the research project, Techniques developed his political interests into his aspiration for a community-based project that is accessible to unemployed youth. He was reflexive about the value of education, but believes that higher education in its current form remains inaccessible to many young people:

There are a lot of things that one can do, though I'm not saying that education is not important. It is important. But the way we go about. . . putting it out there, I think that's the problem. To motivate the youth, to develop them, develop the way we think, the way we see life. Life is more than just the big car, the fancy house, the money. What about those people who are lagging behind, who don't have the resources we have? What are you doing for them? [INT 3].

Another aspect of student capability is the representation of diverse identities in academic content. Aziza reported that she was alienated by Eurocentric experiences embedded within academic content:

> *In a sense they [are] making us a little bit inferior [by implying] that maybe our [African] academic information is not good enough. If they add the African element [and] a bit of realism into it, when someone else is reading, [they] can relate to it. Because most of the articles in [the developmental module], we can't really relate.*
>
> *If they could add stuff like that ['the African element'], it would be really interesting ... [it] was a total bore to read those things ... [W]hen it comes to English, make it interesting so we can actually interact with words [INT 2].*

In her experience, academic content that offered a balanced representation of diverse identities enabled Aziza to convert content knowledge into academic engagement, as she describes below:

> *So if ever you speak about ... the experience of Black people ... if ever you learn about someone's culture in your [academic literacy] class, and then that same thing is implemented maybe in psychology or sociology ... then [I'll say]: Oh, I did this in class. And then I'm going to [apply] it to my other modules [INT 2].*

Within the institution, Condorrera's capability development was enabled by her agency to pursue personal and academic development despite institutional and social limitations:

> *[At school] I was not interested in reading. [Now] I read more, I research more. When you told me about this digital narrative thing, I said it was new; I wanted to do that. Because then I want to leave university knowing I'm equipped in this and that. So I'll be able to tell others about digital narrative [and] about the importance of knowing your own language, [and] what it's like being at university [INT 2].*

The relevance of education was mediated through her engagement with creative writing, which helped Condorrera make sense of structural constraints in her community. She described her decision to write a book as an act of resistance to the absence of creativity at school, as well as a strategy to enhance capability development:

> *Condorrera is a Venda word; it means perseverance. In the book, I talk about myself; how I grew up; the experiences that I had. So I actually walked to school with holes in my shoes. But I look at it as, yes, those shoes they had holes; it was difficult to walk to school in winter's cold like that, but they took me far in life. So it's a story about hope [INT 2].*

Transformation and student agency

The enabling pedagogical and institutional arrangements in this chapter suggest what is possible when students and staff enact agency and resistance despite systemic inequality. Many opportunities were associated with peer and lecturer affiliation, while platforms for student voice, access to critical knowledge, and the recognition of student capabilities also enhanced the freedom to participate. At a structural level, it is crucial to ensure that students have access to arrangements that cultivate critical academic capabilities while simultaneously offering the psychosocial affiliation necessary for becoming an engaged university student (Pym & Kapp 2013; Barnett 2007). Students who were alienated from lecturers during the early part of their degree such as Clarice, Naledi and Techniques also showed evidence of the enabling benefits of lecturer affiliation. This suggests the importance of ensuring that institutional arrangements are redesigned so that more students have real opportunities for equal participation.

Overall, students reported more constraining than enabling pedagogical and institutional arrangements and there was little evidence of equal participation. Even though most participants described arrangements that enabled participation, these opportunities did not expand most students' freedom to participate as equal members of the university. Most of the enabling experiences described were transient experiences of support that did not always increase secure opportunities for participation. While participants used their agency to access and convert resources, these opportunities did not offer sustained opportunities for support throughout the degree programme (Walton *et al.* 2015). Most participants did not have access to degree-specific support structures throughout the degree programme, and had to compete for lecturer and tutor support and resources that supported learning. Although participants valued activities that developed capabilities for leadership, critical thinking, creativity, and community engagement, the freedom to pursue these opportunities was constrained by the lack of material resources.

References

Barnett, R., 2007. *A Will to Learn: Being a Student in an Age of Uncertainty*. Berkshire: Open University Press.

Boughey, C., 2010. Academic Development for Improved Efficiency in the Higher Education and Training System in South Africa. Development Bank of Southern Africa.

Brooman, S., Darwent, S., & Pimor, A., 2014. The Student Voice in Higher Education Curriculum Design: Is there Value in Listening? *Innovations in Education and Teaching International* 0(0), 1–12.

Burke, P.J., 2008. Writing, Power and Voice: Access to and Participation in Higher Education. *Changing English* 15(2), 199–210.

Cook-Sather, A., 2006. Sound, Presence, and Power: 'Student Voice' in Educational Research and Reform. *Curriculum Inquiry* 36, 359–390.

DHET, 2013. White Paper on Post School Training: Building an Expanded, Effective and Integrated Post-school System. Pretoria: Department of Higher Education and Training, Republic of South Africa.

Fraser, N., 2009. *Scales of Justice: Reimagining Political Space in a Globalizing World.* New York, NY: Columbia University Press.

Freire, P., 1970. *Pedagogy of the Oppressed.* New York, NY: Penguin Books.

Gachago, D., Condy, J., Ivala, E., & Chigona, A., 2014. 'All Stories Bring Hope Because Stories Bring Awareness': Students' Perceptions of Digital Storytelling for Social Justice Education. *South African Journal of Education* 34(4), 1–12.

Gee, J., 2005. Meaning Making, Communities of Practice, and Analytical Toolkits. *Journal of Sociolinguistics* 9(4), 590–594.

Giroux, H.A., 2013. Public Intellectuals against the Neoliberal University. 29 October, 2013. *Truthout.* www.truth-out.org/opinion/item/19654-public-intellectuals-against-the-neoliberal-university

Hockings, C., Cooke, S., & Bowl, M., 2007. 'Academic Engagement' within a Widening Participation Context – a 3D Analysis. *Teaching in Higher Education* 12, 721–733. https://doi.org/10.1080/13562510701596323

Kapp, R., & Bangeni, B., 2005. 'I was Just Never Exposed to this Argument Thing': Using a Genre Approach to Teach Academic Writing to ESL Students in the Humanities, in Herrington, A. & Moran, C. (Eds), *Genre Across the Curriculum* (pp. 109–127). Utah: Utah State University.

Leibowitz, B., 2009. What's Inside the Suitcases? An Investigation into the Powerful Resources Students and Lecturers Bring to Teaching and Learning. *Higher Education Research & Development* 28, 261–274.

Leibowitz, B., 2011. Academic Literacy as a Graduate Attribute: Implications for Thinking about 'Curriculum'. In Bitzer, E., & Botha, N. (Eds), *Curriculum Inquiry in South African Higher Education: Some Scholarly Affirmations and Challenges.* Stellenbosch: SUN MeDIA, pp. 221–236.

Nkoane, M.M., 2010. Listening to Voices of the Voiceless: A Critical Consciousness for Academic Industrial Complex. *South African Journal of Higher Education* 24(3), 317–341.

Paxton, M., 2012. Student Voice as a Methodological Issue in Academic Literacies Research. *Higher Education Research & Development* 31(3), 381–391.

Pym, J., Goodman, S., & Patsika, N., 2011. Does Belonging Matter?: Exploring the Role of Social Connectedness as a Critical Factor in Students' Transition to Higher Education. *Psychology in Society* 42, 35–50.

Seale, J., Gibson, S., Haynes, J., & Potter, A., 2015. Power and Resistance: Reflections on the Rhetoric and Reality of Using Participatory Methods to Promote Student Voice and Engagement in Higher Education. *Journal of Further and Higher Education* 39, 534–552. https://doi.org/10.1080/0309877X.2014.938264

Sellar, S., & Gale, T., 2011. Mobility, Aspiration, Voice: A New Structure of Feeling for Student Equity in Higher Education. *Critical Studies in Education* 52(2), 115–134.

Tronto, J.C., 2010. Creating Caring Institutions: Politics, Plurality, and Purpose. *Ethics and Social Welfare* 4, 158–171. https://doi.org/10.1080/17496535.2010.484259

Vally, S., & Motala, E., 2014. *Education, Economy & Society.* Pretoria: Unisa Press.

Walton, E., Bowman, B., & Osman, R., 2015. Promoting Access to Higher Education in an Unequal Society: Part 2 – Leading Article. *South African Journal of Higher Education* 29(1), 8–25.

Chapter 7

Capabilities for equal participation

Based on the student narratives, I now introduce a list of capabilities for equal participation. As part of the undergraduate project, I worked closely with students and their narratives in selecting which capabilities to include (Wood & Deprez 2015; Crosbie 2013). The list of capabilities includes the following: practical reason; critical literacies; student research; deliberative participation; critical affiliation; and values for the public good. The capability set responds to structural conditions identified as obstacles to equal participation that are grounded both in the accounts of students' struggles and achievements at university. The aim of this chapter is to design capability praxis for higher education environments where students are vulnerable to unequal participation because of the intersection of resource scarcity and structural inequalities. From a decolonial lens, these capabilities could be incorporated into epistemological and institutional transformation in higher education.

From exclusion to capability development?

Before introducing the principles underlying this praxis, I briefly review an individual narrative to frame the application of these principles within the context of student experiences. In the preceding chapters, Techniques' experiences demonstrated how unequal access to resources and misrecognition worked clustered together to constrain his freedom for equal participation (Wolff & de-Shalit 2007; Fraser 2009). He entered university as a first-generation student from a working-class family and did not have the freedom to pursue his aspirations. Even though he demonstrated critical awareness in response to unfair structural arrangements, he did not have sustained opportunities to resist institutional inequalities while struggling to adapt to academic requirements and worrying about money for food, textbooks, transport and accommodation. Besides first-year developmental modules, which were misaligned to his academic or social needs, in his experience the institution did not offer other accessible support structures. If these structures were available, Techniques did not know about them and was not able to convert them into equal participation. He was also not connected to student leadership networks and struggled to gain recognition as a valued member of the institution. Although he networked with a youth development agency, he did not have the support or resources to develop these connections into valued functionings. Despite changing his degree course, he lost his bursary and was forced to leave the university without completing his degree. How could the university have reallocated resources, opportunities and pedagogical arrangements to enable Techniques to convert his agency, resources into capabilities for equal participation? At what point in his trajectory could appropriate resources or support have been made available to enable participation? What should pedagogical arrangements have looked like to give Techniques the freedom to cultivate the capabilities he needed for equal academic participation? Given the significant resources that were spent to fund his tuition and living costs during these three years, could there have been more enabling alternatives that would have allowed him to leave the institution with both a recognised qualification and the capabilities needed to achieve his aspirations to contribute to the public good?

The praxis developed in this chapter responds to these questions. It proposes a capability-informed pedagogy that could address the constraints to equal participation faced by Techniques and other first-generation and socioeconomically vulnerable university students. The chapter is organised as follows: the first section briefly defines my conceptualisation of praxis; the second section focuses on a minimum threshold of basic resources required for the conversion of resources into capabilities; and the third section outlines the six capabilities for equal participation.

Designing capability praxis

Given the evidence of constraining and enabling arrangements for participation identified by students, how could these principles be translated into practice in university pedagogy? The six capabilities in Table 7.1 were selected in participation with students as we analysed their narratives (Deneulin 2014; Pick & Sirkin 2010; Smith, Sheppard, Johnson, & Johnson 2005). Building on the principle of education as freedom outlined in Chapter 3, this model of praxis operationalises six capabilities for pedagogical arrangements, with reference to the student narratives I used on Freire's definition of praxis as a simultaneous processes of 'reflection and action directed to the structures to be transformed' (Freire 1970: 120). Drawing on this convergence of reflection and action, I conceptualised praxis as capabilities that enable students and lecturers to collaboratively redesign pedagogical arrangements for academic capability development (Hart 2015, personal communication; see also Waghid 2001).

Another aspect of Freirean pedagogy that aligned to this design is the focus on egalitarian practices that think critically about hierarchies between students, lecturers and institutional structures (Freire 1976). Freire and other critical pedagogy scholars maintain that the purpose of less hierarchical arrangements is

Table 7.1 Capabilities emerging from student narratives and literature

	Capability	Evidence in narratives	Evidence in literature
1	**Practical reason** Making well-reasoned and informed choices; becoming an independent and critical thinker	Valued opportunities to be challenged and to have access to rigorous learning environments; students resisted 'dumbed-down' pedagogy	Walker 2006; Wilson-Strydom 2015
2	**Critical literacies** Incorporating student resources into pedagogical environments; confidence to speak and contribute	Valued opportunities that incorporated existing individual resources and capabilities; discipline-specific opportunities for writing, reading, thinking and speaking	Hart 2012; Pym and Kapp 2013; Leibowitz 2011
3	**Undergraduate student research** Undergraduate student research to promote agency and ownership	Valued the opportunity to be involved in research aligned with aspirations, which increased ownership of the learning process	Appadurai 2006; Neary & Winn 2009; Wood and Deprez 2012
4	**Deliberative democracy** Participatory platforms for engagement with the broader university community	Valued opportunities to be listened to by lecturers and management, and consulted in decisions about pedagogy and curriculum, and democratic processes in the classroom	Meier 2008; Wood & Deprez 2015
5	**Critical affiliation** Affiliation as social networks, recognition, identity and belonging	Valued supportive affiliation with faculty and peers and to be recognised as members of the academic community	Walker 2006; Wilson-Strydom 2015; Fraser 2013
6	**Values for the public good** Commitment to social change through community engagement	Valued opportunities to contribute to community engagement and to form aspirations for the public good	Wilson-Strydom & Walker in press; Boni & Walker 2013

to expand students' freedom for critical education (Burke 2015; hooks 2003; Siry & Zawatski 2011). The outcome of this praxis would be policies that enable equal participation for vulnerable students. Instead of imagining a 'perfectly just university', these capability-informed practices work pragmatically towards the ideal of a just university (Sen 2009).

Resources and pedagogy

A foundational aspect of a capability-informed praxis is a threshold of material and academic resources required for equal participation. The narratives suggested that even when arrangements were enabling, students without financial resources for transport to campus, for instance, were less able to convert resources into capabilities or functionings. In this way, the absence of financial resources acted as corrosive disadvantage that decreased students' freedom for equal participation (Sen 1999: 10; Wolff & de-Shalit 2007). When students had to find work part-time or find alternatives ways to raise income, their fragmented attention was misframed as apathy, boredom and academic disengagement (Bozalek & Boughey 2012; Fraser 2009).

Pedagogy emerged as an important starting point for resource distribution since for some commuter students, classrooms and tutorials were the only places where they had regular contact with staff and other students. Yet the classroom has been side-lined as 'most institutional efforts have been situated at the margins of students' educational life' (Tinto 2012: 5; see also Engle & Tinto 2008). By reinstating the classroom as the central point of engagement, lecturers committed to an egalitarian ethic could use the opportunity to redesign arrangements so that vulnerable students benefit more equally from existing academic resources. For instance, interactions in the capability-informed classroom could become catalysts for debates and information-sharing.

In practice, this requires lecturers, peer allies and support staff who are committed to engaged pedagogy and public deliberation at a pedagogical and institutional level. For instance, if knowledge related to issues of resource scarcity is more effectively integrated into pedagogical practices and curricula, it could be possible to create an informational database and communication platforms that would help the institution identify and support students who are excluded due to resource insecurity. Another practical implication would be a stronger collaboration between academic teaching staff and student support services.

To address resource scarcity, lecturers could also create platforms to identify student needs, while being sensitive to the fact that some students will need more resources to reach the same level of participation. In this way, classrooms could be critical spaces to identify students who require more academic resources, while avoiding a deficit approach to 'less-prepared' students. For instance, while access to a textbook is critical, even if a student is able to afford a textbook, he might require sustained, discipline-specific lecturer and tutor input to convert the contents of the textbook into capabilities for critical academic participation (Nussbaum 2011). When these resource clusters were available, for example in Condorrera's narrative, it created a fertile environment for her to convert knowledge resources into academic capabilities. But when these resource clusters were not available, capability development was compromised and functionings were precarious and unsustainable, as Techniques described in his narrative. For this reason, it is crucial to ensure the alignment between financial and academic resources required for equal participation, because the stakes are higher for students with fewer resources.

Another short-term intervention to address resource insecurity is to ensure that students know where to find free resources such as good-quality MOOCS, online books, legitimate downloadable articles, accessible academic blogs, reputable and good quality news sources, videos, and other content with a Creative Commons licence. While participants valued these resources, they reported that lecturers mostly focused on rushing through curricula instead of facilitating access to knowledge resources that could benefit students with fewer resources and opportunities. An important caveat is that pedagogical practices and teaching staff can only play a limited albeit important role in redistributing knowledge resources. Once resource scarcity has been identified, the university would need to ensure that available resources are then distributed to meet the needs of vulnerable students. Individual efforts are unsustainable without resource distribution for the most vulnerable students at an institutional level, which depends on a commitment to resource investment from the state (Bozzoli 2015).

Capabilities for equal participation in pedagogy

I now turn to the six capabilities that emerged during the longitudinal research. These capabilities are a pedagogical response to inequalities identified in student experiences that constrained their freedom to participate equally. These capabilities have been identified as alternatives to the constraining arrangements, which include:

1 Practical reason
2 Critical literacies
3 Student research
4 Deliberative participation
5 Critical affiliation
6 Values for the public good.

These broad capability clusters have a number of possible functionings embedded within each cluster. For instance, the capability for critical literacies would include a number of corresponding capabilities associated within discipline-specific communication and research practices required. Specific capabilities cannot be determined without consulting students and knowledge experts within disciplinary fields. Therefore, although the capability development below suggests practical steps that students and staff could take to challenge inequality, this is not a 'problem-solution model' for unequal participation (Boughey 2010). Instead, the capabilities reflect principles of justice to be negotiated in consultation with students to reflect diverse pedagogical and discipline-specific contexts.

These practical proposals reflect the contributions of student narratives while also drawing on the normative language of the capability approach which moves from judging a situation towards a 'certain type of action to transform that situation' (Deneulin 2014: 47). Although the evidence focuses on both pedagogical and institutional arrangements, the praxis focuses particularly on conditions within teaching and learning. In resistance to a deficit approach to pedagogy, these capabilities challenge hierarchies, encourage critical thought, facilitate democratic deliberation, and align with values for the public good.

Practical reason

The capability for practical reason was identified as an opportunity that all participants valued, but that was thinly spread across pedagogical arrangements. From a capability perspective, practical reason is defined as 'being able to form a conception of the good and to engage in critical reflection about the planning of one's life' (Nussbaum 2002: 41–42). The definition has been expanded in relation to higher education as: 'Being able to make well-reasoned, informed, critical, independent, intellectually acute, socially responsible, and reflective choices. Being able to construct a personal life project in an uncertain world. Having good judgment' (Walker 2006: 128). In relation to the transition from high school to university, practical reason is '[B]eing able to make well-reasoned, informed, critical, independent, and reflective choices about post-school study and career options' (Wilson-Strydom 2015: 115).

When students become clients in massified institutions, an important task is to identify the student less to be rewarded by the system, recognised as a producer of knowledge, to achieve her aspirations or to cultivate the capabilities that enable participation in the world as a critical citizen. From a transformative perspective, practical reason would enable a student to interrogate 'beliefs, statements, and arguments' that create uncritical acceptance of authority and systemic arrangements (Nussbaum 2006: 388). Instead of being silenced, marginalised students would claim platforms for agency and voice in response to structural injustices (Bozalek & Boughey 2012; Pym & Kapp 2013). Practical reason in higher education would allow students the freedom to become producers of knowledge, in resistance to student as consumer:

> [I]f students are to become critical members of, and contributors to, the discourse, rather than instrumental reproducers, they have to be allowed the time and space to engage with the messy process of exploring (through talking, reading and writing) who they are (and who they are becoming) in relation to the authoritative voices in the field.
>
> (Kapp & Bangeni 2005: 114)

Student narratives confirmed that in some cases, pedagogical arrangements perpetuated an uncritical approach when lecturers taught students how to memorise and regurgitate knowledge instead of enabling intellectual autonomy. In particular, participants reported that pedagogical arrangements offer few opportunities to seek alternatives to rote learning, which some students experienced as negative, demotivating and less likely to encourage deep engagement with learning. Instead, some developmental modules taught generic 'study skills' that encouraged students to summarise and memorise information for assessment. As part of curriculum transformation, lecturers could cultivate classrooms where students have the freedom to convert resources into critical engagement with knowledge. Achieving practical reason depends on a university curriculum that 'enhances the capability of students to develop as independent and critical thinkers' (MacFarlane 2012: 724).

An equal distribution of academic resources means that pedagogy should not be 'dumbed down' because students have not yet developed access to academic discourses. Instead, lecturers could cultivate practical reasons for vulnerable students by mediating complex knowledge instead of assuming that students do not have the potential to learn (Lawrence 2002; Pym & Kapp 2013). Instead of being subjected to low expectations, lecturers could be aware of homogenising messages about student ability and provide a supportive environment to cultivate critical freedoms (Walker 2006; Wood & Deprez 2012). Access to strategic information is important to help students negotiate the university space (CHE 2010). Lecturers could use their authority, social capitals and pedagogical spaces to share strategies about how to navigate intellectual culture and support structures (Walker 2006).

Critical literacies

The capability for critical literacies builds upon practical reason as forms of expression such as the confidence to speak publicly and the freedom to read and research outside the boundaries of prescribed course material. Being critically literate includes the ability to distinguish between corporate marketing and independent sources of information, while being able to make sense of your world without undue coercion by religious or academic influences, social media or other social structures (Nussbaum 2010; Gee & Hayes 2011). In higher education, it means being aware of bias embedded within curricula, such as embedded stereotypes about race or gender that are normalised within disciplinary content. A critically literate student would be able to offer sound reasoning for the choices she has made using a diverse variety of sources, including own experience, academic texts and informal sources of knowledge.

Literacy remains a contentious debate in higher education research. While the new literacies movement enabled a theoretical shift away from conventional text-based practices as the standard measure of literacy, there is still much emphasis on student 'illiteracy' with its emphasis on generic language-based practices (Bock & Gough 2002; Gee & Hayes 2011; Henderson & Hirst 2007; Hurst 2015; Jacobs 2005; McKenna 2010).

While all the participants were second-language English speakers, accessing knowledge was not a general deficit of grammar or vocabulary. Rather students need access to the complex academic disciplinary discourses, including theoretical concepts and ways of writing, thinking, reading and speaking specific to their degree courses, which did not improve with the additive language course offered by the bridging degree programme (Leibowitz 2011; Eybers 2015; Boughey 2010):

> [B]ecause limited proficiency in the dominant language often co-occurs with inadequate mastery of the written academic register, it is easy to understand why many educationists refer to difficulties with the additional language as the problem, when it is only one among the many challenges facing multilingual students
>
> (Leibowitz 2005: 676)

Since the pedagogy, curriculum and assessment prescribed by a literacy course were described or perceived by students as disconnected from the academic requirements of their mainstream programme, participants felt that they were not able to transfer competencies from the literacy course to their mainstream modules. At the same time, participant responses confirmed that decontextualised language skills did not develop critical capabilities (Boughey 2010). Instead of pedagogy that is designed around 'formalized, monolingual, monocultural, and rule-governed forms' (Gee, Courtney, Cope, & Fairclough 1996: 61) critical literacy should be 'creating access to the evolving language of work, power and community, and fostering the critical engagement necessary for [students] to design their social futures and achieve success through fulfilling employment' (Gee *et al.* 1996: 60). It would be important to 'work with' the literacies that students bring to the classroom, while keeping in mind that the literacies required by workplaces are different from the academic literacies required for academic study, which lecturers who have not worked in the field may not be as familiar with as academic researchers (Leibowitz 2011).

In response to this limitation, I included critical literacies as a capability based on the analysis of student literacies throughout the research project. While there was some evidence of critical engagement with knowledge, this was thinly spread across the narratives. At the same time, there was almost no evidence that pedagogical conditions were encouraging students to develop critical literacies that acknowledged student resources, identities and capitals. If these opportunities existed, participants did not have the freedom to convert these resources into critical academic capabilities. In response to this absence, opportunities to develop critical literacy could be expanded and embedded within disciplinary practices. In practice, the development of critical literacies could incorporate students' multilingual resources in order to enhance access to disciplinary knowledge (Newfield, Andrew, Stein, & Maungedzo 2003; Pavlenko & Blackledge 2004; Paxton 2009; Stein 2000). In this way, critical literacy could design curricula using the knowledges, cultures, languages and identities that diverse students bring to the university (Cross & Carpentier 2009; Crosbie 2013; Gandin & Apple 2002; Leach & Moon 2008; Meier 2012).

Instead of producing students who comply with uncritical pedagogy, curricula and assessment practices, developing this capability for literacy could also enable students to recognise and respond constructively to constraining arrangements. Across narratives, students described the function of university education to prepare them for the existing labour market. The primary purpose of a degree was to enable formal employment and an income; students described little evidence that education had a critical, transformative function.

In a normative sense, critical literacies could serve the purpose of:

> enhancing the ability of the individual autonomously to realize, understand, recognize, articulate and act towards or follow their own formed (through education), informed and reasoned values through deep discussion, sustained engagement and critical scrutiny of a range of perspectives among fellow students, client groups and knowledge resources.
> (Vaughan & Walker 2012: 506)

Another practical function of critical literacy could develop understanding the complex and ever-shifting power relations underlying systems of knowledge (Gee 2005). In this way, instead of generic skills development, critical literacies would make explicit the normative content of disciplinary and popular texts. Critical access to complex multimodal reading, writing, speaking and listening skills would weave critical literacy into the identity work of becoming an independent thinker and 'to negotiate norms, values, attitudes and beliefs different from their home discourses' (Pym & Kapp 2013: 274).

Student research

Students valued the opportunity to approach learning as research (Appadurai 2006; Neary & Winn 2009; Smith-Maddox & Solórzano 2002; Brown 2009; Hunter, Laursen, & Seymour 2007; Siry & Zawatski 2011):

> *In the sessions we had, Talita would give us questions, and then she would say we should go and research with it. Today I am able to do my own research and I can say I am in a better position* [Pedagogy colloquium].

Undergraduate research has been found to improve the quality of learning, particularly in the development of critical academic skills, while also enabling an active approach to learning (Neary & Winn 2009: 198; see also Neary 2010). Undergraduate research was also found to address the dichotomy between scholarship and teaching and challenges the 'traditional archetypes of teacher and student with a collaborative investigative model', while using a mentorship based model of teaching and expanding students' analytical and communicative skills (Healey & Jenkins 2009). Positioning students as collaborators also has the potential to increase retention rates for students who are at risk of drop out (Taylor & Wilding 2009), while student participation in curriculum development showed that 'meaningful engagement requires a revision of the culture and processes of university curriculum decision making' (Carey 2013). Instead of a passive approach to learning, undergraduate research could help students to engage in the production of knowledge (Hordern 2012; Guertin 2015), while involving student researchers in cognitive, personal and professional development (Hunter *et al.* 2007). Other studies showed that students were more likely to engage with learning when lecturers used collaborative learning techniques (Ewald 2007; Fielding 2001; Seale *et al.* 2015; Schlicht & Klauser 2014).

These findings confirm the value that students attached to collaborative opportunities throughout the duration of our research project. For example, although Techniques was disengaged from academic content in some of his subjects and struggled to pass assessment, he articulated well-reasoned and socially engaged aspirations for education targeting vulnerable youth. Based on the findings above, it is possible that if he had been given more engaging and active forms of learning, together with a basic threshold of resources, he could have developed an approach to learning that may have increased his chance of equal participation. Moreover, Kea reported that being involved in research helped her think critically about her role at the university and as a future graduate:

> *I became empowered in that I realised that the project was about the struggle to success. I used to talk more and listen less. It improved my confidence ... I gained the skill of becoming a researcher, and I am proud to say that I am now a researcher.*

The transfer of capability development from the research platform outside the classroom also helped create a pedagogical environment where students expanded their freedom to engage with knowledge and cultivate reasoned academic voices. In this way, the research team played a role in cultivating conditions that benefitted their capability development, as Clarice described:

> *And after the first few months, we spoke to each other more, we interacted more. The class just became a place where, that's where you always wanted to be. 'Cos you felt like you're not just being given a lecture, and then you leave, you haven't asked questions or you haven't interacted [INT 3].*

Deliberative participation

The fourth capability that emerged in connection with equal participation was a participatory platform for consultation and decision-making to address 'the need for greater institutional engagement with students in order to address their needs' (Manik 2014: 148). The freedom for deliberation operationalises the importance of education as freedom developed in the conceptual framework.

Despite institutional barriers, limited resources and unjust practices, I argue that a participatory approach could create conditions that expand the freedom for equal participation. I define the three aspects of participatory freedom as 1) a rigorous process of participation that works to 2) increase access to critical knowledge and 3) expands student agency and opportunity freedoms (Sen 1999; Deneulin 2014; Crocker & Robeyns 2010; Drydyk 2008). For example, instead of generic skills interventions designed to remediate literacy deficits, students and lecturers could engage in a consultative process to co-design a pedagogical approach to academic literacy aligned with students' mainstream disciplinary knowledge and their existing literacy resources to increase opportunities for critical learning (Boughey 2010; Leibowitz 2009).

Recognising student agency as ownership and active engagement (Crocker & Robeyns 2010) within pedagogy could reframe education as a *process* of freedom for expanded capability development. I draw this conclusion based on findings in the student narratives that a lack of consultation and decision-making decreased students' commitment to learning. Participants reported arrangements that reflected un-participatory approaches to education that decreased individual agency and isolated students from decision-making processes related to their academic development. It was also evident across student experiences that when pedagogical arrangements were imposed onto students without consultation, the potential benefits and perceived value of resources were diminished. Moreover, participants took a less critical and more passive approach to learning when arrangements were devalued and perceived as coercive.

Instead, participatory classrooms could offer students the freedom to engage in processes of decision-making as well as opportunities to achieve valued outcomes (Sen 1999: 291). In this sense, capability praxis would create pedagogical spaces that model democratic processes. For example, a deliberative process of consultation could determine how to make these structures accessible to individual students and to negotiate a fair distribution for the most vulnerable. Sen writes that 'the freedom to participate in critical evaluation and in the process of value formation is amongst the most crucial freedoms of human existence' (Sen 1999: 287). Student experiences confirmed their need for flexible processes that enable them to re-negotiate modules that are misaligned to their academic needs (Walton, Bowman, & Osman 2015). Instead of being alienated from learning, it would have been helpful if Clarice had had access to a participatory platform that did not compromise her academic performance or push her to leave the institution. Her participation could have been enhanced if she had had more freedom to participate in choosing modules and designing the structure of her course.

Finally, participatory parity could enable students to actively challenge unequal arrangements. Lecturers could enable students to negotiate and design constructive ways to challenge arrangements that are not conducive to learning which reflects an ethical responsibility to create pedagogical environments in collaboration with their students, where students feel free to engage with knowledge, ask questions and cultivate reasoned academic and individual voices: 'Current student protest is a direct consequence of the manner in which the university governance has underestimated proper consultation with students and other constituencies of our universities' (*Mail & Guardian* 2015).

Importantly, Freire writes that '[d]emocracy and freedom are not a denial of high academic standards. On the contrary, to live an authentically free life means engaging in adventure, taking risks [and] being creative' (Freire & Freire 1992: 34). This freedom should be available to all university students regardless of the constraints that they face.

Critical affiliation

The fifth capability is the opportunity for critical affiliation, which I define as a form of social support with staff and other mentors, while being critical of hierarchies within these support structures. Across the divergent disciplinary communities reviewed in Chapter 2, the opportunity to become integrated as part of a challenging and supportive learning community was a requirement for epistemological access, recognition and the development of a learning disposition (Tinto 2014). Another crucial point is that students' perceptions of whether they are valued members of the university community have an impact on their engagement with learning, and even on decisions to leave the university (Tinto 2014: 9). From a social justice perspective, it is worrying that students like Naledi were unable to convert academic resources into the critical affiliation associated with learning (Leibowitz 2009; Leach & Moon 2008):

> *Before being on the research team my idea of getting a degree was just to get a degree, go work. . . . Before being on the team, it was just going to a class for two hours, dragging my feet [INT 3].*

Naledi's experience of her department was alienating and meant that she moved between home and campus without the opportunity to make friends, access support or participate in enriching opportunities. This degree of isolation was not conducive to equal participation; for this reason, students like Naledi should be given priority when opportunities for capability development are allocated across the student cohort. In practice, this would mean reviewing selection criteria to include students who are not given the same opportunities for capability development, or proving access to alternative platforms for capability development. On the other hand, while Condorrera faced challenges associated with poverty, there was convincing evidence to suggest that she was integrated as a valued member of the university who benefitted from available academic and social resources and opportunities, in contrast to other participants. Evidence of her participation was found in the fertile range of capabilities and functionings that she reported during the project. In follow-up interviews, Condorrera was pursuing a Master's degree.

Further research would need to establish how many students remain on the margins of university life without opportunities to establish critical pedagogical connections with lecturers and peers. According to student narratives, it would be important to determine the extent to which constraints created by resource scarcity, alienation and discriminatory practices converge in the experiences of commuter students in non-selection courses. In student narratives, it was evident that commuter students facing resource scarcity were particularly vulnerable to weak forms of institutional affiliation, which decreased their access to networks and opportunities for academic capability development.

I have framed this capability as a critical version of affiliation because it should not only enable students to cope with the academic and social side effects of exclusion, but also increase constructive and collaborative alternatives to structural challenges. The critical function of affiliation would extend beyond social support to include platforms to critique less enabling student–staff interactions. Although some participants had been socialised into a school culture with exaggerated hierarchies, the narratives showed that they valued opportunities for collaborative alliances with faculty. Instead of alienating authority structure, classrooms can challenge the alienation, fear and silence created by strong academic hierarchies. Creating alliances emerged as an important condition for engaged classrooms. Student narratives revealed misunderstanding between students and faculty based on deficit assumptions around class, race, gender, ethnicity and language. Instead of silencing conflict, lecturers can use their authority to challenge stereotypes and use conflict as opportunities to develop critical consciousness. Lecturers could then create a pedagogical climate to resist institutional power structures while educating students about how different forms of power and potential for collaboration permeates relationships between people.

Keeping in mind the importance of affiliation in capability lists for higher education, the absence of opportunities for meaningful affiliation across the student body is a remediable institutional failure. I have identified critical affiliation as a capability that can be cultivated within pedagogical settings by fostering a sense of affiliation that strengthens students' confidence and agency and enables 'the development of social connectedness, identity and agency [which] strongly assists academic success' (Pym & Kapp 2013: 278; Gachago *et al.* 2014). Recognition could be cultivated by students' contribution to the teaching and learning environment:

> It is part of our task to help [students] to work reflexively, to reflect on current priorities, and develop future goals that are meaningful to them. They have engaged in agentic ways in the past. We provide them with the time and space to reflect on how and why they have engaged in particular subject positions rather than others, and to consider how those roles may or may not change in the future.
>
> (Pym & Kapp 2013: 281)

In practice, critical affiliation could also nuance lecturers' assumptions around poverty, schooling and experiences of female, working-class and African identities by focusing on the life histories of individuals (Janse van Rensburg & Kapp 2015; Marshall & Case 2010). At the same time, instead of encouraging interpersonal competition for resources or recognition, lecturers could encourage cooperation amongst students by steering away from a sole focus on measurable outcomes. This could mean taking an active role in identifying vulnerable students who have less confidence to demand attention and support, as Condorrera pointed out:

> *But I think if [lecturers] see something that can benefit us, it's better if you tell us in time. Because we are still learning and we want to move forward [INT 2].*

Affiliation embedded within pedagogical arrangements could take into account students' need for opportunities for mentorship, regular feedback sessions, the development of self-esteem and voice, and platforms for communication that emerged in the data. Although social and emotional aspects of learning are often neglected in the classroom, a critical praxis would create a platform that distributes these aspects more equally (Christie *et al.* 2008: 579; Pym, Goodman, & Patsika 2011; Nussbaum 2010). The narratives suggested that vulnerable students who have regular opportunities to connect with lecturers and peers expanded their freedom to participate.

As illustrated throughout the research, students converted the opportunity to listen to the lives of others into narrative imagination when the visibility of suffering in the lives of their peers cultivated empathy. The capacity to imagine the lives of other people involves 'developing students' capacity to see the world from the viewpoint of other people, particularly those whom their society tends to portray as lesser, as "mere objects"' (Nussbaum 2010: 45).

Values for the public good

The final capability for equal participation is the cultivation of values for the public good. This capability reflects a normative stance which argues that the purpose of education is not only to empower individuals with knowledge, but also to address local and global injustices (Boni & Walker 2013; Nussbaum 2010; Walker 2006; Wilson-Strydom 2015; Walker & McLean 2013). The capability approach is founded upon *ethical individualism*, which translates into an examined life with concern for others, which could lead to individual actions that enhance collective well-being. For this reason, capability praxis would enable individuals to convert education into capabilities and functionings that expand their freedom to live an ethically engaged life. This means 'conceptualizing education as an active space that may enable an individual to learn and to develop their values and agency goals' (Vaughan & Walker 2012: 496; see also Walker

& McLean 2013; Boni & Walker 2013; Deneulin 2014). The long-term measure of equal participation would be well-being achievement that benefits individuals, protects the natural environment, and decreases inequality, in alignment with the values of equity, sustainability, participation and productivity (Alkire 2005). As such, this is a long-term vision of human development that incorporates education as a site where values for the public good can be cultivated. As I discussed in my introduction, these values would extend the function of education as a private commodity or a driver of national economic growth.

A focus on cultivating socially just values could challenge instrumental discourses associated with higher education:

> According to Aristotle . . . we learn to be virtuous by acting in virtuous ways, we learn to live well by living well. We then need to ask what we are all learning to become and be as we currently 'live' and 'do' in our schools, colleges and universities; through discourse we end up producing the kind of education system desired by government policy makers, while non-market values get squeezed to the margins.
> (Walker 2012: 391; see also Walker & McLean 2013).

From a human development perspective, pedagogy should enable a platform to nurture the ideals of sustained interventions to social justice and values that enable students to convert educational resources into 'social and moral consciousness' (Wilson-Strydom & Walker 2015: 18). The role of capability pedagogy would be to incorporate social justice values that prioritise the well-being of people and the environments into curricula. In the 1997 White Paper, the following policy statement connects the role of higher education to the public good alongside the knowledge-driven and human development functions of higher education:

> To contribute to the socialisation of enlightened, responsible and constructively critical citizens. Higher education encourages the development of a reflective capacity and a willingness to review and renew prevailing ideas, policies and practices based on a commitment to the common good.
> (MoE 1997: 4)

Institutions have the potential to provide resources and to shape agency and values (Vaughan & Walker 2012: 499). From a Freirean perspective, students who learn mostly by parroting information are unlikely to develop critical consciousness (Freire 1970; see also Gasper 2013). This requires mentorship from peers and faculty who are committed to modelling ethical, value-laden practices and knowledge(s) in pedagogical spaces. Michael Sandel argues that people who have not been given the opportunity for ethical action may have difficulty cultivating ethical ways of being (Sandel 2010).

Yet, while most participants valued opportunities to address social inequality, they were disillusioned by the disconnection between curriculum and social justice aspirations. Although students valued opportunities to contribute to community projects they were confused by the mixed signals sent by the institution. Some participants reported that they were being socialised into the idea of individual success and personal development without alternative views of what success might mean. For example, Kea was frustrated that she was being taught how to 'work for someone else' instead of being taught how to start her own business. Clarice, Aziza and Naledi were overwhelmed by inequality in their families and communities, but did not think they had the freedom to develop capabilities that could help them convert information into social transformation. The pedagogical challenge would be to create pedagogical and institutional practices that provide opportunities for individual capability development despite resource constraints faced by first-generation students.

Conclusion

In this chapter, I have outlined a basic resource threshold as the means to capability achievement and six capabilities as foundational requirements for a capability-informed praxis relevant to socioeconomically vulnerable, first-generation university students. These capabilities also bear relevance to students who are not first-generation, and who face different vulnerability. Previous chapters have outlined the necessary conversion factors for freedom to achieve. The capabilities are intended to reflect enabling pedagogical arrangements in which students would be able to convert available academic resources into equal participation. These capabilities would have to be publicly debated and empirically tested using a larger and more representative sample of the first-generation student cohort to establish their relevance and applicability, which is beyond the scope of this book. Yet, based on the findings and corroborated by evidence in literature, I propose that these capabilities could be applied to diverse pedagogical contexts in consultation with student cohorts who face accumulative resource scarcity and misrecognition in higher education.

References

Alkire, S., 2005. Why the Capability Approach? *Journal of Human Development and Capabilities* 6, 115–135.

Appadurai, A., 2006. The Right to Research. *Globalisation, Societies and Education* 4(2), 167–177.

Bock, Z., & Gough, D., 2002. Social Literacies and Students in Tertiary Settings: Lessons from South Africa. *Australian Review of Applied Linguistics* 25(2), 49–58.

Boni, A., & Walker, M., 2013. *Human Development and Capabilities: Re-imagining the University of the Twenty-first Century.* Oxon: Routledge.

Boughey, C., 2010. Understanding Teaching and Learning at Foundation Level: A 'Critical' Imperative? In *January 2009 Rhodes University Foundation Seminar.*

Bozalek, V., & Boughey, C., 2012. (Mis)framing Higher Education in South Africa. *Social Policy & Administration* 46(6), 688–703.

Bozzoli, B. (2015, October 19). Behind the University Funding Crisis. *Politics Web*. Retrieved from www.politicsweb.co.za/news-and-analysis/behind-the-university-funding-crisis?utm_source=Politicsweb+Daily+Headlines&utm_campaign=3b24c3e2df-DHN_20_Oct_2015&utm_medium=email&utm_term=0_a86f25db99-3b24c3e2df-140192113.

Brown, R.N., 2009. *Black Girlhood Celebration: Toward a Hip-hop Feminist Pedagogy*. New York, NY: Peter Lang.

Burke, P.J., 2015. Re/imagining Higher Education Pedagogies: Gender, Emotion and Difference. *Teaching in Higher Education* 20(4), 388–401.

Carey, P. 2013. Student as Co-Producer in a Marketised Higher Education System: A Case Study of Students' Experience of Participation in Curriculum Design. *Innovations in Education and Teaching International* 50(3), 250–260.

CHE, 2010. *Access and Throughput in South African Higher Education: Three Case Studies. Higher Education Monitor*. Pretoria: Council on Higher Education. www.che.ac.za/sites/default/files/publications/Higher_Education_Monitor_9.pdf

Christie, H., Tett, L., Cree, V.E., Hounsell, J., & McCune, V., 2008. 'A Real Rollercoaster of Confidence and Emotions': Learning to be a University Student. *Studies in Higher Education* 33, 567–581. https://doi.org/10.1080/03075070802373040

Crocker, D.A., & Robeyns, I., 2010. Capability and Agency. In Morris, C. (Ed.), *Amartya Sen*. Cambridge: Cambridge University Press.

Crosbie, V., 2013. Capabilities and a Pedagogy for Global Identities. In Boni, A., & Walker, M. (Eds), *Human Development and Capabilities: Re-imagining the University of the Twenty-first Century*. Oxon: Routledge.

Cross, M., & Carpentier, C., 2009. 'New Students' in South African Higher Education: Institutional Culture, Student Performance and the Challenge of Democratisation. *Perspectives in Education* 29(1), 6–18.

Currie, J.K., & Newson, J., 1998. *Universities and Globalization: Critical Perspectives*. New York: SAGE Publications.

Deneulin, S., 2014. *Wellbeing, Justice and Development Ethics*. London and New York: Routledge.

Drydyk, J., 2008. How to Distinguish Empowerment from Agency. Paper presented at the 5th annual conference of the HDCA, New Delhi, India.

Engle, J., & Tinto, V., 2008. *Moving Beyond Access: College Success for Low-Income, First-Generation Students*. Pell Institute for the Study of Opportunity in Higher Education. Retrieved from http://eric.ed.gov/?id=ED504448.

Ewald, J.D., 2007. Foreign Language Learning Anxiety in Upper-Level Classes: Involving Students as Researchers. *Foreign Language Annals* 40(1), 122–142.

Eybers, O., 2015. From Mechanist to Critical Realist Interrogations of Academic Literacy Facilitation in Extended Degree Programmes. *South African Journal of Higher Education* 29(1), 79–90.

Fielding, M., 2001. Students as Radical Agents of Change. *Journal of Educational Change* 2(2), 123–141.

Fraser, N., 2009. *Scales of Justice: Reimagining Political Space in a Globalizing World*. New York, NY: Columbia University Press.

Fraser, N., 2013. *Fortunes of Feminism: From State-Managed Capitalism to Neoliberal Crisis*. New York, NY: Verso Books.

Freire, P., 1970. *Pedagogy of the Oppressed.* New York, NY: Penguin Books.
Freire, P., 1976. Education: *The Practice of Freedom.* London: Writers and Readers.
Freire, P., 1998. *Pedagogy of Freedom: Ethics, Democracy, and Civic Courage.* Lanham, MD: Rowman & Littlefield.
Freire, P., & Freire, A.M.A., 2004. *Pedagogy of Hope: Reliving Pedagogy of the Oppressed.* London: A&C Black.
Gachago, D., Condy, J., Ivala, E., & Chigona, A., 2014. 'All Stories Bring Hope Because Stories Bring Awareness': Students' Perceptions of Digital Storytelling for Social Justice Education. *South African Journal of Higher Education* 34(4), 1–12.
Gandin, L.A., & Apple, M.W., 2002. Can Education Challenge Neo-Liberalism? The Citizen School and the Struggle for Democracy in Porto Alegre, Brazil. *Social Justice* 29(4), 26.
Gasper, D., 2013. Education and Capabilities for a Global 'Great Transition'. In Boni, A., & Walker, M. (Eds), *Human Development and Capabilities: Re-Imagining the University of the Twenty-First Century.* London and New York: Routledge.
Gee, J., 2005. Meaning Making, Communities of Practice, and Analytical Toolkits. *Journal of Sociolinguistics* 9(4), 590–594.
Gee, J.P., & Hayes, E.R., 2011. *Language and Learning in the Digital Age.* London: Taylor & Francis.
Gee, J., Courtney, C., Cope, B., & Fairclough, N., 1996. A Pedagogy of Multiliteracies: Designing Social Futures. *Harvard Educational Review* 66(1), 60–92.
Giroux, H.A., 2005. The Terror of Neoliberalism: Rethinking the Significance of Cultural Politics. *College Literature* 32(1), 1–19.
Guertin, E., 2015. Helping Students Design an Education. *The Journal of General Education* 64(2), 131–138.
Hart, C.S., 2012. *Aspirations, Education and Social Justice: Applying Sen and Bourdieu.* London: Bloomsbury.
Hart, C.S., 2015. Personal communication at HDCA conference 2015, Washington, DC, USA.
Henderson, R., & Hirst, E., 2007. Reframing Academic Literacy: Re-Examining a Short-Course for 'Disadvantaged' Tertiary Students. *English Teaching: Practice and Critique* 6(2), 25–38.
hooks, bell, 2003. *Teaching Community: A Pedagogy of Hope.* New York and London: Routledge.
Hordern, J., 2012. The Student as Producer within a Productive System. *Enhancing Learning in the Social Sciences* 4(3), 1–12.
Hunter, A., Laursen, S. L., & Seymour, E., 2007. Becoming a Scientist: The Role of Undergraduate Research in Students' Cognitive, Personal, and Professional Development. *Science Education* 91, 36–74. https://doi.org/10.1002/sce.20173
Hurst, E., 2015. 'The Thing that Kill Us': Student Perspectives on Language Support in a South African University. *Teaching in Higher Education* 20(1), 78–91.
Jacobs, C., 2005. On Being an Insider on the Outside: New Spaces for Integrating Academic Literacies. *Teaching in Higher Education* 10(4), 475–487.
Janse van Rensburg, V., & Kapp, R., 2015. 'So I Have to Be Positive, No Matter How Difficult It Is': A Longitudinal Case Study of a First-Generation Occupational Therapy Student. *South African Journal of Occupational Therapy* 44, 29–33.
Jenkins, A., & Healey, M., 2009. Developing the Student as a Researcher through the Curriculum. *Innovations in Practice* 2, 3–15.

Kapp, R., & Bangeni, B., 2005. 'I was Just Never Exposed to this Argument Thing': Using a Genre Approach to Teach Academic Writing to ESL Students in the Humanities, in Herrington, A. & Moran, C. (Eds), *Genre Across the Curriculum* (pp. 109–127). Utah: Utah State University.

Lawrence, J., 2002. The 'Deficit-Discourse' Shift: University Teachers and Their Role in Helping First Year Students Persevere and Succeed in the New University Culture. Presented at the First Year in Higher Education Conference 2002: Changing Agendas, University of Canterbury.

Leach, J., & Moon, R.E., 2008. *The Power of Pedagogy*. London: SAGE Publications.

Leibowitz, B., 2005. Learning in an Additional Language in a Multilingual Society: A South African Case Study on University-Level Writing. *TESOL Quarterly* 39(4), 661–681.

Leibowitz, B., 2009. What's Inside the Suitcases? An Investigation into the Powerful Resources Students and Lecturers Bring to Teaching and Learning. *Higher Education Research & Development* 28, 261–274.

Leibowitz, B., 2011. Academic Literacy as a Graduate Attribute: Implications for Thinking about 'Curriculum'. In Bitzer, E., & Botha, N. (Eds), *Curriculum Inquiry in South African Higher Education: Some Scholarly Affirmations and Challenges* (pp. 221–236). Stellenbosch: SUN MeDIA Stellenbosch.

Macfarlane, B., 2012. Re-framing Student Academic Freedom: A Capability Perspective. *Higher Education* 63(6), 719–732.

Mail & Guardian. 2015. Academics Support Student Struggle: Democratise Higher Education Now. *Mail & Guardian*. http://mg.co.za/article/2015-10-22-academics-support-student-struggle-democratise-higher-education-now/

Manik, S., 2014. Shifting the Discourse: Student Departure in the Context of Relative Deprivations. *South African Journal of Higher Education* 28(1), 148–163.

Marshall, D., & Case, J., 2010. Rethinking 'Disadvantage' in Higher Education: A Paradigmatic Case Study Using Narrative Analysis. *Studies in Higher Education* 35, 491–504. https://doi.org/10.1080/03075070903518386

McKenna, S., 2010. Cracking the Code of Academic Literacy: An Ideological Task. In Hutchings, C., & Garraway, J. (Eds), *Beyond the University Gates: Provision of Extended Curriculum Programmes in South Africa*. January 2009 Rhodes University Foundation Seminar.

Meier, D., 2012, June. *Creating Democratic Classrooms*. University of the Free State.

MoE, 1997. Education White Paper 3 – A Programme for the Transformation of Higher Education. Pretoria: South African Ministry of Education.

Neary, M., 2010. Student as Producer: Bringing Critical Theory to Life through the Life of Students. *Roundhouse: A Journal of Critical Social Theory*, 36–45.

Neary, M., & Winn, J., 2009. The Student as Producer: Reinventing the Student Experience in Higher Education. In Neary, M., Bell, L., & Stevenson, H. (Eds), *The Future of Higher Education: Policy, Pedagogy and the Student Experience* (pp. 192–210). London: Continuum.

Newfield, D., Andrew, D., Stein, P., & Maungedzo, R., 2003. 'No Number Can Describe How Good It Was': Assessment Issues in the Multimodal Classroom. *Assessment in Education: Principles, Policy & Practice* 10(1), 61–81.

Nussbaum, M., 2002. Education for Citizenship in an Era of Global Connection. *Studies in Philosophy and Education* 21(4/5), 289–303.

Nussbaum, M.C., 2006. Education and Democratic Citizenship: Capabilities and Quality Education. *Journal of Human Development* 7(3), 385–395.
Nussbaum, M.C., 2010. *Not for Profit: Why Democracy Needs the Humanities*. Princeton, NJ: Princeton University Press.
Nussbaum, M.C., 2011. *Creating Capabilities*. Harvard, MA: Harvard University Press.
Pavlenko, A., & Blackledge, A., 2004. *Negotiation of Identities in Multilingual Contexts*. Clevedon, UK: Multilingual Matters.
Paxton, M., 2009. 'It's Easy to Learn When You Using Your Home Language But with English You Need to Start Learning Language Before You Get to the Concept': Bilingual Concept Development in an English Medium University in South Africa. *Journal of Multilingual and Multicultural Education* 30(4), 345–359.
Pick, S., & Sirkin, J., 2010. *Breaking the Poverty Cycle: The Human Basis for Sustainable Development*. Oxford: Oxford University Press.
Pym, J., & Kapp, R., 2013. Harnessing Agency: Towards a Learning Model for Undergraduate Students. *Studies in Higher Education* 38(2), 272–284.
Pym, J., Goodman, S., & Patsika, N., 2011. Does Belonging Matter?: Exploring the Role of Social Connectedness as a Critical Factor in Students' Transition to Higher Education. *Psychology in Society* 42, 35–50.
Sandel, M.J., 2010. *Justice: What's the Right Thing to Do?* New York, NY: Farrar, Straus and Giroux.
Schlicht, J., & Klauser, F., 2014. Improving Higher Education by Linking Research with Teaching and Learning Processes. *South African Journal of Higher Education*, Part 2: HELTASA 2012 Special Section 28, 1017–1032.
Seale, J., Gibson, S., Haynes, J., & Potter, A. 2015. Power and Resistance: Reflections on the Rhetoric and Reality of Using Participatory Methods to Promote Student Voice and Engagement in Higher Education. *Journal of Further and Higher Education*, 39(4), 534–552.
Sen, A., 1999. *Development as Freedom*. Oxford: Oxford University Press.Sen, A., 2009. *The Idea of Justice*. London: Penguin Books.
Siry, C.A., & Zawatski, E., 2011. 'Working with' as a Methodological Stance: Collaborating with Students in Teaching, Writing, and Research. *International Journal of Qualitative Studies in Education* 24(3), 343–361.
Smith, K.A., Sheppard, S.D., Johnson, D.W., & Johnson, R.T., 2005. Pedagogies of Engagement: Classroom-Based Practices. *Journal of Engineering Education* 94, 87–101. https://doi.org/10.1002/j.2168-9830.2005.tb00831.x
Smith-Maddox, R., & Solórzano, D.G., 2002. Using Critical Race Theory, Paulo Freire's Problem-Posing Method, and Case Study Research to Confront Race and Racism in Education. *Qualitative Inquiry* 8(1), 66–84.
Stein, P., 2000. Rethinking Resources in the ESL Classroom: Multimodal Pedagogies in the ESL Classroom. *TESOL Quarterly* 34(2), 333–336.
Taylor, P., & Wilding, D., 2009. Rethinking the Values of Higher Education: The Student as Collaborator and Producer? Undergraduate research as a case study. University of Warwick.
Tinto, V., 2012. *Completing College: Rethinking Institutional Action*. Chicago, IL and London: University Of Chicago Press.
Tinto, V., 2014. Access without Support Is Not Opportunity. *Community College Week* 26(15), 4–4.

Vaughan, R.P., & Walker, M., 2012. Capabilities, Values and Education Policy. *Journal of Human Development and Capabilities* 13(3), 495–512.

Waghid, Y., 2001. Reflexivity, Democracy and Praxis: Reflecting on a Critical Moment in Classroom Pedagogy. *Perspectives in Education* 19(1), 29–38.

Walker, M., 2006. *Higher Education Pedagogies: A Capabilities Approach.* Berkshire, UK: Open University Press.

Walker, M., 2012. A Capital or Capabilities Education Narrative in a World of Staggering Inequalities? *International Journal of Educational Development* 32, 384–393. https://doi.org/10.1016/j.ijedudev.2011.09.003

Walker, M., & McLean, M., 2013. *Professional Education, Capabilities and the Public Good: The Role of Universities in Promoting Human Development* (1st edn). New York, NY: Routledge.

Walton, E., Bowman, B., & Osman, R., 2015. Promoting Access to Higher Education in an Unequal Society: Part 2 – Leading Article. *South African Journal of Higher Education* 29(1), 262–269.

Wilson-Strydom, M., 2015. *University Access and Success: Capabilities, Diversity and Social Justice.* London and New York: Routledge.

Wolff, J., & de-Shalit, A., 2007. *Disadvantage.* Oxford: Oxford University Press.

Wood, D., & Deprez, L.S., 2012. Curricular Implications for the Capability Approach. *Journal of Human Development and Capabilities: A Multi-Disciplinary Journal for People-Centered Development* 13(3), 471–493.

Wood, D., & Deprez, L.S., n.d. Re-Imagining Possibilities for Democratic Education: Generative Pedagogies in Service to the Capability Approach. *Learning for Democracy* 5, 5–31.

Chapter 8

Creating just universities

In the previous chapter, I outlined six capabilities for equal participation, in the context of higher education pedagogy. In this final chapter, I broaden my focus on pedagogy to the university as an institution. Given the individual and structural challenges that students shared in their narratives, how could universities expand arrangements that enable vulnerable students to convert available resources and opportunities into equal participation? We know that universities invest extensively in programmes and interventions to widen access, participation and success, but how do we ensure that students facing structural disadvantage benefit equally from such opportunities and resources? How do we ensure that academic interventions combine the technical rigour required by underprepared students with a critical participatory approach that takes into account student voice and resources?

Since unequal participation is not limited to the most vulnerable students, what could these capabilities for equal participation offer to students who may have attended well-resourced schools, but face other constraints that erode their participation? Clarice is an example of this paradox. Even though a superficial reading of Clarice's narrative suggests that her schooling and supportive family have prepared her for higher education, I found complex factors that decreased her participation. Her disengagement was not only due to lack of academic preparation or financial pressure, but also because she was keenly perceptive and therefore adversely affected by the deficit approach to students on the access programme. Her experience of being misrecognised as deficient and subjected to low expectations eroded her self-confidence, created a negative perception of the university, and contributed to her alienation, disengagement and early departure from the university.

Like disadvantage, advantage also clusters, so that a privileged student entering the university with a bundle of valued capabilities, resources and attributes for higher education is more likely to succeed, even if she is from a poor family and attending an 'under-resourced' school. This clustering was clear in Condorrera's narrative: despite poverty and other challenges, she entered university as a mature student who is highly motivated, aspirational, fearless in creating affiliation with lecturers, with an inherent curiosity and love for learning. She is the 'ideal student' who seeks out resources, uses all available opportunities, challenges unfair treatment, stays motivated despite challenges, and cultivates a passion for learning.

Condorrera's success is a cause for celebration, and evidence that a deficit approach to poor students is unhelpful and limiting. But what about students who enter the university with similar academic potential and aspirations, but do not enter a degree programme where their unique bundle of resources, capitals and capabilities can be converted in capabilities? Instead of simply blaming the individual, how could we re-arrange the university's structures and resources to enable students with the most serious disadvantage clusters an equal opportunity to succeed? Instead of accepting undergraduate attrition, disengagement and alienation as inevitable, could universities find and implement sustainable and innovative ways to distribute resources and opportunities more equitably?

From deficit discourse to enabling structures in higher education

At the beginning of the book, I argued that undergraduate students are vulnerable to the consequences of massification and resource constraints at higher education institutions. In response, we need to understand which institutional and pedagoical arrnagements deepen inequality for vulnerable students. Instead of only trying to 'fix' students, my capability-informed approach examines the university as a complex system in which embedded cultures, values, practices and power imbalances perpetuate unequal participation. Much research and resources continue to be invested in implementing, funding and improving student support, academic programmes, curriculum delivery and design, and assessment practices. Many factors that complicate participation could be addressed with practical interventions, such as redesigning or improving academic support programmes. However, my reading of student narratives suggests that we need more research to understand the psychological aspects, embedded discourses, power structures and relationships in higher education that contribute to student misrecognition and unequal participation. As such, universities would benefit from pedagogical interventions that give the most vulnerable students an equal chance to succeed. This means taking into account the often invisible logistical challenges and layers of discrimination that a Black, working-class student will face in navigating university life.

Under an increasingly stressed higher education system, efficient and workable problem-solution interventions are more likely to be the institutional response to unequal participation because they can be evaluated as part of performance management. For instance, quantifying success as the percentage of students passing a course is more manageable that quantifying the degree of recognition and belonging that students cultivate in the classroom. These interventions are an important yet insufficient response to the vulnerable students whose freedom for equal participation is eroded by structural inequalities. If we are concerned with higher education as a public good, cultivating spaces in which students are able to cultivate voice, recognition and belonging has important consequences not only for their academic performance, but is also aligned with the need to continue transforming higher education and the societies within which universities are situated.

For the complex reasons that I have outlined in the book, Black, poor and rural students are often framed as academically underprepared, passive and disengaged under-achievers. Instead of pathologising students, or only celebrating the 'outliers' who excel in academic pursuits and leadership, how do we enable participation for individuals who are flying 'below the radar', while struggling against structures that make it difficult for them to flourish? How do universities ensure that vulnerable students have equal freedoms to cultivate the academic capabilities to engage as students, future professionals and citizens? Instead of unwittingly perpetuating systemic inequalities, how could universities enable more of their vulnerable undergraduate students to flourish as equal and valued members of the academic community? In the section below, I discuss five areas of institutional and pedagogical response that could be re-designed in response to these questions.

Implementing a resource threshold

A basic resource threshold is a foundational requirement that should precede other pedagogical and institutional interventions, depending on the circumstances of individual students. A close reading of student narratives confirms that without a threshold of resources, it is difficult or impossible for students to enjoy a meaningful experience when they are fighting daily hunger, cannot access university textbooks, and live so far from campus that they are unable to attend regular lectures. According to Alexander (2008: 12):

> unless a radical redistribution of material resources is realised within the lifetime of the present generation, all the glib rhetoric of social transformation, national democratic revolution and African Renaissance will come to mock their authors and exponents in the years ahead.

Access to basic resources is about dignity, survival and well-being. From a capability perspective, access to resources can be justified as an end in itself. It is deeply unjust that some students have access to three meals a day, the freedom to travel, to cultivate social lives and extracurricular interests, to live in safe and comfortable accommodation, to build professional networks with academic staff, while others spend time and energy surviving and retaining their place at the university, forced to make trade-offs that leave them vulnerable to a diluted academic and social experience.

Resources are a means to survival, and also a means to academic engagement. Added to the stress and indignity of poverty, when resource scarcity clusters with other disadvantages, students are less likely to have the freedom to cultivate deep, rewarding and sustained engagement with knowledge. The consequence is not simply a concern with low academic results, but the fact that students do not have the opportunity to cultivate valued academic capabilities, for which the student, her family or the state have paid a high price. If we are interested in producing competent scholars, professionals and citizens, then a more fair redistribution of resources should be an urgent priority. In South Africa's current funding crisis, the challenge will be how to distribute resources to universities across the competing national demands, and to allocate resources equitably within the higher education system so that the most vulnerable students have a fair opportunity for equal participation. The announcement of free education for poor students in 2018 may be a step in the right direction.

From a capability lens, equal participation requires a minimum level of resource security that could enable *capability security*, which Wolff and de-Shalit (2007) define as knowing that a capability will be reliably available in the future. This resource threshold would depend on the needs of an individual student and should ensure that students have access to a minimal threshold of resources needed to participate equally. In practice, a threshold would also identify students who need a greater bundle of resources to achieve equality, such as for example students with disabilities or commuter students with fewer opportunities for social integration (Nussbaum 2011). In Techniques' narrative, when historical poverty, family unemployment and resource scarcity intersect, his freedom for academic participation and social integration was impossible to maintain, and he eventually dropped out of university. If Techniques had had access to at least the basic resources needed to live and study, could he have achieved a more equitable level of participation?

In Table 8.1, I list the components of a basic resource threshold to ensure that all students have a fair chance to succeed with the basic requirements of living costs and academic materials. Implementing a basic resource threshold would require both institutional and state commitment to ensure that students like Techniques 'who need more help to get above the threshold get more help' (Nussbaum 2011: 24). As a commuter student on a non-specialist degree course, an early warning system embedded in pedagogical and/or institutional arrangements might have offered resources before socioeconomic vulnerability resulted in drop out (Christie, Munro, & Fisher 2004).

Table 8.1 A minimum resource threshold

Basic resources for equal academic participation
1 Reliable and decent nutrition
2 Safe and reliable transport to campus and extracurricular activities
3 Access to textbooks and other academic materials required by the degree course
4 Resources needed for academic printing and photocopies
5 Access to information technology, especially reliable data connectivity and the software/hardware required for academic assignments
6 Safe housing that is located at a reasonable distance from campus
7 Resources for minimal participation in extracurricular activities
8 Access to basic medical care, including access to mental health care
9 Access to basic toiletries and to clothing that does not cause shame to the individual

We know that poverty is not an inevitable barrier to academic participation and success (Marshall & Case 2010; Janse van Rensburg & Kapp 2015). For instance, Condorrera, Kea and Aziza all faced resource insecurity and still completed their degrees. Their narratives suggest that despite resource insecurity, students attained a threshold of minimum resources to survive, however precarious and unstable their situation, and despite a compounded burden of stress and anxiety that accompanied the balancing act of university study and poverty. But being successful at university without a minimum threshold of financial support, in combination with fragmented family and institutional support and unreliable opportunities and resources left students particularly vulnerable to exclusion. Student narratives confirmed that the freedom for equal participation is constrained by the intersection of individual resource scarcity and higher education institutions that are under pressure to meet demands for quality education and for expanding student numbers, despite decreased state funding in real terms (USAf 2016).

Equalising opportunities

The second cluster of findings in student narratives was that some participants entered university with fewer valued capabilities than more privileged peers. Finances were not the only conversion factor that determine participants' freedom to convert available resources into capabilities and functionings. For example, Naledi and Techniques entered the university with a smaller bundle of recognised resources, while at the same time their freedom to pursue academic, extracurricular or social opportunities was constrained. The freedom was further eroded by the struggle to meet minimum academic requirements without embedded and reliable support structures. Instead of advantage clustering for those who already have the capitals and resources to succeed, how do we ensure that available resources, opportunities and structures are converted into capabilities by competent yet economically vulnerable students?

Some participants needed more opportunities to get to the same threshold of participation. For instance, while Dante reported a university experience filled with opportunities for academic and personal development, Naledi was alienated from academic and social engagement in university life (Wilson-Strydom 2015). It was striking how Dante's involvement in residence life, campus-based activities and community projects, which cultivated a social life, enabled capability development and showed evidence of fertile functionings, while Naledi did not have real opportunities to achieve the same capabilities and functionings. Tracking Dante's experiences suggests that the resources offered by an elite schooling system prepared him for participation at university. On the other hand, Naledi's social environment, combined with poor quality schooling and the failures in her first two years at university, positioned her precariously at the institution. This disparity of experiences requires a closer investigation into the way that not only resources but also opportunities are unequally distributed.

Another important aspect of opportunity distribution is an institutional response to evidence that even when academic support structures exist, there are complex reasons why students do not access or benefit from these resources (see also Walton, Bowman, & Osman 2015). When opportunities for capability development were available, some students were unable to afford the additional costs associated with participation (Rivera 2015). An example is the resource shortage that made it difficult for Techniques to gain access to campus for academic and extracurricular activities. To resist an inequitable model of opportunity distribution, all students should have sustained opportunities for capability development regardless of their status at the university. Ideally, such opportunities would incorporate existing resources and capabilities that students bring to the institution. Universities could create platforms where students who are unable to benefit from available opportunities have access to accessible alternatives. If these processes are participatory and deliberative, they could bring the academic expertise of lecturers and institutional planners to an engagement with resources and capabilities that students bring to the university. In practice, this could mean creating collaborative spaces where vulnerable students and undergraduate teaching staff find solutions to problems with teaching and learning arrangements that adversely affect students' potential to succeed. This could also include finding a more effective way to track students who face complex forms of academic, extracurricular and social exclusion (Yu & Jo 2014; see also Coolbear 2014; Gašević, Dawson, Rogers, & Gasevic 2016).

Equal opportunities for commuter students

We should be concerned that commuter students like Naledi had not accessed any opportunities for extracurricular capability development, peer affiliation, faculty mentorship, student association or other leadership programmes. Therefore, another important policy intervention would be to ensure that commuter students in particular are not excluded from opportunities for capability development. In practice, this could mean creating pedagogical networks that connect students to support services. The university could ensure that affiliation is cultivated with at least one supportive staff member or academic advisor available to students who live off campus and who have fewer resources or time to participate in activities that foster the development of academic capabilities. It was evident in the narratives that even isolated instances of enabling interaction with a supportive lecturer, or a subject with which the student was critically engaged, mitigated some negative effects of discrimination and exclusion. Increasing access to qualified mentors could give more students the freedom to navigate systemic constraints, even while structural conditions remain resistant to transformation (Tinto 2014). However, keeping in mind the warnings against fragmentation and irrelevance to academic purpose (Leibowitz & Bozalek 2015), this form of affiliation could be embedded within disciplinary spaces and ideally connected to learning, in order to prevent the proliferation of additive programmes that demand additional time and resources to which students, staff and departments do not have equal access. At the same time, these programmes would depend on the availability of qualified staff and funding, which reiterates the need for increased state funding to higher education institutions.

Restructuring academic support programmes

For universities that have support structures in place, how are these addressing the needs of the most vulnerable and do they enable equal participation for students facing accumulative disadvantage? Academic support programmes may be fertile spaces for academic engagement but are also complex spaces that could perpetuate stereotypes and deepen power imbalances. In this study, there were examples of how academic support programmes reiterated negative beliefs about student intelligence and potential based on race, home language and class. Some students experienced academic development as a constraining environment in which they felt isolated from their peers, patronised and subjected to low expectations. Some students were less likely to question low expectations, which deepened their vulnerability to unfair treatment.

Instead of offering freedom for engagement with knowledge, perceptions of low expectations eroded students' status as valued members of the institution, and diminished their capabilities for equal participation (Fraser 2009). This was illustrated in Clarice's narrative, where her experiences and perceptions of deficit treatment by staff members decreased her motivation to engage academically. Although at the beginning of the project she expressed aspirations for academic participation and belonging, she left the university before completing her degree with a very negative perception of the institution (Tinto 2014). Due to a series of personal challenges and systemic failures, she was unable to join the final year cohort in her degree major, which decreased her motivation to engage academically. As a result, Clarice became increasingly isolated and distracted from her studies, while being forced to spend an additional year completing first-year elective courses without access to the supportive mainstream lecturers and peers. In what way could Clarice's experience been different? At what point in her trajectory could enabling arrangements have enabled participation?

Unequal participation may be exacerbated by academic support programmes that were misaligned with the capabilities that students needed for academic participation. There was little evidence that students valued these courses, attended them regularly, or that academic capabilities were cultivated. Instead, students were postponing developmental modules until their final year, reporting concerns about academic quality, low expectations and a deficit approach to students. Academic support programmes face immense pressure in articulating with the academic development required by students on extended degree programmes. This reflects the resource and staffing constraints, which suggests a potential waste of resources created by ineffective programme design. For these and other interrelated reasons, additive programmes 'seldom result in systemic change' and had a limited impact of student participation (Walton et al. 2015: 267).

To prevent these programmes from eroding the freedom for critical engagement with knowledge, one institutional response could be designing and implementing theoretically appropriate and discipline-specific programmes instead of offering fragmented, generic courses that fail to increase academic participation (Zepke 2016). Academic support should be incorporated into departments and/or faculties and facilitated by staff members who offer discipline-specific academic development (see Pym & Kapp 2013). Because structural inequalities affected not only poor and/or first-generation students, all students must be integrated into a supportive learning community.

Developmental interventions risk reproducing misrecognition and perpetuating a real or perceived deficit approach to undergraduate students. The marginal status of students on academic support programmes, combined with resource scarcity, had a negative effect on some students' ability to engage with knowledge, to seek and expect challenge, to cultivate academic identity as valued members of the institution, or to claim ownership of her academic project. In response to these limitations, academic support programmes could decide not to separate bridging students from the mainstream and instead consider alternative approaches to develop the academic capabilities that students need within mainstream provision, while ensuring that the curriculum enables meaningful engagement with learning. Universities could design programmes aimed at 'restructuring the underlying generative framework' without 'creating stigmatized classes of vulnerable people perceived as beneficiaries of special largesse' (Fraser 1995: 82). This requires investigating the epistemological assumptions underlying pedagogical arrangements.

From a social justice perspective, it would be ideal if all students had access to sustained, well-resourced, and good-quality pedagogical arrangements on undergraduate programmes. Universities could ensure that existing resources in earmarked grants are allocated to transform academic support programmes (Hendricks & Leibowitz 2016). This could include redesigning developmental curricula and pedagogy while resisting the status injuries of developmental programmes that diminish student freedom, agency and critical reason.

Transforming knowledge and institutional cultures

As part of expanding participation for vulnerable students, significant transformation of pedagogy is necessary (Hendriks & Leibowitz 2016; Le Grange 2016; Luckett & Naicker 2016; Smith 2012). Part of this process is to cultivate critical spaces to interrogate the histories, embedded beliefs and assumptions that lecturers and students bring to the classroom (Vorster 2016; Keet, Sattarzadeh, & Munene 2017). Because many students in academic development programmes face accumulative vulnerability, how do these resist slipping into disempowering models that frame students as passive recipients of knowledge? How do arrangements nurture critical thinking instead of encouraging compliance and assimilation into existing knowledge constructs? How do we recognise and draw on student resilience and agency despite vulnerability?

Recognition requires knowledge systems that incorporates knowledge from the African continent and the global South alongside contributions from the global North (Connell 2014). Including indigenous knowledge means challenging the value hierarchies that have pushed African and indigenous epistemologies to the margins of the university. Bringing students into the research process is one way to begin expanding academic knowledge beyond the theories based on unchallenged hierarchies about who is able to produce knowledge, whose knowledge counts, and whose knowledge is included in curricula and pedagogy.

Part of institutional transformation will be challenging and finding alternatives to the deficit approach found in pedagogical interventions aimed at vulnerable students, as summarised below:

> We would suggest that tertiary institutions have to consider not just the arrangements made to support students, but also to reflect on the institutional cultures and practices that compound the barriers that perpetuate patterns of unequal access to success. If they do not, interventions that provide only the financial means to access may inadvertently destroy the very bridges to belonging that they are designed to build.
> (Walton *et al.* 2015: 267)

It may be necessary for pedagogy and curricula to distribute academic resources more fairly, while being sensitive to students' need to be recognised as valued members of the community. This could mean that institutional structures and pedagogical arrangements should be transformed in consultation with students who are disengaged and excluded. As reflected in #Feesmustfall, is necessary to distinguish between the urgent need for providing financial support to students who are unable to afford higher education, and the transformation of institutional cultures, curricula, pedagogies and relationships at the university (Booysen 2016; Pithouse 2015; Dickinson 2015; O'Halloran 2016).

Another implication is the need for more research that deepens our understanding of the complex factors that affect students' capability for equal participation (Walker 2012). At an institutional level, this would mean improving the quality and competence of academic staff by providing adequate funding for the university to employ a sufficient number of qualified lecturers across degree programmes. This could include implementing pedagogical measures associated with equal participation across the curriculum, such as lower student–staff ratios, tutorials for every module, seminars from the first-year level and the intensive development of critical academic literacies for all students, in particular academic writing embedded within disciplines.

The interventions above will be difficult to achieve given the major financial constraints in the system, which is another reason why higher education institutions need a commitment to the stable and sustained forms of funding required to ensure quality education for the growing student body. Without these systemic interventions, the proliferation of additive forms of teaching and learning may continue to be marginally effective.

Cultivating recognition

An important theme in all the narratives is students' need to be recognised as valuable members of the university. All students shared experiences of misrecognition, which resulted in alienation, lack of motivation and disengagement. Cultivating recognition requires addressing the effects of status injury and the perceptions that students draw from lecturers' dismissive or discriminatory treatment (Fraser 2013). Recognition must be formalised as part of an institutional culture, and should be embedded into academic programmes.

In order to enable misrecognition, institutions need alternatives to conditions that silence vulnerable students. Challenging hierarchies is a particular challenge in the South Africa context where hierarchies spill over into education and are enforced by religious and cultural norms across racial groups. Transforming higher education would need to enable recognition and collaboration between students and staff, without disregarding cultural nuances.

Undergraduate research

The participatory research included aspects of undergraduate research, which contributed to participants' capability development. Investing in more opportunities where students not only participate in but also benefit from undergraduate research is an important way to enhance the status of undergraduate students. How many students value deep engagement with knowledge, and given real opportunities, affiliation with lecturers and peers and sufficient resources, would cultivate meaningful academic capabilities? How many students that leave the university with a mediocre qualification, a negative view of learning, or who drop out before graduation, had the potential, but were denied these freedoms because of poorly designed programmes? How could pedagogical arrangements enable more students to be engaged and captivated by knowledge, and to play an active role in creating new knowledge?

Based on the positive feedback from the research project, cultivating more opportunities for undergraduate student research could contribute to capability development. Involving more undergraduate students in rigorous, discipline specific participatory research (Appadurai 2006) may have the potential to address the conflict between teaching and research so often expressed by academic staff (Mouton, Louw, & Strydom 2013). Expanded freedom for inquiry-based, active and critical research also has the potential to cultivate capabilities associated with engaged learning, as was evident in this project. As the narratives suggest, creating platforms for undergraduate research has the potential to respond to the constraints identified by first-generation students. This includes challenging the student–lecturer hierarchy using participatory collaboration.

In practice, academic staff could identify vulnerable first-generation students who could be affiliated with supportive lecturers and postgraduate students in discipline-specific, participatory research projects. Such initiatives could bring together the capability development of students with the creation of learning communities that increase recognition for vulnerable undergraduate students. These projects would have to be carefully structured and planned, and sufficiently funded. It would also be important to align these projects with research output requirements so that researchers and/or lecturers involved are able to align such projects with the demand for research outputs.

Participatory decision-making

It is critical to expand the quality and sustainability of platforms that recognise, consult and include undergraduate students as valued members of the institution. In the narratives, it was evident that such platforms increased individual autonomy, ownership and the incentive to engage with knowledge. Sustainable participatory platforms for students to participate in decision-making was a resource that participants valued, but that was frequently inaccessible due to lack of genuine opportunities. Given the pedagogical structure of large classrooms and the subsequent distance between lecturers and students, the narratives pointed to a need for sustained dialogical spaces where collaborative interaction is allowed to flourish between students and staff.

As a response to misframing first-generation students and undergraduate students more broadly, students should have the opportunity to cultivate the capabilities they need to resist structural injustice using practical reason and critical literacy. This means that platforms in which access to knowledge could increase confidence to contribute should be a critical priority. This recommendation builds on Sen's idea of development as freedom, not as unbridled critique, but an evidence-based and socially embedded engagement that takes divergent student voices seriously. To enable students requires creating opportunities to develop reasoned and well-informed critique so that they are prepared for engagement in public fora and so that important demands are not compromised by the absence of critical information. Using the human development value of participatory democracy, this could mean institutional platforms that amplify student voice in a way that enables a reasoned, articulate voice, while taking seriously the concerns and inequalities raised by these protests.

There is also evidence that although students recognised constraining pedagogical conditions, their resistance to these arrangements was compromised by a corrosive cluster of personal and structural limitations. As a policy response, the institution could include first-generation students in decision-making processes to ensure that these problems are addressed in a participatory way. For instance, students in this project made pertinent suggestions for improving pedagogical conditions, which are potentially valuable to staff and policymakers who are addressing unequal participation. A long-term response to the issues raised by the participants highlights the importance of consulting and collaborating with undergraduate students in the design of pedagogical, curricular and other institutional interventions that influence the way students learn and participate in academic life.

Inequality and transforming higher education

In this book, I have used a capability approach to argue that universities could expand their contribution to the public good by challenging socioeconomic and status hierarchies in their own structures. Despite policies in higher education that aim to equalise participation, for many students university offers hardship and confusion, loneliness and disappointment, fear of failure and misrecognition of potential. For the student who travels from her accommodation far from campus, to a crowded classroom, to a library desk and then home again, while facing the daily stress of poverty, the university is less likely to offer opportunities to develop critical academic capabilities, and to be integrated as an equal member. There is a high economic and social cost for students who could have cultivated capabilities at university, but who flounder in an environment where resources and support are thinly spread, and where intersectional discrimination act as barriers to equal academic participation. Student narratives show that clustered moments of discrimination, exclusion and resource deprivation erode participation: discriminatory treatment by a lecturer combined with dismissive attitudes of administrative staff, hunger, illness, poor accommodation and low academic expectations. Agency, opportunities and resistance also cluster: being registered on a smaller degree programme, engaging with a lecturer who is supportive, meeting friends at residence and having a family member who helps with tuition fees. Yet these individual clusters of advantage are precarious, unreliable and unevenly spread. While higher education has offered some students access and opportunities, the student narratives in this project suggest that we need to pay attention to persistent redistributive inequalities. To participate in higher education, the individual must enter armed with social capitals, financial resources and sustained support. Yet these are resources that students are less able to access when they are dividing their energy to meet minimum academic requirements, fighting against the precarious living conditions associated with poverty, working part-time and caring for families and relatives.

Sites that are urgently in need of resource redistribution include pedagogy and curricula in non-elite, large undergraduate programmes, because many students who are most vulnerable to unequal participation, financial exclusion and status injury are registered on these degrees. This includes academic and social support structures, initiatives and programmes that, unlike high-status research projects in higher education, are under-theorised, underfunded and at risk of offering academic provision and technical solutions with limited impact (Walton *et al* 2015).

Transforming higher education

The macro-economic and social forces that create inequality have shaped the contours of universities in South Africa. In light of these inequalities, there is anxiety about the future of the South African higher education and complex questions about how to enable affordable or free education for poor and 'missing-middle' students. At the same time, scholars and students in the global South are resisting higher education that has become 'a marketable product bought and sold by standard units' (Mbembe, 2016). Disrupting the way that university students are encouraged to 'seek private solutions to socially generated troubles' (Bauman 2009: 161) requires structural interventions that interrogate how erodes students' freedom for participation.

The student narratives in this book reiterate the importance of creating transformation that is defined, negotiated and constructed in partnership with students. #Feesmustfall, despite its controversies and tensions, has re-energised debates about untransformed structures, cultures and relationships at universities, and called attention to colonial and apartheid-era ideologies and practices that are complicated by universities under pressure to respond to market demands. Although the protest focused on tuition fees, students are also calling for decolonised higher education as part of institutional transformation, especially in Africanising the curriculum and challenging institutional racism, classism and gender-based discrimination. The narratives in this book show that students have been articulating what a transformed university might look like, both during #Feesmustfall and in the years leading up to the protests (Luescher, 2016; Nwadeyi, 2017). Yet even though these protests were platforms for students to articulate their exclusion, aspects of these processes were not participatory as defined by the principles of deliberative democracy. Universities also need participatory platforms in pedagogy, curricula and institutional transformation where issues of exclusion are addressed while challenging the misrecognition of students. Instead of becoming disruptive and steering attention away from learning, universities could ask how to channel activism into productive spaces that enhance freedom for academic participation.

In the aftermath of student protests, new vocabularies are emerging around questions of knowledge, race, redistribution and mutuality in a post-colonial, post-apartheid context (Keet *et al*. 2017; Kamanzi 2017; Mama 2016; Nkopo

2015; Nwadeyi 2017). The conversation around decolonisation is complex, but there is some agreement that it demands the integration of devalued languages, cultures, identities and knowledge eroded by colonialisation and apartheid (Fataar 2017; Mama 2016). Finally, given the urgency of the social and environmental crises within which society and higher education is embedded, higher education must work with students and communities to create 'a non-racial university [which] is truly about radical sharing and universal inclusion. It is about humankind ruling in common for a common which includes the non-humans, which is the proper name for democracy' (Mbembe 2016).

References

Alexander, N., 2012. Race is Skin Deep, Humanity is Not. In Vally, H., & Isaacson, M. (Eds), *Enough Is a Feast – A Tribute to Dr Neville Alexander*. Foundation for Human Rights, Braamfontein.
Alexander, N., 2008. EDUCATION FOR MULTICULTURALISM: The challenge for institutions of higher learning. Nelson Mandela Metropolitan University public lecture, 19 November 2008. Nelson Mandela Metropolitan University.
Appadurai, A., 2006. The Right to Research. *Globalisation, Societies and Education* 4(2), 167–177.
Bauman, Z., 2009. *Does Ethics Have a Chance in a World of Consumers?* Cambridge, MA: Harvard University Press.
Booysen, S., 2016. *Fees Must Fall Student Revolt, Decolonisation and Governance in South Africa*. Johannesburg: Wits University Press.
Christie, H., Munro, M., & Fisher, T. (2004). Leaving University Early: Exploring the Differences between Continuing and Non-continuing Students. *Studies in Higher Education* 29(5), 617–636.
Connell, R., 2014. Rethinking Gender from the South. *Feminist Studies* 40, 518–539.
Coolbear, P., 2014. Enhancing the Impact of Projects Designed to Enhance Tertiary Teaching and Learning. *HERDSA News* 36, 26.
Dickinson, D., 2015. Fee Protests Point to a Much Deeper Problem at South African Universities. *The Conversation*. http://theconversation.com/fee-protests-point-to-a-much-deeper-problem-at-south-african-universities-49456
Fataar, A., 2017. Towards a Teacher Education Pedagogy of Recognition as a Response to the Decolonizing Education Imperative, in: *Decolonization of Teacher Education and Educational Research*. Potchefstroom Campus, NWU.
Fraser, N., 1995. *Social Justice in the Age of Identity Politics: Redistribution, Recognition, and Participation*. Presented at the Tanner lectures on Human Values, Stanford University.
Fraser, N., 2009. *Scales of Justice: Reimagining Political Space in a Globalizing World*. New York, NY: Columbia University Press.
Fraser, N., 2013. *Fortunes of Feminism: From State-Managed Capitalism to Neoliberal Crisis*. New York, NY: Verso Books.
Gašević, D., Dawson, S., Rogers, T., & Gasevic, D., 2016. Learning Analytics Should Not Promote One Size Fits All: The Effects of Instructional Conditions in Predicting Academic Success. *The Internet and Higher Education* 28, 68–84. https://doi.org/10.1016/j.iheduc.2015.10.002

Hendricks, C., & Leibowitz, B., 2016. Decolonising Universities Isn't an Easy Process – But It Has to Happen. 23 May, 2016. *The Conversation*. https://theconversation.com/decolonising-universities-isnt-an-easy-process-but-it-has-to-happen-59604

Janse van Rensburg, V., & Kapp, R., 2015. 'So I Have to Be Positive, No Matter How Difficult It Is': A Longitudinal Case Study of a First-Generation Occupational Therapy Student. *South African Journal of Occupational Therapy* 44(3), 29–33.

Kamanzi, B., 2016. Decolonising the Curriculum: The Silent War for Tomorrow. *Daily Maverick*. https://www.dailymaverick.co.za/opinionista/2016-04-28-decolonising-the-curriculum-the-silent-war-for-tomorrow/#.Wr-aCohubIV

Keet, A., Sattarzadeh, A., & Munene, A., 2017. An Awkward, Uneasy (De) Coloniality: Higher Education and Knowledge Otherwise. *Education as Change* 21.

Le Grange, L., 2016. Decolonising the University Curriculum. *South African Journal of Higher Education* 30(2) 1–12. https://doi.org/10.20853/30-2-709

Leibowitz, B., & Bozalek, V., 2015. Foundation Provision – A Social Justice Perspective: Part 1: Leading Article. *South African Journal of Higher Education* 29(1), 8–25.

Luckett, K., & Naicker, V., 2016. Responding to Misrecognition from a (Post)/colonial University. *Critical Studies in Education* 0, 1–18. https://doi.org/10.1080/17508487.2016.1234495

Luescher, T., 2016. Towards an Intellectual Engagement with the #studentmovements in South Africa. *Politikon* 43, 145–148. https://doi.org/10.1080/02589346.2016.1155138

Mama, A., 2016. [film] *Decolonizing Knowledges 101: In the Master's House* by Prof Amina Mama, filmed by Wandile Kasibe, 2016. University of Cape Town.

Marshall, D., & Case, J., 2010. Rethinking 'Disadvantage' in Higher Education: A Paradigmatic Case Study Using Narrative Analysis. *Studies in Higher Education* 35(5), 491–504.

Mbembe, A., 2016. Decolonizing the university: New directions. *Arts and Humanities in Higher Education* 15, 29–45. https://doi.org/10.1177/1474022215618513

Mouton, N., Louw, G., & Strydom, G., 2013. Present-Day Dilemmas and Challenges of the South African Tertiary System. *International Business & Economics Research Journal* 12(3), 285–300.

Nkopo, A., 2015. We Still Don't Belong Here! *The Star*. https://www.iol.co.za/the-star/we-still-dont-belong-here-1912238

Nussbaum, M.C. (2011). *Creating Capabilities*. Harvard, MA: Harvard University Press.

Nwadeyi, L., 2017. *Decolonising the Curriculum: Justice, Humanisation and Healing through Education*. University of Pretoria.

O'Halloran, P., 2016. The African University as a Site of Protest: Decolonisation, Praxis, and the Black Student Movement at the University Currently Known as Rhodes. *Interface: A Journal on Social Movements* 8.

Pym, J., & Kapp, R., 2013. Harnessing Agency: Towards a Learning Model for Undergraduate Students. *Studies in Higher Education* 38, 272–284. https://doi.org/10.1080/03075079.2011.582096

Rivera, L.A., 2015. *Pedigree: How Elite Students Get Elite Jobs*. Princeton, NJ: Princeton University Press.

Simpson, L.B., 2017. *As We Have Always Done: Indigenous Freedom through Radical Resistance*. Minneapolis, MN: University of Minnesota Press.

Tinto, V., 2014. Access without Support Is Not Opportunity. *Community College Week* 26, 4.

USAf, 2016. Universities Funding in South Africa; A Fact Sheet. Universities South Africa.
Vorster, J., 2016. *Curriculum in the Context of Transformation: Reframing Traditional Understanding and Practices.* Rhodes University.
Walker, M. 2012. A Capital or Capabilities Education Narrative in a World of Staggering Inequalities? *International Journal of Educational Development* 32(3), 384–393.
Walton, E., Bowman, B., & Osman, R. (2015). Promoting Access to Higher Education in an Unequal Society: Part 2 – Leading Article. *South African Journal of Higher Education* 29(1), 262–269.
Wilson-Strydom, M., 2015. *University Access and Success: Capabilities, Diversity and Social Justice.* London and New York: Routledge.
Wolff, J., & de-Shalit, A., 2007. *Disadvantage.* Oxford: Oxford University Press.
Yosso, T.J., 2005. Whose Culture has Capital? A Critical Race Theory Discussion of Community Cultural Wealth. *Race Ethnicity and Education* 8(1), 69–91.
Yu, T., & Jo, I.-H., 2014. Educational Technology Approach toward Learning Analytics: Relationship Between Student Online Behavior and Learning Performance in Higher Education. In *Proceedings of the Fourth International Conference on Learning Analytics and Knowledge*, LAK '14. ACM, New York, NY, pp. 269–270. https://doi.org/10.1145/2567574.2567594
Zepke, N., 2016. *Student Engagement in Neoliberal Times: Theories and Practices for Learning and Teaching in Higher Education.* New York, NY: Springer.

Index

absenteeism 72
abuse 78, 86, 90
academic literacy 32, 34, 103–4, 107, 111; and constraints 121; and equality 154, 157; and just universities 177; and student agency 129, 131–2, 137, 140–1, 144
academics 1, 7, 29–32, 57
access 2–8, 10, 12–13, 15, 29; access to knowledge 138–41; and alienation from lecturers 114; and aspirations 86, 89; and capabilities 46, 48, 50, 54, 57–9, 61–2, 143, 147, 149–51, 153–5, 157–9; and constraints 96–8, 100; and decision-making 109, 112; and distribution 138–41; and just universities 168, 170–1, 173–4, 176; and misrecognition 118–19; and platform creation 137; and school systems 71–3, 75, 79; and structural conditions 32, 34–5, 96–8, 100; and student agency 130, 132, 134–5; and student narratives 70, 92; and transformation 123, 179; and uncritical engagement 102–4, 106–7
accommodation 13, 35, 88, 99–100, 140, 147, 170, 179
accountability 25
achievement 8, 11, 23, 27–8, 45; and capabilities 48, 53, 62; and constraints 97, 101, 110, 116, 118; and equality 147, 161–2; and student agency 128, 135; and student narratives 74, 81, 85, 92
activism 107, 157, 171, 178, 180
adaptive preference 55
affiliation 58, 114, 116, 123, 139; and equality 147, 149, 151, 158–60; and just universities 168, 173, 177–8; with lecturers 127–32; with peers 132–6; and student agency 145

Africa 8–9, 25–6, 30, 72, 85, 144, 160, 170, 176, 180
African Americans 4
agency 1–2, 6, 15–16, 24, 29; and alienation from lecturers 115; and aspirations 87, 89–90; and capabilities 45–6, 48, 51–4, 59–62, 148–9, 152, 157, 159–61; and constraints 99–100; and decision-making 111–12; and just universities 175–6; and school systems 73, 76–80, 82; and structural conditions 32–4, 36; and student narratives 68, 70, 92; of students 127–46; and transformation 122–3, 179
Alexander, N. 170
alienation 33, 35, 56–7, 77–8, 96; and capabilities 142–3, 157–9; and constraints 100, 106, 111, 116, 121–3; from lecturers 113–16; and just universities 168–9, 172, 177; and student agency 130–2, 136, 145
alliances 33, 116, 127, 131, 138, 159
apartheid 1, 7, 10, 13, 25, 34, 45, 53, 58, 71–2, 85, 180–1
apathy 108, 122, 150
Aristotle 161
Arts subjects 30, 84
aspirations 2, 6, 11, 15–16, 33; and capabilities 53, 56, 59; and constraints 100, 109, 114, 123; developing 83–92; and equality 147–9, 152, 156, 162; and just universities 168–9, 174; and student agency 130, 134–5, 138–40, 142–3; and student narratives 67, 70, 73–6, 78–80, 82
assessment 30, 45–6, 79, 101–5, 107, 113, 118, 130, 138, 153–6
attrition rates 5, 9, 169
audit cultures 26
Australia 5

autonomy 24–5, 53–4, 57, 111, 121–2, 132, 152, 155, 178

banking system 57–8, 104–5, 136, 138–42, 161
Berg, G.A. 5
bias 57, 153
Black students 1, 9–13, 26–8, 31, 35; and capabilities 144; and constraints 101; and just universities 169–70; and misrecognition 117, 119, 121; and student agency 135; and student narratives 67, 71, 74–5, 78, 81, 85, 90; and transformation 122
boredom 76, 110, 116, 118, 122, 139–40, 150
brain drain 30
bridging programmes 29, 97, 103, 107–9, 112, 129, 154
bullying 133
bureaucracy 51
bursaries 9, 13–14, 35, 77, 85, 88–90, 98–9, 104, 109, 123, 140

capability approach 2, 14–16, 24, 32–3, 45–66; and access to knowledge 138, 140–1; and alienation from lecturers 113–14; and aspirations 83–5, 87–9; capability praxis 15–16, 147–51, 157, 160, 162; capability security 171; and constraints 96, 100–1; and decision-making 109, 111–13; development of 147–8; and equal participation 147–67; framework for 47–56; and Fraser 58–61; and Freire 56–8; and just universities 168–9, 171–4, 176, 178; and misrecognition 116–17, 120–1; and platform creation 137; and recognition 142–4; and school systems 75–6, 79–81; and student agency 127–36; and student narratives 68–70, 92; and student research 177; and transformation 122–3, 179; and uncritical engagement 105–7
capitalism 25, 59
Carpentier, V. 4
caste 6
censorship 51
citizenship 1
class structure 4–6, 28, 31, 35–6, 59; and capabilities 61, 158–9; classism 13, 27, 180; and just universities 174–5; and misrecognition 117, 119–21; and student narratives 72, 90; and transformation 121–3

climate change 139
coercion 79, 110, 112, 153, 157
Coleman Report 72
collaboration 137, 147–8, 150, 155, 173, 177–9
colonialism 7, 13, 71, 180–1
Coloured students 11–12, 71, 74, 79, 91, 119
commuter students 132, 150, 159, 171, 173–4
conceptual framework 61–3
constraints 1, 5, 7, 10, 15–16; and access to knowledge 141; and aspirations 84, 86–7, 90–1; and capabilities 50, 52–3, 57, 61, 144, 148, 151, 155, 158, 162; and conversion factors 55; and just universities 168–9, 172–3, 178–9; and school systems 73, 75, 77–9, 81–3; and structural conditions 23, 27–30, 33, 36, 96–126; and student agency 127, 130, 133, 135; and student narratives 68–70, 92; and transformation 121–4
consumerism 47, 152
conversion factors 54–5, 61–3, 67–8, 70, 73–82; and access to knowledge 138–9, 141; and alienation from lecturers 113–15; and capabilities 142, 147–8, 150, 153–4, 158, 160–2; and constraints 99–100, 102; and decision-making 107, 109–10, 112; and just universities 168, 172; negative conversion factors 96; and platform creation 137–8; and student agency 127–9, 132, 134–5, 145; and student narratives 86, 89–90, 92; and transformation 123; and uncritical engagement 103, 106
corporatism 1, 24, 26, 108, 153, 159, 162
corrosive disadvantages 49, 73, 116, 150, 179
Council on Higher Education (CHE) 11
counsellors 85
Creative Commons 151
critical consciousness 56–8, 80, 111, 113, 142; and affiliation 158; and capabilities 159, 161; and equality 159; and platform creation 137; and transformation 179
critical engagement 57, 80, 96, 102–7, 145; and access to knowledge 138–41; and capabilities 142, 153–4, 158–9; and equality 149–50, 152–5; and just universities 173, 175–8; and student agency 128, 130–4, 141
critical literacy 14, 58, 86, 131, 147, 149, 151, 153–5, 178

Crocker, D.A. 52, 89, 112
curricula 12, 31, 46, 72, 82; and constraints 103, 105, 111, 121, 123; and equality 149–51, 153–6, 161–2; and just universities 169, 175–6, 179–80; and student agency 140, 142

de-Shalit, A. 171
debt 25
decent work 2, 24
decision-making 25, 33, 51–2, 56, 62, 73, 96, 107–13, 121, 156–7, 178–9
deficit approach 13–15, 23, 26–36, 45–6, 52–3; and capabilities 59, 150, 152–3, 157, 159; and constraints 97, 102; and conversion factors 54; and just universities 168–9, 174, 176; and misrecognition 116, 121; and school systems 73, 77; and student agency 127–9; and student narratives 67–8; and uncritical engagement 103
deliberation 51–3, 56, 61, 70, 80; and constraints 104, 109; deliberative participation 157–8; and equality 147, 149–52, 156; and just universities 173, 180; and student narratives 89
democracy 1–2, 7–8, 10–12, 33, 51–2; and capabilities 58, 62; and equality 149, 152, 157–8; and just universities 170, 179–81; and student agency 134
Department of Basic Education 71
Department of Education 11
Department of Higher Education and Training (DHET) 11
developmental modules 105–8, 110, 116–17, 121–2, 128–9, 138, 141, 144, 147, 153–4, 157, 174–5
distribution/redistribution 24, 48, 52, 54, 56, 59, 130, 132, 138–41, 150–1, 153, 170–1, 179–80
Drèze, J. 112
drop outs 5, 11–12, 15, 27, 34, 98, 156, 171

economic growth 2, 8, 28
economic policies 3, 23, 25–6
egalitarian theory 45, 50, 56, 58–9, 108, 147–8, 150, 170
elites 4–6, 8, 13, 23, 28; and capabilities 59; and constraints 110, 123; and just universities 172; and student narratives 74–5, 79, 81–2, 91
empathy 47, 58, 77, 133, 160

employment 2, 13, 24–5, 30, 49, 76, 79, 84–6, 90, 100, 123, 154–5
enabling factors 15, 27, 46, 54–6, 58; and capabilities 63; and constraints 110–11, 114–15, 124; and equality 148–50, 152–3, 155, 162; and just universities 169–70, 173–4; with lecturers 127–32; with peers 132–6; and student agency 139, 145; and student narratives 75, 80, 85, 88
endowments 4, 9
English language 34, 77–8, 80, 92, 107, 111, 120, 142, 144, 153
entrepreneurship 27
environment 161
epistemology 6, 13, 29, 35, 57, 112, 122, 147, 158, 175–6
equality 2, 45–51, 53, 55, 57; and access to knowledge 138; and alienation from lecturers 113–15; and aspirations 83, 85, 90; and capabilities 60–3, 147–67; and constraints 98, 100; and decision-making 110, 112; equal opportunities 172–4; and just universities 168–71, 174, 176; and misrecognition 116–17, 121; and student agency 127, 131–2, 145; and student narratives 68–70, 92; and transformation 179; and uncritical engagement 103, 107; and well-being 56
ethics 24, 35, 56, 92, 131–2, 157, 161
ethnicity 4–8, 53, 121, 136, 159
Eurocentrism 6, 13, 143
Europe 6, 25
examinations 13, 99–100, 102–4, 113
exclusion 2, 6, 9–11, 27–8, 33–5; and capabilities 48–50, 59–61, 63; and constraints 100, 104, 108–9, 112, 115–16, 119, 121, 123; and equality 147–8, 150, 159; and just universities 172–3, 176, 179–80; and student agency 132, 140, 143; and student narratives 67, 73, 77, 81, 83, 85–6, 89
exploitation 24, 71–2, 90–1, 118, 139
extracurricular interests 14, 71–2, 79, 82, 123, 170–3

facilitation sessions 103, 108, 135, 139
failures 6, 9, 11, 14, 24; and capabilities 47, 51, 54, 59–60; and constraints 104–5, 108, 110, 112, 114–16, 118–19, 121; and individualism 96–102; institutional failure 105, 132, 159; and just universities 172, 174–5, 179; and structural conditions 27–8,

188 Index

31–3, 36; and student agency 128, 132, 134, 140; and student narratives 68, 71–3, 75–6, 78, 81–3, 90
families 2, 4–5, 7, 10, 13–14; and constraints 97–101, 119, 122–3; and equality 147, 154, 162; and just universities 168, 171–2, 179–80; and structural conditions 27; and student agency 131, 143; and student narratives 69–70, 73–5, 77–9, 82–4, 86–92
Fees Must Fall 25, 176, 180
feminism 59
first-generation students 1, 4, 13, 28–9, 31; and capabilities 50–3, 147, 162; and constraints 97–9, 101; and just universities 175, 178–9; and structural conditions 34–5; and student agency 131–2, 136; and student narratives 67, 82; and transformation 122
focus groups 68, 123, 136
food 1, 13–14, 88, 91, 97, 147
foundational programmes 12–14
Fraser, N. 45, 48, 58–61, 83
freedom 45–9, 51–2, 55, 57–61, 63; and access to knowledge 138–9, 141; and alienation from lecturers 114; and aspirations 83–4, 87–8, 90–1; and capabilities 142, 145, 147–54, 160, 162; and constraints 96–7, 99–100, 102; and conversion factors 55; and decision-making 107–8, 111–13; and education 50–1, 56–8, 62; and just universities 169–70, 172–3, 175, 178, 180; and misrecognition 116–20; and platform creation 136–7; process of 157; and school systems 72, 80–3; and student agency 128, 130–2, 134; and student narratives 67–8, 70, 92; and transformation 180; and uncritical engagement 103–7
Freire, P. 45, 48, 56–8, 112, 148, 158, 161
functionings 48–50, 54, 56, 58, 62; and access to knowledge 138–9; and capabilities 148, 150–1, 155, 158; and student agency 127–8, 133–5; and student narratives 68, 79
further research 159, 162, 169–72, 176

gap years 87–8, 90, 100
gated communities 1
gender 4–7, 12, 28, 35–6, 61; and constraints 121–2; and equality 153, 158–60; and just universities 175, 180; and student narratives 72, 85, 88, 90

Giroux, H. 23
globalisation 3–4, 57, 107
governance 158
graduates 2–3, 9, 11–12, 14, 26, 57–8, 107, 138, 156, 177
gross domestic product (GDP) 8, 47

health 2, 49, 52, 55, 97, 171
Heher, J. 9
hierarchies 10, 28, 34, 36, 47; and capabilities 53, 56, 58; and constraints 108–9, 111, 117, 119, 121; and equality 148, 152, 158–9; and just universities 176–9; and student agency 127, 129, 132; and student narratives 67–8, 79
higher education 1–22; and capabilities 45–66, 147–67; and constraints 96–126; and deficit approach 169; and equality 147–67; as freedom 50–1, 56–8, 62; and inequality 45–66, 179–80; and just universities 168–84; mapping of 3; and massification 7–8; overview of 3–4; and structural conditions 96–126; and student agency 127–46; and student narratives 67–95; and transformation 179–81
homophobia 59
housing 2, 13, 171
human capital 2, 27, 47
human development 16, 24, 45, 48, 51; and capabilities 56, 58; and equality 161; and just universities 178; sustainable human development 3, 9, 47, 169, 173
Humanities subjects 30, 84, 100

identity 6, 12, 28, 32, 70; and capabilities 54, 60, 143–4, 149, 154–5, 160; and constraints 115; and equality 159; and just universities 175, 181; and student agency 131, 137; and student narratives 76, 82, 86, 91
imperialism 59
implementation 170–2
India 6
Indian students 11, 71
indigenous communities 4
individualism 13–15, 23, 26–7, 33, 45–6; and capabilities 56; and constraints 96; and equality 160, 162; and failure 96–102; and just universities 169; and student narratives 76, 78
inequality 2–3, 15–16, 45–66, 92, 96; and access to knowledge 139; and aspirations

83, 89–90; and capabilities 142–3, 147, 151, 157, 159, 161–2; and decision-making 108; in higher education 1–22; and just universities 168–70, 173–6, 179; and misrecognition 120–1; and participation 23–44; and school systems 71–3, 76–8; and structural conditions 23–44; structural inequality 13–15; and student agency 130; and student narratives 67–72; and transformation 121–3, 145, 179–80
infrastructure 7–8, 10, 12, 30, 71–3, 102
injustice 45–7, 52–3, 58–60, 92, 170; and aspirations 83, 90; and capabilities 152, 157, 160; and constraints 96–8; and decision-making 112; and just universities 168–84; and school systems 73, 75; and student narratives 67–9; and uncritical engagement 104
institutional cultures 15, 23, 96, 107, 121, 129, 175–7
institutional demographics 6, 10–12
institutional failures 105, 132, 159
instrumentalism 24, 46–7, 50, 76, 79; and access to knowledge 141; and capabilities 143, 152, 161; and constraints 100–1, 104–5, 122; and student agency 130; and student narratives 85
internalisation 78, 97, 102
international students 81–2, 135
Internet 14, 54
intersectionality 12–13, 15, 29, 35–6, 47, 72, 75, 96, 147, 172
investment 9–10, 26–7, 31, 35, 47; and alienation from lecturers 115–16; and capabilities 151, 155; and constraints 99; and just universities 168–9; and school systems 71; and student agency 132; and student research 177; and transformation 123
isolation 74–5, 82, 88, 91, 99, 131–3, 157–8, 173–4

Kapp, R. 34
knowledge economy 24, 57, 102, 107, 177

laboratories 71, 75
language issues 32–4, 77–8, 80, 84–5, 92; and constraints 107, 111, 120; and equality 151, 159; and just universities 181; and student agency 142, 144
laptops 1, 123, 138
Latin America 25

leadership 14, 50, 59, 61, 82; and constraints 107–8; and decision-making 109–10, 112; and just universities 170, 173; and student agency 135, 143, 145; and student narratives 90; and transformation 123
lecturers 1, 14, 57–8, 96, 101–2; and access to knowledge 138–41; and alienation 113–16; and capabilities 148–54, 157, 159–60; and constraints 104–8; and enabling factors 127–32; and just universities 168, 173–4, 176–8; and misrecognition 116–18, 120; and student agency 136; and transformation 122, 145, 179
Lesotho 81
libraries 1, 14, 54, 71–2, 79, 179
limitarianism 48
literacies 33, 46, 50, *see also* academic literacy; critical literacy
loans 5, 9, 35
low expectations 13, 55, 72, 103–4, 108, 116, 118, 122, 153, 168, 174

macro-economics 23, 36, 180
Mamdani, M. 30
managerialism 25–6, 169
marginalisation 6, 10, 32–3, 36, 55, 73, 116, 139, 152, 175, 177
marketing 85, 130, 153
massification 3–4, 7, 26–30, 36, 56, 152, 169
mature students 97, 113, 140–1, 168
memorisation 104, 122, 130, 152–3
mentorship 12, 14, 88, 106, 112; and constraints 114, 117; and equality 155, 160–1; and just universities 173; and student agency 127, 135, 140
meritocracy 13, 27–8, 48–9, 58, 78, 82, 98, 121, 160
middle-class students 2, 4, 6, 9, 12, 35, 59–60, 82, 91, 98, 123, 132
misrecognition 12, 15, 27–8, 36, 53; and capabilities 59–61; and constraints 96, 101, 103, 108, 114, 116–21; and equality 147, 162; and just universities 168–9, 175, 177, 179–80; and student agency 127, 132, 137, 139, 142; student narratives 75, 77, 81, 83, 85
misrepresentation 61, 108
Model C schools 75, 81–2, 86
multilingual students 154
multimedia 67

National Student Financial Aid Scheme (NSFAS) 9
neoliberalism 3, 23–6, 59, 98, 121; and capabilities 45, 47–8, 50; and constraints 102; and decision-making 108; and student agency 132
normalisation 57, 153
normativity 32, 35, 45, 56, 112, 130, 151, 153, 155, 160, 177
North 3–8, 23–4, 29, 32, 176
North America 6, 89
numeracy 72, 107
Nussbaum, M.C. 48, 52
nutrition 2, 13–14, 35, 49, 52, 171

OECD 9
ontology 175
outsiders 13, 29
outsourcing 25

participation 1–8, 10–16, 23–4, 27–31, 33–6; and access to knowledge 138, 141; and adaptive preference 55; and aspirations 83, 85, 88, 90; and capabilities 45–51, 56–61, 142, 147–67; and conceptual framework 61–3; and constraints 96–126; and conversion factors 55; and decision-making 178; deliberative participation 156–8; and democracy 51–2; and inequality 23–44; and just universities 145, 168–76, 178–9; lack of participation 107–13; participatory parity 59, 83, 157; and school systems 70–3, 76–7, 79; and structural conditions 23–44, 96–126; and student agency 127–31, 133–4, 136; and student narratives 67–9, 92; and transformation 179–80
paternalism 158–9
patriarchy 177
pedagogy 1, 6, 12, 15–16, 23; and access to knowledge 138, 140–1; and alienation from lecturers 113–15; and aspirations 84; and capabilities 46–7, 50, 52, 56–8, 61, 63, 142, 148–55; and constraints 96, 99–100, 102; and conversion factors 54; and decision-making 107, 109–12, 178; and just universities 168–9, 171, 174–9; and misrecognition 116–18, 120–1; and platform creation 136; and research threshold 170; and resources 148–51; and school systems 80; and structural conditions 29–34; and student agency 129–33, 135; and student narratives 68, 92; and transformation 122–3, 145, 180–1; and uncritical engagement 102, 104–6
performance/performativity 26, 29, 71–2, 79, 96; and constraints 98, 101, 108, 116; and equality 157; and just universities 169; and student agency 130–1
planners 173
platform creation 136–8, 145, 173, 178, 180
poor students 2, 4, 9–10, 14
post-colonialism 180
Post-School Sector 12
postgraduates 9, 14, 28–9, 128, 178
poverty 1–5, 8, 15, 25, 32; and alienation from lecturers 114; and aspirations 84, 86, 88–9, 91; and capabilities 48, 60, 158, 160; and constraints 97, 99; and just universities 168–70, 172; and misrecognition 117; and school systems 77, 79; and student agency 132, 135; and student narratives 71–2, 78; and transformation 122, 179–80; and uncritical engagement 104–5
power relations 28, 33, 36, 67, 104; and capabilities 56, 59, 154–5, 159; and constraints 121–2; and just universities 169, 174; and student agency 132
practical reason 51–2, 57, 147, 149, 151–3, 178
praxis 15–16, 147–50, 152, 157, 160, 162
precarity 25–6, 29, 45, 57, 59; and constraints 101, 104, 107; and equality 150; and just universities 172, 179–80; and student narratives 77–8, 83–4, 90
pregnancy 87–8, 91
private schools 79, 81, 83, 92
private sector 26
privatisation 7
privilege 5, 7, 27, 32, 34–5; and capabilities 46, 48, 59; and constraints 98–9, 102, 117, 123; and just universities 168, 172; and student agency 128; and student narratives 72–5, 86, 89
productivity 47, 67, 161
professional development 30, 156
professionalism 72, 170–1
professors 14, 30, 58, 119
profit 25, 28, 47
programme restructuring 174–7
protests 25, 158, 180
psychology 13, 28, 78, 83, 136, 144
public good 23–4, 45, 58, 92, 143; and just universities 169, 179; and student agency

147–9, 151–2; values for 61, 147–9, 151–2, 160–2
public speaking 34, 49, 82, 134, 149, 153–5
Pym, J. 34

quintile system 71–2

race 5–8, 10–12, 28, 31–2, 90–1; and capabilities 61, 153, 158–9; and constraints 102, 117; and just universities 174–5, 177, 180–1; and misrecognition 119–21; racism 4, 13, 26–7, 59, 180; and student agency 135–6; and student narratives 71–2, 75; and transformation 121–2
recognition 29, 35–6, 69–70, 87, 96; and capabilities 53–5, 59–60, 62, 142–4; cultivation of 177–9; and equality 147–9, 152, 155, 158–60; and just universities 169, 176–8; and school systems 73–83; and student agency 127, 129–30, 137, 145
recommendations 73
reflexivity 33–4, 77, 89, 97, 133, 143, 148, 151–2, 159, 161
religion 6, 153, 177
representation 59–61, 108
research threshold 170–2
residence committees (RC) 109
resilience 2, 29, 78, 86, 89, 127, 133, 176
resistance 32–6, 47, 50–2, 57–8, 68; and alienation from lecturers 115; and aspirations 83, 85–6; and capabilities 142, 144, 147, 149, 152, 157, 159; and decision-making 108, 112; and just universities 175–6, 178; and misrecognition 116–17; and school systems 73, 75, 77–8, 81–2; and transformation 145, 179; and uncritical engagement 103, 105
resource scarcity 2, 4, 8, 15, 23; and access to knowledge 141; and capabilities 143, 147, 150–1, 157, 159, 162; and constraints 96, 98–100, 122–3; and decision-making 109; and equality 147, 159, 162; and just universities 170–3, 175; and structural conditions 29, 34; and student agency 127, 130–1; and student narratives 76–8; and transformation 122, 179; and uncritical engagement 102
resources 4–5, 7–10, 12–13, 15, 26–31; and access to knowledge 140–1; and adaptive preference 55; and alienation from lecturers 113–16; and aspirations 83–4,
86–9, 91; and capabilities 45–9, 51–2, 57–63, 142, 147–51, 153–8, 160–2; and conversion factors 54–5; and decision-making 109–10; and families 86; free resources 151; and just universities 168–9, 171, 173–4, 176–7; and misrecognition 118–19, 121; and pedagogy 150–1; and platform creation 138; and research threshold 170; and school systems 71–83; and structural conditions 33–6; and student agency 131–2; and student narratives 68–70, 92; and transformation 122–3, 179; and well-being 55–6
Robeyns, I. 48, 89, 112
rural students 1, 9–10, 13, 26, 120, 170

safety nets 123
Sandel, M. 161
school systems 10, 28, 34, 67, 92; and access to knowledge 139; and alienation from lecturers 113, 115–16; and aspirations 86; and capabilities 142, 144, 152, 159–60; and constraints 101–2, 120; and decision-making 108; and just universities 168, 172; and misrecognition 116, 119–20; and student agency 142; and student narratives 69–83; and transformation 123; and uncritical engagement 104–5
segregation 1, 10, 15, 26, 31, 159, 177
Sen, A. 48, 50–2, 56, 58, 112, 157
sexism 13
short cuts 122
sign language 84–5, 89, 129
smartphones 1, 123
social capital 14, 86, 153, 179
social justice 24, 29, 31, 149, 151, 160–1; and capabilities 45–9, 52, 54, 56, 58–9, 158, 162; and structural conditions 33, 35; and student agency 132, 135, 138; in universities 168–84
social media 153
social mobility 3, 5, 15, 24, 50, 82–3
social sciences 69, 84, 102, 111
social theory 16, 45, 61
socialisation 50, 112, 159, 161–2
socialism 59
socioeconomic status 4–5, 7, 12, 63, 72; and access to knowledge 139–40; and capabilities 162; and constraints 96, 116–17, 122–3; and just universities 171; and student narratives 83–4, 92; and transformation 179

sociology 34, 144
solidarity 58
South 2–4, 6–8, 23, 25, 28, 30, 36, 176, 180
South Africa 1–2, 4–11, 15–16, 45, 53; and constraints 96, 108; and just universities 171, 177; and school systems 70–2; and structural conditions 23–6, 28–9, 31–2; and student agency 139; and student narratives 89–90; and transformation 121, 180
standardisation 13, 30, 50, 55, 101, 122, 180
state 4, 8–9, 25–6, 71–2, 75, 81–3, 99, 102, 151, 171–5
STEM subjects 30, 84
stereotypes 31, 116, 119, 121, 153, 159, 174
stigmatisation 31, 60–1, 74, 103, 121–2, 142, 175, 181
stress 14, 77–8, 96–100, 131, 170, 172, 179
structural conditions 2, 5, 7–8, 12–13, 15–16; and access to knowledge 140–1; and adaptive preference 55; and aspirations 89; and capabilities 49–50, 53, 58–63, 144, 147–8, 152–3, 157, 159; and constraints 96–126; and conversion factors 54–5; and democratic participation 51; and inequality 13–15, 23–44; and injustice 45–7; and just universities 168–9, 172–3, 175, 178; and neoliberalism 47; and school systems 71, 73, 75–80, 82–3; and student agency 127, 130–1, 135; and student narratives 67–70, 72, 92; and transformation 121–4, 179–80
student experiences 1, 15, 29, 49, 53–5; and agency 127, 129–30, 136; and capabilities 59; and constraints 101, 112, 114; and equality 147, 151, 157; and just universities 172; narratives of 67–95
student narratives 1, 15–16, 45, 50, 67–95; and agency 127, 129–30, 136, 138; and capabilities 59–63, 147–9, 151–2, 157, 159–60; and constraints 96, 102, 106, 108, 114, 122; and cultivating recognition 177–9; and decision-making 178; and equality 147–9, 151–2; and just universities 168–75, 178; and transformation 179–80
student representative council (SRC) 107, 109, 135
student voice 34, 49–50, 52, 67–9, 108; and constraints 120; and equality 152, 158, 160; and just universities 169, 179; and student agency 127, 136–8, 145

student-staff ratios 8, 13, 106, 176
students 1–3, 15–16, 33–4, 36, 142–4; and affiliation 127–36; and agency 33–4, 127–46; and decision-making 107; and just universities 168–84; and lecturers 57–8, 127–32; and misrecognition 118–19; and peers 132–6; student research 147, 149, 151, 155–6, 176–8; students with disabilities 171; and transformation 145, 180–1; and uncritical engagement 102–3
sub-Saharan Africa 4, 8
substance abuse 75, 79
support structures 23, 27, 31–2, 34, 49; and access to knowledge 138; and alienation from lecturers 114, 116; and capabilities 147, 153, 157–8; and constraints 96–8, 100–2; and decision-making 110; and inequality 1, 4–5, 10, 12, 14; and just universities 168–9, 172–3, 175–6; and misrecognition 117; and programme restructuring 174–7; and student agency 128, 131, 134; and student narratives 83, 88; and transformation 179–80; and uncritical engagement 102–3, 106
sustainable development 3, 9, 47, 169, 173

tests 14, 72, 99–100, 102, 104, 113, 122
textbooks 10, 13–14, 35, 97, 99; and constraints 105–6, 109, 122; and equality 147, 150; and just universities 170–1; and student agency 141
townships 69, 74–7, 82, 86, 91, 120
trade-offs 8–10, 15, 28, 122–3
transformation 6, 10–12, 24, 28, 31; and aspirations 88; and capabilities 49, 52, 55, 57–60, 143, 147–8, 152–5, 162; and constraints 108, 121–4; and decision-making 113; and inequality 179–80; and just universities 170, 174–5, 177, 180–1; of knowledge 175–7; and misrecognition 121; and school systems 73, 77; and student agency 130, 145; and student narratives 68
transport 1, 13–14, 35, 91, 99–100, 123, 140, 147, 150, 171
travel 71, 80–1, 84, 100, 113, 122, 129, 170, 179
tuition fees 2, 5, 9–10, 25, 89, 92, 99, 107, 148, 179–80
tutorials 13–14, 54, 97, 103, 113, 138, 150, 177
tutors 102, 107, 110, 113–15, 129, 145, 150

Uganda 30
undergraduate students 1, 4–5, 9, 11–12, 14–15; and capabilities 147; and constraints 96; and just universities 169–70, 173, 175, 179; and misrecognition 119; and structural conditions 26, 28–31, 35; and student agency 128; and student narratives 67–8; and student research 155–6, 177–8; and transformation 180; and uncritical engagement 102
underpreparation 7, 10, 12–13, 26–30, 32–3; and capabilities 54, 150; and constraints 103, 107, 113–14, 116; and just universities 168, 170; and uncritical engagement 107
unemployment 2, 8, 25, 75–7, 79, 83, 89, 91, 143, 171
United Kingdom (UK) 5–6
United States (US) 4–5, 84, 89
universities 1–22; and aspirations 83, 85, 87–90, 92; and capabilities 45–66, 147–67; and constraints 96–126; and equality 23–6, 147–67; and just universities 168–84; and school systems 70–3, 76–82; and structural conditions 23–44; and student agency 127–46; and student narratives 67–95; and transformation 180–1
Unterhalter, E. 4

values for public good 61, 147, 149, 151–2, 160–2
vice chancellors 112
violence 6, 56, 68, 72, 89–91, 122
vulnerable students 1, 5–6, 9–10, 12–13, 15–16; and capabilities 47–8, 50, 52, 55, 58–60; and constraints 97, 100–1, 109–10, 115, 117–19, 122; and equality 147–51, 153, 156, 159–60, 162; and just universities 168–78, 180; and structural conditions 23–4, 26–31, 34–5; and student agency 132, 143; and student narratives 72, 76–8, 83, 85, 88–90

Walker, M. 51
wealth 1–2, 10
well-being 24, 45–7, 49–50, 55–6, 62, 70–1, 135, 160–1, 170
wellness syndrome 53–4
white students 9, 11–12, 73–4, 77, 120–1
Wilson-Strydom, M. 33
Wolff, J. 171
work experience 90, 92, 114
working-class students 1, 4–7, 9, 13, 27–9; and capabilities 59–60, 147, 160; and just universities 169; and misrecognition 116–17; and structural conditions 35; and student narratives 67, 86; and transformation 122–3
World Bank 2

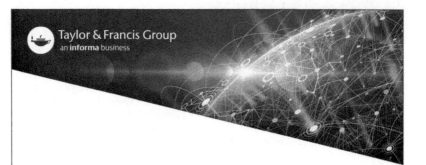

Taylor & Francis eBooks

www.taylorfrancis.com

A single destination for eBooks from Taylor & Francis with increased functionality and an improved user experience to meet the needs of our customers.

90,000+ eBooks of award-winning academic content in Humanities, Social Science, Science, Technology, Engineering, and Medical written by a global network of editors and authors.

TAYLOR & FRANCIS EBOOKS OFFERS:

- A streamlined experience for our library customers
- A single point of discovery for all of our eBook content
- Improved search and discovery of content at both book and chapter level

REQUEST A FREE TRIAL
support@taylorfrancis.com